THRUST

Through the Sound Barrier

THRUST
Through the Sound Barrier

RICHARD NOBLE

and David Tremayne

with contributions from

Andy Green

and others

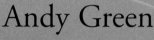

PARTRIDGE

London   New York   Toronto   Sydney   Auckland

Rhodes Oct-19th 1998

contents

TRANSWORLD PUBLISHERS LTD, 61-63 Uxbridge Road, London W5 5SA. TRANSWORLD PUBLISHERS (AUSTRALIA) PTY LTD, 15-25 Helles Avenue, Moorebank, NSW 2170, TRANSWORLD PUBLISHERS (NZ) LTD, 3 William Pickering Drive, Albany, Auckland. Published 1998 by Partridge a division of Transworld Publishers Ltd. Copyright © R. Noble Ltd, Andy Green, David Tremayne and SSC Programme Ltd 1998. The right of Richard Noble, Andy Green, David Tremayne and SSC Programme Ltd to be identified as the authors of this work has been asserted in accordance with sections 77 and 78 of the Copyright Designs and Patents Act 1988. A catalogue record for this book is available from the British Library. ISBN 185225 2685.
Designed by the Senate. Printed in England by Butler and Tanner.

INTRODUCTION

More than two hundred years ago, the celebrated but lamentably unimaginative Dr Johnson remarked to his sidekick, James Boswell, 'Fie, sir – twenty miles in one hour upon a coach? No man could rush so fast through the air and continue to draw breath!'

In 1990, when I began to suggest that a supersonic car might be a serious possibility, similar doubters reacted with the late-twentieth-century equivalent of such scepticism, though most of them did not dignify their derision with the title 'Sir'. A supersonic car? Impossible! It just wasn't on.

Being told what can and can't be done has always been a spur to me. Such negative thinking merely added jet fuel to an ambition already fired by the American Craig Breedlove. He was hoping to break the land-speed record of 633 m.p.h. I had set with *Thrust2* seven years earlier, and to push on past 700 m.p.h. We both knew this would mean encountering the sound barrier at ground level. I decided it was a challenge that simply could not – should not – be resisted.

On 14 October 1947 Charles 'Chuck' Yeager had become the first man to fly at supersonic speed. Breaking the sound barrier on land would be an historic landmark, comparable to the conquest of Mount Everest in 1953, or the 'one small step for man, one giant leap for mankind' taken by Neil Armstrong when he first set foot on the surface of the moon in 1969.

We stood on the brink of an enormous global achievement. There just weren't too many of those fabulous things left.

Back in 1943 the Ministry of Aircraft Production had commissioned the Miles Aircraft Company to build a supersonic aeroplane. Subsequently a powered model achieved Mach 1.38. But then in what became known as 'Ben's Blunder' Ben Lockspeiser, the Director General of Scientific Research at the Ministry, had cancelled the project. At a stroke we had given away our lead in supersonic flight research to the Americans.

Now was the time to redress the balance. A supersonic land-speed-record car would be a fantastic challenge, one that might help to correct what I saw as an endemic lack of confidence in our ability as a nation to do the great things we once did. Fifty years after Ben's Blunder we, too, were tilting at a supersonic windmill, but fortunately we were a little team and the government couldn't get at us!

On 15 October 1997, Andy Green and the *ThrustSSC* team, working on a desert playa 6,000 miles from home, established the world's first official supersonic land-speed record, at a speed of 763.035 m.p.h., Mach 1.02.

This world first will for ever stand as a lasting tribute to British engineering, ingenuity, courage and determination. I am desperately proud of what our small, dedicated team and our loyal supporters achieved in the face of scepticism, industrial indifference and a continuous financial battle that every day threatened to bankrupt us.

It was Theodore Roosevelt who said, 'It is not the critic who counts; not the man who points out where the strong man stumbled or where the doer of deeds could have done them better. The credit belongs to the man who is actually in the arena, whose face is marred with dust and sweat and blood. At best, he knows the triumph of high achievement; if he fails at least he fails while daring greatly, so that his place shall never be with those cold and timid souls who knew neither victory nor defeat.'

This is the real story of a determined team, which entered the arena, dared greatly and returned home triumphant.

PROLOGUE

Wednesday, 15 October 1997. I rose at 5 o'clock that morning, still feeling incredibly tired, but nonetheless aware of the promise of a crisp dawn.

Gerlach is often missed off maps. A tiny hamlet on the edge of Nevada's Black Rock Desert, it is 125 miles north of Reno, the second largest gambling metropolis in the American West. For a small place it does well for bars; there are five of them. Not bad for its 350 souls. The town is usually quiet at such an hour, but the *Thrust* and *Spirit of America* teams, and the associated pressmen, had temporarily swelled its population, and all along Main Street the place was stirring with anticipation. I knew that down at Bruno's Country Club the other team members would be breakfasting ready for another day on the desert, but my wife Sally and I were staying in a house belonging to a great friend of ours, Bev Osborn, just on the outskirts of town. When we ran into trouble over the limited hotel accommodation available, Bev had immediately turned her house over to us, while she slept in the back room of her popular bar, the Miners' Club. It was typical of the enduring kindness of the local people, who helped us so much over the years.

Neither Sally nor I were sleeping well at this stage, dulled by the grind of operating *ThrustSSC* on the desert by day, and administering the project by night. Five hours' sleep was a luxury rather than the norm.

I had time to snatch a quick bowl of cereal and, as I ate, I eyed the increasing glow of the sun struggling into the sky. It was going to be another fine day. *ThrustSSC* would run, and once again we would try to go supersonic in both directions, within the hour allowed by the regulations. But whether it really would be *the* day was totally unpredictable. If it happened, it happened. You couldn't rush it just by wanting it to be so. All that mattered was going through the same painstaking routines, pushing the car that little bit faster each time, without overstepping the safety margin.

The Black Rock Desert is one of the world's most spectacular places. It has its own disarming beauty, with its dark mountain ranges shielding the golden playa that seems to go on forever. Once the summer sun causes the winter floods to evaporate, the flattened surface dries and cracks into distinctive, irregular-sized polygons of mud, which crumble beneath the heel of your foot. The surface nevertheless remains hard, while far beneath it is primeval ooze, endowing the place with the forgiving compliance of a mattress. It's perfect for the pursuit of very high speeds.

I drove the few miles out of town to the slip road onto the desert with my head full of thoughts, and with little inclination to take in the beauty of the surrounding countryside or the steam rising gently from the hot pools on the edge of the road. For out there, further up the endless yellow highway onto which I turned my car, *ThrustSSC* sat waiting to take aim at the sound barrier.

ThrustSSC was designed for a maximum speed of 850 m.p.h. The aerodynamic forces on a vehicle travelling at that speed at ground level are truly enormous. If the nose of ThrustSSC were to lift by even half a degree from its correct trim attitude, the car would be thrown into the air with a vertical acceleration of about 30g, which would clearly be catastrophic. Setting the car into an excessively nose-down attitude might seem like a simple way of countering this, but that would be just as dangerous, as the same enormous forces would now push downwards and simply crush the suspension.

It was clear that, simply to survive at these speeds, the car had to be extremely strong and rigid, as well as being very stable and tightly controlled in pitch attitude. But as a car approaches the speed of sound (which is approximately 750 m.p.h. at ground level, but varies with temperature), shock waves are created and the situation becomes very complex. While the car is accelerating from high subsonic speeds to supersonic speeds, the shock-wave pattern is constantly changing, so the enormous forces on the car are also changing.

In the case of an aeroplane such as Concorde in supersonic flight, the shock waves take up a natural cone shape, and when the outer edges of this cone fan out and hit the ground the sudden change in air pressure is detectable as a sonic boom. Sometimes two sonic booms may be heard.

Nobody had previously investigated the 'supersonic ground effect', so nobody knew how a car would react when it created a sonic boom. At 30,000 feet altitude there is plenty of room for a plane's shock waves to dissipate. For *ThrustSSC*, travelling at ground level, there was no such margin. Would the shock waves lift the vehicle as they bounced back from the ground? Might they be strong enough to damage its structure? Might they actually prove fatal to the car and its driver? There was no shortage of experts who told us we were attempting the impossible and that disaster would occur if we pressed ahead. Only one thing was certain. The already complicated flow pattern around the car would be made even more complicated by the close proximity of the ground, so the huge aerodynamic forces would be even more difficult to predict and control.

Even that did not exhaust the hidden dangers of the transonic region. In some circumstances, as a result of complex inter-reactions between shock waves and boundary layers, the whole flow pattern can become unstable. The local areas of subsonic flow and supersonic flow, which co-exist in the transonic region, appear to vie for supremacy. The resulting unsteady airflow can result in violent vibrations that may destabilize control systems or damage structures.

In the early stages of supersonic flight, many aircraft were destroyed by such phenomena, and this no doubt contributed to the reputation of the dreaded sound barrier. In truth, of course, the sound barrier doesn't exist, and aircraft now routinely, and safely, exceed the speed of sound.

Since the 1960s many contenders had spoken of their plans to make a supersonic car. None had succeeded. When we achieved the record of 633 m.p.h. with *Thrust2*, the local airflow over the cockpit screen was supersonic. And, of course, the tops of the wheels would also have been travelling at supersonic speed!

Thus our problem was to design a car that was impeccably stable in an airflow that was itself unstable and constantly changing throughout the transonic region. How big is this transonic region? It isn't clearly defined, but transonic phenomena can be quite significant at Mach 0.7, and it may be Mach 1.3 or more before supersonic flow is fully established over the whole vehicle surface.

Would the driver actually hear a supersonic boom? No. Imagine you are driving a speedboat along a river and creating a bow wave. The boats you pass will bob up and down as a result of your bow wave, but, being in the middle, you do not experience it.

It was clear that designing a supersonic car would be extremely difficult. It was also clear that testing the car would be very hazardous, as we were exploring totally uncharted territory, so, in addition to coping with the risks we had identified, there was always the possibility of encountering new problems that were essentially unforeseeable. To complete the stark picture, we also knew the project would be completely unforgiving. Even a small mistake at transonic speeds would lead to a fatal accident.

A two-year programme of research was dedicated to studying the physics of the problems that confronted us. Everything was aimed at maximizing the margin of safety. The initial attack on the complex aerodynamic problems was carried out using computational fluid dynamics (CFD) – a simulation technique that required the full power of the largest supercomputer in the country. The results were validated in a unique experiment that involved blasting an instrumented model of the car along a test track at Mach 1.1. Eventually our aerodynamicist,

Ron Ayers, was satisfied that an attempt on the sound barrier was feasible. He was confident that he understood the transonic ground effect well enough for the aerodynamic forces on *ThrustSSC* to be predicted and controlled.

I'm absolutely sure that, had we planned just another solo attack on our 1983 record, we would never have got as far as we did. The sponsors didn't want to do another car, and nor did the public. This all changed in 1990, when Craig Breedlove announced that he was going to try to reach speeds of over 700 m.p.h. The McLaren Formula One team began making similar noises. In Australia, Rosco McGlashan thought he had a chance, too. So it would become a race for Mach 1, and competition gave us our only hope of creating the car that now stood ready for its ultimate challenge.

We had the best design team in the world: Ron Ayers, the man who had come up with the whole shape of *ThrustSSC*; Glynne Bowsher, who had designed the structure and the mechanical components to fit within the shape Ron's research had determined; and Jeremy Bliss, who had designed all the electronic and hydraulic systems, including the car's computer-controlled active suspension.

We had the most highly qualified driver in land-speed-record history in Andy Green, who time and again had demonstrated his calm brilliance. He is an RAF squadron leader and fighter pilot, not a devil-may-care hot-rodder, and he exuded a controlled and intelligent attitude that was: always push ahead, so long as it is safe to do so.

By mid-October, we had already set a new land-speed record at over 700 m.p.h., but we were running out of time and money. Many of our key people were perilously close to the end of their annual leave from their regular jobs, and our debts were mounting.

I felt this incredible fear in the pit of my stomach every time *ThrustSSC* ran. I had never felt like this when I was driving *Thrust2*, but now that I was no longer the man in the cockpit, such emotions intruded no matter how I tried to suppress them. I had witnessed the horrifying power of the forces involved when one of our rocket test models had exploded as it went through the sound barrier.

Watching *ThrustSSC* run was an unnerving experience. It was my obsession with speed that had brought us all to this point in our lives. Ultimately I was the one responsible for it all. I kept asking myself over and again, 'Are we really OK? Are we doing this right? Should I stop it now, before we have a terrible accident?'

The reality was, if we had got it wrong, we had created a monster that could kill Andy Green.

1 FROM LOCH NESS TO CITY ROAD

I owe my obsession with speed to my father, which is ironic since I'm not sure he ever really approved of my land-speed-record attempts. But I would follow a very roundabout route before I finally did something about it.

I was born on 6 March 1946 at Comley Bank in Edinburgh, and the first thing I ever learned about speed came when I was six years old. We were living in Scotland, and one afternoon we happened to go for a drive in the family car round Loch Ness. Father was a big burly man, a colonel in the Army. He drove, with Mother sitting in the front alongside him, while I was in the back with my one-year-old brother, Andrew.

Suddenly we pulled up by the edge of the loch. Father had spotted something. He and Mother turned round in their seats with big smiles on their faces. Father said, 'Let's see what all this is about, shall we?'

I had no idea what he meant, but I sensed from his manner that he was excited. Something special was going on. As we clambered out of the car I didn't know what it was. Father and Mother were looking at something down by the water. I remember being excited, too, without really knowing why as we edged forward. And there it was: a great big streamlined silver boat, edged with goldfish red. It seemed to dwarf everything else around.

Father's smile grew even bigger. 'That's John Cobb's *Crusader*,' he said. And he told me how Cobb had set the land-speed record, and was now going after the water-speed record with this fantastic boat.

John Cobb in the cockpit of his Crusader jet-powered hydroplane.

Crusader begins a run on Loch Ness.

Suddenly I felt myself gripped with this tremendous excitement. The whole thing was just so fabulous.

It wasn't the boat itself that was to prove my inspiration, though *Crusader* was a sleek beauty with torpedo-shaped floats or sponsons outrigged at the back, which made it look as if it would run on skis. It was the enormous power that was so appealing, especially to a six-year-old. This was the 1950s, remember, and there we were, in our little Hillman Minx, which had maybe 30 horsepower, if that. And there was this great big boat with an aeroplane engine. And not just any aeroplane engine, but one of the new jets with more than 5,000 horsepower!

Cobb was killed a few days later when *Crusader* broke up while travelling at well over 200 m.p.h., the first time anyone had achieved such a terrific velocity on water. But I never forgot that day, or the intense thrill I felt. In later life, when I heard land-speed record-breaker Art Arfons describe getting 'the chills', I knew

Crusader breaking up at more than 240 m.p.h.

exactly what he meant. From that day at Loch Ness onwards I started collecting anything I could find on speed attempts, with the land-speed record uppermost in my thoughts. I'd sketch record cars in my school exercise books; when I was a bit older, I used to go crawling round in scrapyards, trying to find spark plugs that were just the right shape for a cardboard jet-engine mock-up I'd built. By my tenth birthday I'd read Eric Burgess's book *Rocket Propulsion* from cover to cover many times. It's a bloody good book, and I have that copy to this day. Almost without realizing it, I had become obsessed with the land-speed record.

Speed attempts don't happen overnight, though, and I had a lot of ground to cover before I ever went near a fast car.

Thanks to Father's job in the Army we had a very weird, itinerant sort of existence. When I was three we went to live in Libya, before going back to Scotland. Then Father was posted to Austria, and we went out there with him for a short time. From around 1955, the year before my second brother, Charles, was born, Father was based at the School of Infantry in Warminster. Andrew and I had a lot of fun playing on the tanks there. We lived in Malta from 1958 to 1960, and then came back to Greenwich, so all told we moved about a fair bit.

To begin with I went to a little school in Nairn, run by a wonderful lady we called Sharpie and her husband, Dr Gruber. They were very tough. Anything wrong and you got your knuckles rapped with a ruler. A pretty hard sort of place!

Prep school came next, one called Horris Hill in Newbury. It was a very good school, which produced some excellent results. But that was another very tough place.

After that I went to Winchester College. I sneaked in there and was bottom of the school in mathematics for a whole year! I didn't do very well academically, but I had an awful lot of fun and made some great friends. It was an interesting environment. After years of being restrained by rules I found Winchester very free and relaxed in

The Highlands featured strongly in my early upbringing, as the kilt testifies.

some ways, though it could be extremely unpleasant if you weren't sufficiently robust. Fortunately, I was. Mother was convinced I was too robust, because I was always something of a rebel. On one occasion we tear-gassed the headmaster's party! It was his first parents' cocktail party, something of a public relations exercise by a very formal headmaster. There were all sorts of important people there, looking pompous: cabinet ministers, bishops, judges, and so on – and suddenly, because of us, there they were all crying. It was incredibly funny!

Of course there was hell to pay. We were threatened with expulsion, but for some reason it never happened.

Father was very keen that I follow him into the Army, especially as I was the eldest son. But I felt that really the military had had its day. There wasn't a problem as such about it, because whenever he tried to impose anything on me I'd generally got my own ideas.

Father was also very keen that I should become a musician, but that didn't happen either, which I'm very sad about. It was a big mistake. He wanted me to study music, at least play the piano or something like that, and I missed the opportunity there. Andrew, however, is a brilliantly accomplished pianist, so at least one of us is musically inclined.

As a schoolboy at Winchester I suddenly became aware of pop music, and quickly adjusted to a more liberated lifestyle.

Eventually, in the contrary manner that adolescents tend to have, I decided to study the guitar. Father said he would only support that if I learned classical music. There was to be no pop. So I went my own way. When I was fifteen I made a guitar, and not long after that I got a rock group going. It was 1964, the time when everyone wanted to be The Beatles. Our group was called The Vampires, and then came The 4 Gears! We were very poor indeed, but we played at a lot of dances and we had plenty of laughs.

After Winchester it was tomatoes! I'd reached the stage where I had to get to grips with the world and decide what the hell I was going to do. So to begin with I worked as a gardener, in charge of 13,000 tomato plants for ICI's Plant Protection offshoot. I needed money while I decided what I wanted to do as a career, and the job was in Fernhurst, just a short distance down the road from home.

Father became rather impatient about this somewhat slow self-education process, and partly at his bidding I eventually went on an Army Outward Bound course in Towyn in Wales. I had been getting nowhere with job applications and was making no progress. Father said, 'This is a good idea. This will be a very, very good thing to do.' He was right. What happened there was an extraordinary and valuable experience.

Before that, however, I had another remarkable offer. I was downstairs at six in the morning, ready for my last day at Plant Protection, when the phone rang. It was a friend of Father's, the managing director of a huge shipping line. 'Richard, what are you doing these days?' he asked. When I told him I was in charge of thousands of tomato plants, he said, 'Well, you're wasting your time. Would you be interested in this opportunity? Our chairman is Sir William Kaiser; his yacht has got itself to France and the Maltese crew has walked out. We need to recrew it quickly

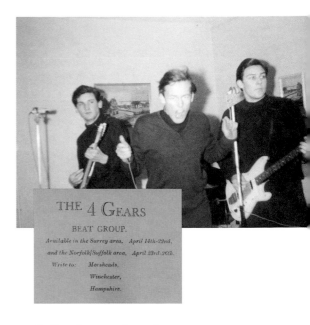

Before long, a few of us formed our own group. I wouldn't pretend that The 4 Gears presented any threat to the established industry, but we tried hard and made a hell of a lot of noise.

and we'd like you to be barman. We'd like you to catch the ten o'clock plane to Paris today, and then you've got a four-month cruise in the Mediterranean. Are you on?'

So I went and woke Father and said, 'What the hell do I do?' And he said, 'It's your decision. You've got to decide what you want to do. But if I were you I'd go for the Army Outward Bound course.'

The whole thing focused my mind wonderfully, so I rang back and told this guy thanks, but I was going to stick with the Outward Bound option. Somehow, having the luxury of an alternative simply seemed to endorse the rightness of my original decision.

The camp in Wales was a seriously tough place. We were all living in corrugated-iron Nissen huts and were woken at six every morning by a guy banging a steel bar along the outside, before running down to the sea for an April swim. When I turned up there I thought I was pretty fit. I'd been labouring at Plant Protection, carting things round, and was in the sort of pretty good health one would expect of a robust teenager. But at this place I was nobody, absolutely hopeless. The standard was incredibly high, and I struggled to keep up. These boy soldiers were very, very tough indeed. For me things got so bad that one morning I just couldn't get out of bed! My stomach muscles hurt so much I couldn't sit up.

There I was, eighteen going on nineteen, and I just couldn't cope with it all. I'd never been very sporty at school; I was good at long-distance running, and very good at the long jump, but otherwise I hadn't taken much interest. I was starting at a standard that was far below these guys, so it was a constant fight to keep up. It was seriously difficult.

I actually bought my return rail ticket home, but I never used it. In the end I stuck it out and won through. I was very proud of that. I just kept going and eventually it got better, so that in the final big exercise I was actually leading our little group.

It was all an astonishing experience. One of the instructors there, Sergeant Gregg, was absolutely dedicated. He wouldn't even take a holiday because his fitness would have suffered.

One day I had to climb a 300-foot cliff face in the middle of Snowdonia. I'd never done anything like that in my life, and I kept falling off. I was totally incompetent. Sergeant Gregg said, 'We've had fourteen thousand people up this cliff face, Noble, and you're not going to be the one that lets us down.' Fortunately we were all on ropes, so the only damage I sustained was to my dignity.

Sergeant Gregg was at the top – I could hear him whistling cheerfully – and he was taking in the rope as I clambered up. I thought I could see an easy way out of this. Suddenly he saw the rope start moving to his left, and he called down, 'Well, Noble, what are you doing?' I shouted back, 'I can see an easy way round this, so I'm going to try it.' I worked up until I got to this huge overhang. And there I was, holding on like a spider, with the overhang right out above my head. I realized I had to go for it. And the way to do that was to lean back into space, with the best part of 300 feet below, kick out with my feet and grab for the overhang, in the frantic hope that I'd reach it and be able to pull myself up. Of course I missed, and I was left hanging in space.

'Right, Noble,' Sergeant Gregg's voice came floating down, 'I could have told you it wouldn't work, so I'm going to lower you a hundred feet and you'll swing in and do it again.'

I came to admire this quiet man enormously. He led people in a very friendly way, which was much more effective than just ordering them around. He did everything: he led us through all-night sessions on the moors, he was brilliant with canoes. Then he was killed about a year later on the same course when something went terribly wrong. I never found out exactly what happened.

Another of our instructors was a guy named Foreman, who taught us gymnastics in an old seaplane hangar. You'd run in, grab a rope and climb up 90 feet! Nothing underneath but concrete. Foreman was absolutely amazing. Around the side walls, seven feet up from the floor, was a bar to which you'd normally rope your seaplane; this guy Foreman would put his hands flat on either side of the bar, press his palms together and pull himself up. He couldn't get his fingers over the top; he just used the sheer compressive strength of his arms. Quite incredible.

The outcome of all this was that I eventually came through the course quite well. I certainly didn't fail it as I'd expected to at one stage. And that was one hell of a turning point, because I realized suddenly that I could do these things. It raised my expectations.

I was still unsure of what I wanted to do with my life. There'd been Winchester, which was a highly successful school, but where some people hadn't been able to integrate at all. I had fitted in all right, but it hadn't given me a direction. Now I still didn't have one. And though I had this new understanding of myself and what I could do, I had one hell of a problem, because having committed to this expensive course, and done it, I now had to face the Army's Regular Commissions Board. I hadn't appreciated this initially, but going into the Outward Bound course – and passing it – automatically meant that you had to go before the RCB at Westbury, where they decided whether you were going to be a soldier or not.

Father was beginning to apply the pressure. He'd say, 'It's a good job. Three years in the Army, short commission, good thing to do.' He was in charge of Army recruitment from the universities, so this made the whole thing doubly difficult.

The RCB camp was one of those three-day things where you got woken up with a cup of tea – a real change from Towyn – and the standard was very low. I suddenly realized that if I passed it I was going into the Army. Well, there was absolutely no way I was going to do that. No way. I didn't know what else I was going to do, but I was certainly *not* going into the Army.

What it boiled down to was that I simply had to fail.

If you've ever been into an exam determined to fail you'll know how humiliating it is. You just feel so awful. I sat down and was asked to write an essay on pubs, so I wrote three pages without any punctuation at all. Then I had to do an obstacle course, and I deliberately fell off everything. Then I had to get a team of guys across a bottomless chasm with a 50-gallon oil drum, and I got them all to an island in the middle and let the time run out. Eventually I was hauled up in front of the board. 'What the hell do you think you're doing?' they asked. I said, 'Look, I've got to explain to you: I don't want to pass. I cannot pass. I don't want to join the Army.' So I was duly failed.

Father was desperately upset. Desperately, desperately upset. Because he was the guy who was responsible for recruiting and his son hadn't even passed through the RCB. That was a low point, but for me it was the only way out of a very difficult situation. I was still partially living at home and, though Father and I were on speaking terms, I sensed we were moving further apart. It was 1966, and I had just turned twenty.

Not long after this I managed to get a job with ICI, selling paint. I fancied sales and marketing because I thought I had the right sort of character for it, and I started work in an office in High Holborn.

All of us juniors looked after back-up for four or five reps who were going out actually selling the paint. We were largely dealing with retail complaints, with a vast amount of correspondence on a daily basis. It was actually a very good introduction to business at the lowest possible level: very hard work, not easy at all. But there was one guy there whom I admired because he seemed to find it so easy. I'd be flogging away dealing with these letters for long hours, but whenever I looked up he'd be smoking and looking out of the window. I kept thinking, How does he cope with this? How does he get to grips with it?

One day he was ill and there was an ongoing complaint in his territory. The office manager told us to break open his desk. We discovered that it was filled with great wads of paper going back years. He'd just been chucking everything in his desk and not bothering with it. He never returned to work, and later two great tea-chests arrived, full of correspondence that he'd taken home!

There was one simply wonderful week when, in an inspired move, and with great management skill, ICI sent all the senior managers away on a course. We then discovered that if you took an elastic band and a paper clip, and bent the long loop of the clip over the band and flicked it, it would go a long way. We started attacking the insurance company 200 feet across High Holborn. The clips would bang against their windows.

Well, soon paper clips were going back and forth. It was warfare. We launched off more than 10,000 of them during that week. And we were dinging them off the roofs of taxis when they stopped, watching the cabbies get out, wondering what the hell was going on.

But around that time I realized, perhaps not surprisingly, that this was a dead-end job. I was having a lot of fun in London with all my friends, and a terrific nightlife, but then I got sent up to Birmingham doing very much the same thing. Five of us shared a house in Sutton Coldfield. It was a fairly austere existence, and it dawned on me that I simply had to get on with life. I had a meeting with the management and told them I didn't really think the job was for me. I should be progressing. Instead I was waiting to fill dead men's shoes. They kept urging me to hang on a bit, it would be all right. But I knew it wouldn't be and, since I have limited patience anyway, I wasn't prepared to wait much longer for a decent opportunity.

About this time there was a great moment when the district manager at ICI Paints took me to one side and said, 'Richard, you've got a reputation for wild driving. Mark my words, you never need to drive at more than forty-five m.p.h.' I'd think about that a lot later in my life.

I'd heard of a job going at ICI Fibres, which was the brighter, more successful side of ICI in those days. It was really going some. But the problem within ICI was that you couldn't change divisions. They didn't want all the good people lurching across and migrating to the better jobs. I went for a meeting with a terrific bloke called Ian Brook, who was sales manager of ICI Fibres. 'Would you like to do this job?' he asked. I replied, 'Yes, I really would, and I can do it.' 'OK,' he said, 'we'll give you a month's trial. But to come to us, you've got to leave the whole of ICI, leave all your pension rights. Then you've got to reapply to ICI Fibres and hope that I will honour this conversation. And I may not. So which is it to be?' I said, 'Ian, I'm leaving ICI right now.'

He did honour his offer, and I got the month's trial. The gamble was worth a couple of years' pension rights. I walked out of ICI Paints and doubled my salary overnight. Then things became seriously interesting. I knew it was a good job, but I didn't realize how exciting it was going to be.

What we were doing was selling man-made fibre, a bulked polyester product called Crimplene. It was an extraordinary material, because, when knitted on high-volume machinery, the garment could be washed and didn't then have to be ironed.

Four of us started off based in Leicester, with sales of just under 20 million pounds. And we took it up to 100 million over a period of just under three years.

Absolutely astonishing. We were driving or flying 50,000 miles a year. I was growing up fast. It was precisely the sort of challenge and environment I needed.

Along the way I met a brilliant businessman called Freddy Strasser, a knitwear manufacturer who would play an important role later in my life. Freddy was a terrific entrepreneur, who'd built up his business from nothing, and together we did what was then the biggest deal in ICI Fibres' history.

ICI's marketing was extremely clever, with enormous effort taken to maintain the quality of the product. We had something like 90 per cent of the market, which seemed to have an endless hunger for Crimplene. I had one of the first double-breasted chalk-stripe Crimplene suits, which you could leave on the floor overnight. You'd just jump into it the next morning and there would be no creases whatsoever. It was very smart, but, because it was knitted, there were millions of minute invisible holes in it. On a cold day the wind whipped through it and you felt as if you weren't wearing anything!

By 1969, as I turned twenty-three, two things were happening. What we didn't know was that the ICI licensing agreement on the master patent was due to expire. What I did know was that I was becoming an ICI man, and I didn't want to be part of that.

It seemed that once you were in the ICI machine it seemed you were in it until you were spat out the other end. Somewhere along the line ICI had commissioned a survey which showed that average life expectancy after retirement was actually only eighteen months. So you'd be on this escalator all these years, and eighteen months after getting off it you'd be dead. And I couldn't be part of that. I really couldn't be. You're only here once. I was also very aware that I hadn't really seen the world. And the speed thing was also still in the background.

At this time Ian Brook got promoted. His management philosophy was extremely simple, and I found it easy to relate to. He said, 'I'm interested in going forwards, and I don't want to keep looking over my shoulder. If you guys screw up, I'll fire you. Simple as that. But if you ever get into trouble I'll support you one hundred per cent, all the way down the line. That's how it works.' It was a remarkable experience working for a man with that kind of ability and strength of character.

Things were not the same after he left. On top of that the competition started to come in at prices 60 per cent lower than ours. Suddenly all my customers, with whom I'd so carefully built up relationships, started buying elsewhere. It was emotionally draining and really disappointing. It was clear that the thing was soon going to be dead in the water. Very soon mundane decisions that I'd been taking regularly on a day-by-day basis were being queried, and were going up to the board for approval. That was it. Time to go.

One of the things I'd always wanted to do was to write. I figured there was a good life to be had by writing, and I wanted to sort myself out and see more of the world. But I needed some thinking time for the novel I was planning. So I went to see Freddy Strasser in London and told him I wanted a new job. He was wonderful. 'What do you want, Richard? I'll rearrange the management, we'll find a nice important role for you. What do you want to do?' And I said I wanted to work on his nightshift, making machine-knitted fabrics from the Crimplene yarn I'd been selling. This would give me the time I needed to write. Freddy was staggered. 'Richard, you must be out of your mind!' he said. But to his eternal credit he didn't try to dissuade me.

So in the middle of 1971 I started on the nightshift at Nova Jersey Knit in City Road, London, making pattern discs for knitting machines. It gave me a chance to read and gather my thoughts while the machines were going *ker-clunk*, *ker-clunk* and doing the work. I was working with all these Pakistani guys by night, while planning my book. It was an unusual existence after ICI, but a very liberating one. I based myself at a friend's house in Putney and drove in each night to City Road in my trusty Series II short-wheelbase Land Rover.

The idea of the book didn't last long. It was really a semi-autobiographical novel, as these things often are. But it was an absolute disaster. I couldn't do it, I really couldn't. I had a whole lot of girlfriends who were typing it, and there was one classic day when they all seemed to ring up together to say, 'Richard, this is so awful that we can't go on!' So that was that. I binned it, quickly. Looking back I'm just very ashamed of the whole thing. It was a try, but it was so bad I can't even remember the title! My career as a novelist was over before it had even begun.

This brought me to another crossroads, and I had to question what I was doing all over again. The

I resigned from my job at ICI in 1972, determined to become a novelist. The writing failed, but my Land Rover would play a key role in my immediate future.

raison d'être of working for Freddy had been to make time for the book I now knew I would never – could never – write. But I still had that yearning to see the world. I was very aware that I'd come blundering out of school and then become stuck in industry, and now was the time to broaden my mind a bit. One of the better things I had managed to do, shortly after I'd bought the Land Rover, was to get myself on a maintenance course at the Rover plant in Solihull. There I learned how to strip one down to the last nut and bolt.

Now the next step was to fit mine out to carry six people, because I'd decided that I was going to see Africa. It was time to travel.

2 AM I GOING TO DO SOMETHING, OR SHALL I LET IT GO?

My girlfriend at the time, Sarah, worked for *The Times*, and through her I placed an advertisement that simply said, 'London to Cape Town overland. Small expedition, £200.' That was all. We had 160 replies, but most of them were dreamers who thought it was going to be tarmac all the way. Eventually we ended up with a team of six: two blokes, myself and Mark Masefield, and four women, Sally, Susie, Jane and Maria. We'd worked our way through all of these applications and it had boiled down to a situation where it was either that group or it wasn't going to happen. We simply had to fill every seat, because the economics weren't going to work otherwise.

Father was very concerned about the whole thing, saying that it was absolutely ridiculous and that you don't take women into the desert. Obviously it didn't help that after apparently settling down at last with ICI, and doing well at a chosen job, I had jacked it all in on a whim to work a nightshift. Or that I was now heading off on some wild-goose chase that might endanger people. As a parent, what you obviously want to see, possibly for selfish reasons, is your child well established. And this wasn't happening. One uncle said to me in a rather sneering sort of way, 'Send me a postcard when you get to Fort Lamy in Chad.' As if he didn't believe we ever would.

Mark and I rebuilt my thirteen-year-old Land Rover, engine, gearbox, the lot. It still looked pretty rough, but it was reliable. Eventually, in April 1972, we set off.

By the time we'd reached Madrid, Sally and I seemed to have paired off, and she was steadfast in all the darkest moments, even when the rest of our crew were in danger of losing heart. By the oddest coincidence, her great uncle Erik had been at the Bonneville Salt Flats in 1947, in John Cobb's team, when Cobb had raised the land-speed record to 394 m.p.h. after hitting 403 m.p.h. on one run. Perhaps that was an omen.

Gripped by an urge to see the world, I organized an overland expedition to Cape Town. After advertising for fellow travellers, six of us left London in April 1972. First stop was Folkestone.

Things went pretty well at first, with all the usual variables of weather and road conditions. But when we got to the Sahara Desert in deep Algeria they suddenly turned nasty. By mistake we were on the old Piste Balisée course of 1930, the original French crossing route, which was perhaps less suitable. We hit a very bad rut and the swivel pins in the front suspension sheared, so the front wheels splayed out in opposite directions. Obviously we couldn't continue until the steering was repaired. On board I had spares for everything apart from those.

I was faced with a really serious problem. We were 100 miles from the Algerian border post, which had water, and 200 miles from Agadez, the nearest town. I should think things are very different now, but back then there was no defined route to get there, you just trusted to luck. The temperature was very hot; it went up to 140 degrees by midday. So immediately we had this accident I realized we were in deep trouble. The only thing we could do was put up an awning, put on plenty of clothes to protect us from the sun, ration the water and sit there waiting to be rescued. Fortunately we didn't have to wait too long.

There was a truck that had broken down somewhere near us, and somehow or other the party with it had managed to get a military truck to come up from Agadez. At the same time we found another vehicle, which

Deep in the Sahara.

was on its way up north to the border post, so I asked Jane to go on that to get up there and tell them we were in trouble. At least I knew she'd be safe there, and it was sensible to let people know of our plight.

Then we left Mark and Susie to guard our damaged Land Rover while the rest of us went south in this military truck with the parts that had to be remachined. We made Agadez but then ran into further trouble, because the Saharan Land Rovers were manufactured under licence in Spain, and the only parts anyone had were metric. Ours, of course, were imperial. We got it sorted out eventually, and within a day I hitched a ride back north on a Land Rover that was effectively a kind of bus service. There were twelve of us aboard, and the others were mostly itinerants going north trying to get jobs in Algeria. They were all smoking like hell, despite the open 20-gallon petrol drums between us.

Somehow the driver knew exactly where we'd broken down. It was quite uncanny. He drove 200 miles in the desert, straight to our Land Rover.

There was another British team travelling the same route with, of all things, a caravan, plus a Land Rover and an NSU Wankel car. They'd arrived at our base shortly after we'd left to find that Mark and Susie were very tired. When you're down to minimum water rations you mentally clog up. You get very slow and things become too difficult, and you wind up in a spiral that can lead to death. The new people had looked after them, then fortunately Jane had come back down from the border post, having told the commandant that we were in trouble. She was the freshest of them all, and had taken charge.

I concentrated on getting our Land Rover repaired. Then I said to the other Britons, 'Look, I'm sorry. We have to leave in half an hour. If you're going to come with us you're most welcome to, because I know the way out, otherwise my responsibility is to my people.' And they said no, they would drive at night when it was cooler; they'd be all right. They weren't all right, and it was quite clear that they weren't. By now they were very tired. But they were adamant about it, so I loaded our party into the Land Rover and drove them down to Agadez as quickly as possible.

Once we were all safely there, I felt we should go back to look for the other Britons. I was worried that they weren't in a state to get far on their own. I went to the military and we requisitioned a bigger Land Rover with 200 litres of water on board and plenty of fuel. We roped in some Army guys, and set off back north. Of course we had to pay for all this, which left a huge hole in the budget, but nevertheless these people had helped us by looking after Mark and Susie, and we had to help them. A few days earlier we had met a Mercedes mechanic, his wife and their little dog, who were driving a brand-new car across the Sahara in some sort of factory trial. They subsequently went off the road further south, and we were horrified to learn that they had perished. After six hours without water you die. The desert is an absolutely merciless place.

We had a Saharan guide, a Tuareg in all his blue gear, and he and I got on really well. He told us to drive straight back 200 miles across the desert, without following any discernible tracks, and again we got to the point of the breakdown without any difficulty. It really is amazing how these guys have such a highly developed sense of direction. But when we got back to our old site we found that the other Brits had moved, and we didn't know which direction they had taken. We couldn't follow them because the wind had erased any wheeltracks. We just didn't know where the hell they were. I was very worried now, because we knew that the German couple had died and that we ourselves had only got out by the skin of our teeth. I didn't want more people dying.

To make the situation even worse, just as we were deciding what to do one of the military guys pointed to the back of the Land Rover. A hose had come out of the big tank, and all the fuel had leaked out. So we were now down to just one small tank. I said, 'That's it. We've got to go back to Agadez.'

'No,' our Tuareg said, 'we're going to find them.' And that's precisely what we did.

We drove in 25-mile zigzags across the desert, and we found them at a watering hole. They were drinking green water, which was stagnant as hell. Horrible stuff. But they were alive, which was the main thing. When they reached Agadez they gave up and sold everything. And after all this, in return for our saving them, they gave us a fire extinguisher!

We flogged on and eventually made it down through the Congo and to South Africa without further serious dramas. It had been a terrific adventure. We had left London on 18 April 1972, and arrived in Cape Town exactly four months later, after a trek of 15,500 miles.

Obviously we needed to raise funds to return eventually to England, so while I was working on the Land Rover and trying to get another expedition together, I got a job as the night manager at the Fairmead Hotel in Rondebosche. Sally and I lived in a room right at the top of the hotel. Apartheid was then at its absolute worst. The hotel manager was an aristocratic German who had come to South Africa via South America. My job was to come on shift somewhere around eight o'clock at night, do the accounts, and supervise the black night staff, who were responsible for cleaning up the place. They lived in breeze-block hutches up on

*The Sahara Desert is a cruel and punishing environment – we drove hard
to cross it as soon as possible.*

the top of the hotel, and we became very friendly. In the evenings, once all the
work was done, we would often sit in the bar and talk after the last guests had
retired.

Cape Town has the most incredible storms, which isn't surprising since it's
perched right out there on the Cape. One night there was an enormous one. With
other members of the staff we gathered in the bar out of habit, and while the
storm was going on we had a bit of a session, chatting away and comparing our
lives in Africa and Europe. One by one everybody dropped off in the armchairs.
The hotel manager, meanwhile, was very concerned about his new curtains, and
by unfortunate chance he came racing round to the hotel at four o'clock in the
morning to check that everything was all right. And there he found us all asleep
in the bar.

'I'll see you at nine o'clock tomorrow morning,' he said to me.

The next morning he fired me for fraternizing with the blacks.

This came as a great surprise. I could understand being fired for nodding off, but not for being friendly with black people. I like to think I'm happy working with or talking to anybody of any colour, sex, creed or whatever, and since we had already driven through the Congo and the whole of black Africa to get to Cape Town, we had developed a strong feeling for the continent and its people. I'd never really come across discrimination before, and what I encountered in South Africa was absolutely terrifying. If the guys working in the hotel were caught without their passbooks they could be thrown into gaol for a month, without being fed. The whole situation was outrageous.

I told the manager that we were getting another expedition together and asked how long Sally and I could stay there. 'Stay here as long as you like,' he said. 'You can use your room, but just don't come into the hotel.' That at least allowed us to get the Land Rover finished.

Sally eventually had to fly back to England because she was running out of money, and if the thing was to work, every seat in the Land Rover had to pay. She and I had a very tearful parting in Johannesburg. We'd become very close friends during the trip and had tested each other in the most appalling circumstances.

I then put together another group, which was astonishingly difficult to do. I had started to conceive a plan to set up a business running overland trips in Africa, which was already being done by some companies, but it was very early days. I wanted to get a feel for it and to find out how you actually did it, and if it could be done with large numbers. It's a wonderful existence. You meet fascinating people, you're all over the place, and you live entirely by your wits. Your vehicle has got to be absolutely 100 per cent all the time. With an expedition, the only time it costs is when it stops, but when it does stop, by God it costs money!

Our new crew included Nick and Judy Hodson, who were newly-weds from South Africa. Nick had a British passport but Judy's was South African. The big problem was getting them out of South Africa with acceptable passports for black Africa. Eventually we got her on to a British passport, so she was all right. But before we managed that we took her into Zambia on a South African passport, which I think was something of a first.

There was also a guy called Dieter Pickhardt, a German whose parents had come to live in Cape Town during the war, and despite his right-wing political views, we got on well. Then there was Fi Mills, who took on the cooking, and a Canadian nurse, Clara. The plan was to go up via East Africa, ship to India, then up India through Afghanistan, and drive the long way back through Iran, taking the hippie trail home. It was a terrific expedition. We clicked as a team and it worked brilliantly. It was also incredibly efficient. On the way out it cost each of us £200 a head, plus £50 for food, but on the way back we managed the food budget better by buying and cooking local produce. Whenever we stopped Dieter would dig a hole and make an oven, and Clara would bake bread. In fact, five months later, at the end of the journey, I was able to give each of the others £18 back from their original £50 food stake. When we arrived back in England, I promptly got us lost outside Dover as I hadn't brought any English maps!

My plan to run overland trips as a business came to nothing in the end. Instead, I tried to get into the SAS. I suppose I didn't want to come straight back down to earth after the excitement of the expeditions, and that seemed a good way to prolong the buzz.

I went in at the same time as a mate called Adam Brodie, but then I knackered my knee on the first excursion, and that was that. Adam made it all the way through, which was terrific, but I was wrecked. I twisted my knee in a foxhole on the middle of a Welsh moor, and after that I was out.

I was never really motivated, to be honest. The lifestyle thrilled me, but I wasn't totally sold on the rest, because I wasn't happy with the idea of killing people.

After that setback I got a job working for the American Management Association. I was very interested in management because of what I'd learned from Ian Brook at ICI, and on the expeditions.

The idea was to sell courses on pure management from a London office run by Bob Windham-Bellord, a cheerful fellow who was constantly being chased by the police for the vast number of parking tickets he racked up outside our office in Albemarle Street.

We put an enormous amount of effort into it all and landed the biggest deal they'd ever had. It began to grow quite well, but then the recession really began to bite early in 1974, and suddenly people were cutting back and just didn't want to buy management courses. The business began to die, just as Crimplene sales had done in my last days at ICI. I read the writing on the wall, and when I saw an advert in *The Times* for a job with GKN Floors I applied and got it.

At this stage Sally had a flat in Moscow Road, Bayswater, and, according to her, I'd rather assumed I could move in on some sort of long-term temporary basis when I'd arrived back in England. So there I was, coming up for my twenty-eighth birthday, moving from flat to flat and about to start yet another new job, and all the time this internal conflict was raging.

My parents were saying that I must get on and start a decent job, get married and become responsible, and all that. But the speed thing was still burning away inside on a slow fuse. I'd had a taste of freedom when I'd broken away from ICI, and I'd loved the expeditions. Through them I'd suddenly realized there was a lot more to life than working in a big multinational, a hell of a sight more!

I suppose the land-speed record had always been there in the background, ever since that day back at Loch Ness, more than twenty years earlier. Now I'd arrived at that inevitable point that all aspiring record-breakers reach, when you have to ask yourself a tough question: Am I going to do anything about it, or shall I let it go?

And I simply decided that I *wasn't* going to let it go.

3 A CATHEDRAL ON WHEELS

I chose the name *Thrust* because it seemed appropriate for the vehicle I started out to create: the first pure-jet car to be designed and built in Britain. Thrust is the term engineers use to measure jet-engine power. Britain's last land-speed-record car had been Donald Campbell's *Bluebird CN7*, which first ran in 1960, when the record rules still catered only for cars that transmitted their power through the wheels. Since then American contenders such as Dr Nathan Ostich, Craig Breedlove, Tom Green and Art Arfons had ushered in the era of turbojet-powered cars which were literally propelled along by their own exhaust gases. They had phenomenal power and no need for a complex, expensive, heavy and power-absorbing transmission, so inevitably they went a lot faster. Soon only pure-thrust vehicles were capable of vying to be the fastest of all.

I decided on a three-stage plan of attack for a variety of very straightforward reasons. First, I was completely unknown. Second, I knew that British industry, being what it is, was not going to give me money for nothing. Well, who would? And third, the project had to be British, or at the very worst Common Market. I had to start somewhere, so I planned to build a cheap car, *Thrust1*, to learn the ropes. Longer term, we would graduate to *Thrust2*, which would be a demonstration car to raise interest and source the funding for

Nothing is won without sacrifice, and once I had set my heart on building a jet-powered car the first thing that had to go to finance the project was my beloved Triumph TR6.

Thrust3, the ultimate record car. Such was my thinking at that stage, because I simply had no experience and no credibility, and it seemed the most logical course.

I didn't have any money, either, and I was determined to raise funds from sponsorship. Remortgaging property was out of the question. I was twenty-eight and naturally couldn't afford to give up work to pursue the land-speed record, but in any case, I never made a secret of my aspirations within GKN, so it was soon all too well known what I was doing. It became very much an operation within an operation!

I had a French-blue Triumph TR6, which I loved, but we needed to raise finance, so it had to go. I got 1,100 quid for it. To be honest, the car was starting to get expensive to run and I'd just been caught speeding again, but it was still a wrench to let it go. But at least there was now a little cash in the project.

Besides Sally's invaluable moral support, friends were also helping: my colleague, George Myers, plus Mark Rasmussen and Simon Chapman, who worked for Black & Decker as a consultant. I'd written asking if Black & Decker could help the project by lending us tools, and as a result we got all sorts of kit: drills, welding gear and so on. The whole car was built with real do-it-yourself gusto.

The first thing was to come up with a concept: I chose a straightforward ladder-type chassis frame with a very simple engine, which hopefully I could understand and install and get running myself. Of course it had to be a jet. With pure-thrust cars you have a choice of either jet or rocket propulsion. The turbojet burns a mixture of air and fuel to provide thrust. A mono-propellant rocket makes its thrust through the chemical reaction as hydrogen peroxide is passed over a catalyst mat, which breaks it down into its constituent parts of hydrogen and superheated oxygen. The rocket is light and needs no drag-inducing air intake, but the fuel is less efficient than jet fuel and you thus have to carry a substantially heavier load. This means that at its maximum speed, when it needs to be heavy and stable, your car is getting lighter as the fuel load decreases. Hydrogen peroxide is not always easy to obtain.

The turbojet is heavier because it has many more moving parts, but that weight can be used to enhance stability. Jet engines are easier to source, and they are cheaper. The military sell them off when they are no longer needed.

The simplest engine of them all was the Rolls-Royce Derwent. It was an old-fashioned centrifugal jet, which meant that it had quite a fat girth, but it fulfilled my requirement that I should sit just ahead of the engine. I thought that would help the weight distribution and dynamics of the car, while keeping me clear of the air intake so there wouldn't be any danger of getting sucked in at high speed. The best model was the mark nine, which was almost unobtainable, but the mark eight was available because the RAF were throwing them out in large numbers. I started off at the RAF Museum in Hendon, where you can get all the manuals on these engines, and by just talking to a number of people, in particular a family friend who collects vintage cars and aero engines. I'd studied all these engines, so I had a good basic knowledge of their design and layout.

The problem is that these engines cost a fortune to develop and you can't just turn up and buy them across a counter. So how were we going to get hold of one?

My contacts eventually pointed me towards a place called Portsmouth Marine Salvage. So I went down there and met this wonderful bloke Fred Lewis, who had got about thirty of these Derwents. They were literally just sitting on the ground in his yard. I spent an afternoon checking them all, and I found a really nice one. It had only a few hours' running time on it, which meant it had plenty of service life left. This was very rare, because most jet engines come up for disposal only when they are life expired. With this one went what was probably the only good jet pipe left in the country.

I said, 'Fred, I've got to have that one.' And eventually he came down to £200 for it. He started off a lot higher, but I just kept on at him. With 3,500 pounds of thrust, I thought that wasn't bad horsepower for the money!

'But you've got to understand, Richard,' he said, 'the French Government is coming the day after tomorrow because they fly in the Pacific around the nuclear atolls. Their Gloster Meteors use the Derwent, and they are my best customers. I can't possibly have a situation where that engine is sitting here, because of course they'll want it. And because they are such a good customer I can't possibly tell them it's earmarked for somebody else.'

We went back down there with a truck the next day, craned the Derwent on board, and escaped with it to London. The French never knew what they'd missed! But we still needed a vital component. We had a good engine and a good jet pipe, but we lacked the 'hot' section that joined the two, which goes on the back of the engine's turbine. I'd taken a flier on being able to find one. Without that part, there was no way we could ever run the Derwent.

The thing is, if you're doing this sort of thing on a limited budget, all you can hope to get are the ex-military bits, because you could never afford to buy them new, even supposing that anyone would actually sell them to you. I went up to RAF Stafford at Stone and found a good one there, but the guy in charge said, 'I'm terribly sorry, but this thing is worth fifteen thousand quid. That's what the government paid for it, and that's what you're going to have to pay.'

He wouldn't budge and we seemed to have reached a horrible impasse, but eventually I managed a bit of persuasion. I don't know how he did it, but with Fred Lewis's connivance we swung things round, and suddenly the hot-end exhaust unit was delivered to Portsmouth Marine Salvage, and we got it for an awful lot less than fifteen grand!

In those days RAF Kemble was flying a display Meteor and I needed to check out its systems, so I went down there and started to chat people up. Before long I'd got a fuel pump, but I still lacked the starter panel. This was a great big tray with a whole lot of electronically wound-up clocks on it, and various other bits and pieces. Without one I wouldn't be able to start the engine. I tracked one of these down at Kemble, but then I looked at it and thought, How the hell do I wire all this up? It was an absolute nightmare.

I looked at the manual and went through the wiring diagrams, and I still couldn't understand it. I was terrified, because there was every chance I'd go and mess things up if I continued trying to do it myself. So I went to Lucas Aerospace, and we actually found the guy who designed the panel, a splendid old character, long retired. 'Good God!' he said. 'I designed that in 1940-something.' And after he'd explained I could then see what I had to do and was able to start to wire it all up.

I designed *Thrust1* on Formula One racing-car principles, but as I was to find out, cars that go fast in straight lines and cars that go round corners very quickly do not necessarily have the same technical requirements! It was not the only lesson we'd learn along the way.

Of course my background had nothing to do with engineering, but I knew I had to do all of that myself. Fortunately I'd learned to weld when I was on the nightshift in Freddy Strasser's factory on City Road, and that helped. But *Thrust1* was built to a very poor standard. It was desperately primitive. It was all my design and it was terribly wrong. I didn't know what the hell I was doing!

It was a dreadful car, in retrospect. A cross between a go-kart on steroids and a cathedral on wheels. But the level of technology we could employ was entirely dependent on the finance we could raise.

The next problem was how to make a chassis to take the engine. I was still working for GKN at that stage, and one day I was prowling round the Sankey works at Telford. The works manager was with me on a sort of guided tour, but I didn't see anything that took my fancy until we came back via the research and development department. And there I saw this ladder-type chassis. I blurted out, 'That would be absolutely ideal for the project.' He looked at me, and then he looked at the chassis and said, 'But we couldn't possibly let you have that; it was part of an experimental project. It's a one-off. It cost a fortune to make.'

And then he looked at the chassis again when I said, 'It's about eighteen inches too long for what we want . . .'

All of a sudden his expression brightened. He called over one of the welders who was working near by, and promptly told him to burn eighteen inches off. When the work was done, he turned with a triumphant beam on his face and said, 'You can have it now – it's damaged!' So now we had a chassis to go with the engine.

Gradually everything came together. By now I was export manager at GKN Floors in Maidenhead. I spent my working life travelling all over the world, particularly to South-east Asia, sometimes to Russia, sometimes to Africa. The great thing was that my bosses at GKN were very understanding. When it came to *Thrust* they said, 'Fine, Richard. So long as your sales are all right, we're quite happy for you to use the phone to progress your hobby.' Quite extraordinary!

On the days when I wasn't having to travel abroad I'd try to come home by about half-past six, seven o'clock in the evening, pull on the overalls and get into the garage to start work on the car again.

The major design consideration centred on avoiding positive lift at the nose. I was all too aware of the dangers of excessive lift. Everyone must have seen the footage of Donald Campbell's somersault on Coniston Water when Bluebird crashed in 1967. The last thing I wanted was for air to get underneath *Thrust1* and to flip it over. That's every record-seeker's abiding fear.

Thrust1 had considerable power: 3,500 pounds of thrust. It had the potential to do 180 m.p.h. on only 25 per cent throttle. Lift is a function of the square of air speed, and the car weighed only 2,000 pounds, so I knew that any high lifting moment at the nose could easily result in the whole thing taking off. The problem is exacerbated with a jet, because the thrust maintains its impetus even if the wheels leave the ground. I fitted big nose wings, like a Formula One car would have, to generate negative lift and to keep the nose down.

None of this was remotely scientific, however. It was all done by eye. But I wanted to be sensible about it all, so the next big hurdle was to get *Thrust1* wind-tunnel tested. Fortunately I managed to get a scale model assessed by what was then BAC (now British Aerospace) in Filton.

Ever since, as a twenty-year-old, I first saw the television footage of Donald Campbell's fatal accident on Coniston Water, I was always concerned about the dangers of aerodynamic lift.

Initially they said the front section of the car would probably generate some lift, until they examined the drawings I'd done, and then they said it probably wouldn't, but that you could never be too sure. They offered to do some tests for £400. I said, 'I'm very sorry, but that's forty per cent of our budget. There's no way I can spend that sort of money. I'll just have to try it and see.' Eventually they were very kind and said they could probably do something for £100, but I still had to turn them down. 'I'm sorry, but we're building *Thrust1* on an absolute shoestring and I don't think I can afford even that.'

But they were still keen to help, and I could see I had their interest. Three or four days later the phone rang: a rare opportunity had arisen. I had nine days to get a wind-tunnel model ready. They told me that if I could do that, then they'd run some tests for nothing. Getting that sort of model built in such a short time is a real hassle, but we made it. And we turned another crucial corner. If we'd had to pay a penny, we literally couldn't have afforded to do it. All the way through we were begging for everything. I even managed to persuade the bank, Williams & Glyn's, to buy an ad on the side of the car for a hundred quid. But things were always very precarious financially. That story would have a very familiar ring to it over the ensuing years. I started to assemble *Thrust1* when I had a flat in Thames Ditton, but then we had to move the car to a lock-up garage near Turnham Green when I moved to another flat in Stamford Brook.

There was a wonderful day when we pulled it out of the garage in Thames Ditton and towed it across London at about six o'clock in the morning, to avoid the traffic. We didn't have a trailer, of course, so there we were with this creation rolling on its own wheels, roped to my GKN company car, a Ford Cortina. And of course I was stopped by this copper. 'What in God's name is that?' he asked, appalled.

So I explained what we were doing. 'Well,' he said, 'it's very early in the morning, there isn't much traffic around, and if I were you I'd get on with it. But three things: first of all you never saw me and you never took my number. Second, get there as quickly as you can. And third, for God's sake don't fire it up on the way!'

We finished it off at Turnham Green, and then came the day when we wheeled it outside. I'd been carrying out checks on the ignition and could get the torch igniters going and so on, but I had no intention of actually getting it running there and then. What I did was press the button. All the clocks whirred and the engine began to wind itself up to a scream. It was a great moment. It also woke up the whole of Turnham Green.

At this time, 1975, the land-speed record stood at 622.407 m.p.h. to the Californian Gary Gabelich, who had driven a beautiful pencil-slim rocket-powered car called *Blue Flame* on the Bonneville Salt Flats in October 1970. Now there were two nascent projects in England that aspired to challenge that. There was ours, and there was also a bloke called Barry Bowles in North London who had built a rocket-powered dragster which he called the *Blonde*

Gary Gabelich's car, Blue Flame, at Bonneville in October 1970.

Bombshell. Like me, he intended it to be the forerunner to something more serious. Both of us had our eye on the land-speed record set in Britain, which at that point still stood to Sir Malcolm Campbell at the 174.883 m.p.h. he had achieved in *Bluebird* on Pendine Sands on 4 February 1927. Because *Thrust1* was so terribly basic, I think a lot of people gave Barry a lot more credibility than they gave us, and he had every right to it. *Blonde Bombshell* was well made and had some very professional help. Comparison emphasized the crudeness of *Thrust1*, but there was no time to worry about such niceties. We had to get some experience. It simply wasn't any good talking about it, we just had to do it.

So we took *Thrust1* down to RAF St Athan in South Wales for its first serious test run. I had discovered that Sergeant Jim Matthews, who was the last specialist on the Derwent engine, was stationed there. He took a look at what we had done and initially he was very sceptical, but after a bit of reflection, and much to my relief, he thawed a bit and said, 'Yeah, it's gonna work. It's gonna work.' He told me I'd got a couple of small technical things wrong, but then added more cheerfully, 'We'll soon put them right.' And we fixed them there and then.

Later that afternoon we were ready to fire up our Derwent for the first time, for its initial static test. We tethered *Thrust1* down, and Jim said, 'Right, Richard. Off you go!' I was anxious about this. If you operated the high-pressure fuel cock incorrectly on the Derwent you could generate a lot of resonance, which could damage the engine. 'Well, look, hang on,' I said, 'I've never done this before. I don't want to wreck it . . .' But Jim just said, 'No, you built this damn thing. You're the one that's going to be sitting in it when we fire it up!' So that's what we did.

It was a wonderful moment when it lit up. Terrific. Absolutely wonderful! After all that effort it felt as if we were really making progress. I had rigged things up so that the high- and low-pressure fuel cocks were operated by simple Bowden outboard-motor cable controls, and everything seemed to work well. I was absolutely elated.

The BBC programme *Tomorrow's World* had come down to film us, at the start of what was to turn into a very enjoyable and rewarding relationship that has lasted right through to the present day. Raymond Baxter made a very interesting comment: 'This is the start of a land-speed-record project.' I had never actually said that; I hadn't got the guts to say such a thing at that stage, even if it was precisely what I had in the back of my mind. It was just never something I would say outright. But that's what Ray said, because he'd figured it out.

The same afternoon we ran it up and down the runway at St Athan. We didn't go very fast, probably 70 or 80 m.p.h. No faster than a family car, really. It was

In comparison with the American jet cars, Thrust1 was laughably crude, but I simply had to start somewhere.

just a shakedown run to make sure that everything worked properly and that nothing was in imminent danger of falling off. But it all convinced me that I'd done the right thing. I'll never forget the feeling when I sat in the open cockpit and saw the revs rising. Then I eased the high-pressure fuel cock open, and suddenly there was this bloody great whoomph as she lit up, and then we were away. We were on 40 per cent idle and cruised up and down to get the feel of things. It didn't feel at all quick at that stage, and I'm sure *Thrust1* was one of those peculiar creations you could only dare to drive because you'd built it yourself. But from that moment I was totally hooked!

Our subsequent runs were made with greater and greater power, as we learned how to go much more quickly. On one memorable occasion I actually drove the thing round Brands Hatch. A film crew followed me round the long circuit in a Range Rover. I nearly blew them off the road! I used a bit too much power when they were following me through Paddock Bend as I started to accelerate up the hill to the Druids hairpin, and they got caught in the jet blast. The trouble is that on a circuit a turbojet engine has even more throttle lag than a turbocharged piston unit, so it was very difficult to judge things properly. The guys in the Range Rover told me later they'd had trouble breathing at one point.

Shortly after this I did something much more sensible. Sally was simply far too good to pass up. We'd known each other for four happy years, and I'd come to admire and respect her enormously. We were married on 30 July 1976. We bought a house in Rivermeads Avenue, Twickenham. I don't think Sally liked it that much – but it did have a double garage!

Back in the mechanical world, I'd had a problem routing the steering linkage on *Thrust1*, which had always bugged me because it meant the ground clearance was far too high. So over that winter we set about a complete rebuild. We reduced the ground clearance by three inches, which made the car look much better. And we fitted servo brakes, which meant that I could hold more engine power against the brakes prior to a run without *Thrust1* sliding forward so much.

The next thing was to sort out permission to run *Thrust1* at RAF Fairford down in Gloucester, which has a useful long runway. That was pretty difficult because it was an operational base. Perhaps I should have taken that as an omen.

The Property Services Agency was the government department responsible for granting such permission, so I phoned the Bristol office to discuss things with the superintendent, Tim LaPage-Norris.

'It normally takes us five to six months to process licence applications,' he told us.

'Really?' I said. 'Well, what does the licence look like?'

'Oh,' he said, 'it's your application form with a stamp on it.'

I sensed that my plans were going to get bogged down in bureaucracy, so I stressed the need to move as quickly as possible. 'I've got to run this thing next Tuesday,' I said. 'I'll deliver all these papers and they'll be on your desk at four in the morning.' He chuckled sceptically.

Then he told me I'd also need insurance cover up to a million pounds.

I got all the papers together and delivered them to the night-security man in Bristol at four o'clock in the morning, as promised. I rang Tim from work in London at around half-past nine to check he'd got them, and he said, 'Well done! I didn't believe you'd do it. But I think we can let you have your licence.' And we got it. Tim appreciated our predicament and responded quickly, which was great.

But things were about to go horribly wrong.

I'd seen plenty of film on the land-speed record, and read all the books, so I knew all about the dangers and the men who'd been killed trying to break it. But the whole tenor of *Thrust1* was happy-go-lucky. After fighting our way through Africa, and dealing with danger as a team, I didn't really give any of that much thought. I guess it was just personally important to me to get on and do it, which sounds terribly selfish, but I couldn't help that. I was struggling to achieve something, and this record thing just wouldn't go away. It had got to the point where I'd rationalized it by saying, 'OK, suppose I get to drive something at three hundred m.p.h. at Bonneville. Wouldn't that be fantastic? Somewhere along the line I'm going to settle down, and at least I'll be able to say, "Look what I achieved."'

One of the things that I'd always been really concerned about was that in due course I was going to have a family, and if I had a son he was going to say, 'Daddy, what did you do with your life?'

I was intensely proud of what Father had done in the war. He was wounded twice and he got the Military Cross. I was terribly aware that I wasn't going to be able to say much. 'Well, I sold some man-made fibres and concrete floors' wasn't on the same plane. I also wanted to be able to instil in my family the excitement of life, and the thrill of going out and discovering what you can really do with it, not hiding away in some great big corporation.

I think it was Donald Campbell who once said to his father, Sir Malcolm, 'But, Dad, you had the war.' Whether the fathers had wanted the war or not, they were part of it, and those who survived felt they'd achieved something. And their sons would ask themselves, 'Now, what's *my* challenge going to be?'

My immediate challenge was to drive *Thrust1* quickly at Fairford on 7 March 1977, the day after my thirty-first birthday. The weather conditions were wicked, and I hadn't had much sleep because of the hours spent preparing the car. The record-breaker's perpetual complaint! There had also been a mix-up over who was going to tow it to Fairford. It took us until three o'clock in the morning to locate a tow vehicle.

The Thrust1 story came to an inelegant end at RAF Fairford on 7 March 1977. Thrust1 completed an involuntary triple airborne roll when a wheel bearing seized at 140 m.p.h.

Anyhow, we got it lit up, and did one westerly run down the runway at about 180 m.p.h. despite a severe crosswind. That felt absolutely fantastic. I got a real sense of high velocity, especially with the open cockpit and the wind rasping past my head. At the end of the run I turned *Thrust1* round, ready for another go.

The plan this time was not to start gently, as we'd always done before, but to hold as much power as possible against the brakes, then release them suddenly and do a dragster start to around 140 m.p.h. Afterwards I'd coast for the remainder of the 10,000-foot runway.

The start went well, but at around 140 m.p.h. I suddenly lost control of *Thrust1*. There was no warning, it just went. It was a fearsome feeling. It wasn't an ordinary car, and I had no motor-racing experience, and suddenly here was a situation where it just went sideways and then *crash!* Over and over and over! It finally came to rest upside down after a triple airborne roll.

I was grateful in the end for the Derwent's tremendous girth, because that had acted like a giant roll-over hoop and taken all the bang. I was left hanging in my seat-belt straps. We discovered subsequently that a rear wheel bearing had seized, throwing the car out of control.

And that was that. In those few frantic seconds of drama *Thrust1* had been reduced to a pile of scrap.

OTHER VOICES

SALLY NOBLE

'Richard went charging up the runway and was almost out of sight when we saw something happen. I could see a lot of what I thought was smoke, and I panicked when the fire engine took off.

'Then, long before we finally got to the accident scene, I could see Richard getting out and walking about, so I knew that he was OK.

'Later one of the firemen said to me, "You shouldn't worry, Mrs Noble. We knew it wasn't anything serious. If it was black smoke, then we would have hurried, because that's fire. What you saw was just vapour."'

My wife, Sally, was one of the first to offer a hug of consolation as we surveyed the wreckage. That same evening I decided to push ahead with Thrust2.

4 'WANTED: 650 M.P.H. CAR DESIGNER'

What do you do when you've just rolled upside down along an airfield runway at 140 m.p.h.? When the machine into which you have invested so much effort and ingenuity during the last few years lies smashed and broken?

We did the only thing left open to us: we went to the pub.

We loaded *Thrust1* onto the trailer and headed for the most convenient hostelry to drown our sorrows. It helped. After a few pints we decided to sell the remains. I didn't want a corpse lying around.

I had taken another, far more significant decision. There was no point in hanging about looking glum. Nor were we going to stop just because of an accident; after all, nobody had been hurt. I decided to push right ahead with the second stage of the project. It was time to start *Thrust2*.

That decision was the best thing to come from an awful day, but there was another consolation, too. In any accident your greatest fear is fire, which is why it was so important for me to shut down the engine. To do this, all I had to do was move the outboard-motor control back. What pleased me was that I'd had the presence of mind to think of such a thing while *Thrust1* was beginning its first airborne roll. I was gratified that I'd been thinking clearly during all the drama, and that I hadn't panicked. With these attempts you start off and somewhere along the line you come to a moment of truth. Sometimes lots of them. There had been plenty while building *Thrust1*, but this was my first real one as a driver. I'd had a crisis, and I'd reacted acceptably. I still wanted to continue. It was something very positive to build on.

I don't suppose we'd spent much more than £1,500 on *Thrust1*, and we'd started the project with the £1,100 I'd got from selling my TR6. Now we stopped off at a scrap dealer in Feltham, just up the road from home, and sold him the wreckage. He gave me 175 quid for it. It worried me that a dreamy look came into the dealer's eyes, and that he started mumbling about getting *Thrust1* going again. So I took his money and made damned sure we removed sufficient parts to discourage any ambition he might be harbouring to set up as a land-speed rival!

Back in the mid-1960s, vehicles such as Craig Breedlove's Spirit of America and Art Arfons's dramatic Green Monster (inset, with parachute) had pushed the land-speed record from 400 to 600 m.p.h. in less than two years.

I knew I needed a completely different engineering approach this time. I would need a proper designer, for a start. But until we found one I based sketches for a new car around a British engine, and the concept Art Arfons had employed in his *Green Monster* jet car. In 1964 and 1965 Arfons had set the land-speed record three times in a gripping duel with Bonneville rival Craig Breedlove. Breedlove's *Spirit of America* three-wheeler had crashed into a brine lake when he lost his braking parachutes on a run at well over 500 m.p.h. in October 1964, and for 1965 he'd built a new four-wheeler. This was a long, Coke-bottle-shaped car, where the driver sat ahead of the engine, *Thrust1* style. That was an option open to us, but I preferred Arfons's concept of a simple air intake for the engine, with the driver sitting alongside it, midway down its length. It was safer because you could build a shorter, stronger structure, and positioning the driver over the centre of gravity helped you to 'feel' the car. This layout would be easier to build and transport. We opted for right-hand drive, however.

This layout also held the attraction of including a passenger seat on the other side of the engine. Building credibility and awareness of what we were trying to do was going to be crucial, and taking journalists, sponsors and other passengers for a high-speed ride seemed an eminently sensible way of going about this.

There was nothing left of *Thrust1*, so we needed an engine. Shortly after the accident at Fairford I met Air Commodore Paddy Hine, later Air Chief Marshal Sir Patrick Hine. Back then he was director of public relations for the RAF. I approached him cold, and explained what was needed. He set up a meeting at Adastral House, in Whitehall. I found myself in the small cinema in the basement. I showed Paddy's group of RAF brass some footage of *Thrust1* and Gabelich's *Blue Flame*, and explained what the new project was all about. They were very enthusiastic, and at the end one of them said, 'OK, Richard, we'd like to help you. What do you want?' I told him, 'I need a Lightning.'

This was the fighter aircraft built in the 1950s by English Electric, and later BAC; I knew the RAF was taking them out of service and breaking them up. It was powered by two Rolls-Royce Avon 210 turbojet engines, each with around 15,000 pounds of thrust – four times more powerful than *Thrust1*'s old Derwent. Once the RAF chaps had recovered from their initial shock, they said yes. I was thus able to buy an Avon from the Ministry of Defence, which was once again sourced from our friends at RAF Stafford. I borrowed the money to buy it, around £2,000. I found a Lightning, too, in a scrapyard at Stone, and we stripped it for valuable systems. All this was done within three months of the crash at Fairford, which further demonstrated our seriousness.

There was a wonderful day when the Avon engine was delivered to Rivermeads Avenue. It was nearly 27 feet long, but by splitting it where the tailpipe joined the main engine we were able to accommodate it.

Not everyone shared our gung-ho enthusiasm. My bank manager of the time told me I should be more responsible, sell insurance, and look after my wife and family. A senior RAC official said to me, 'Donald

With just a few flying hours left, the Rolls-Royce Avon 210 turbojet engine from a Lightning aircraft arrives at our house in Twickenham.

Campbell spent so much of the gross domestic product on Bluebird that British industry will never support such a thing again. Don't bang your head against a brick wall.'

I told them both that they were wrong, and that I was going to prove they were wrong.

My cleaned-up sketch of Arfons's basic design was a squarer version with a great big shark-fin tail, a huge aerofoil at the front and four front wheels; at the time Tyrrell was using something similar in Formula One. We had to start somewhere, and it was important that we had something to show people, even if the real car ended up looking different. But there was no way I had the skill actually to design anything; *Thrust1* had convinced me of that. So now it was time to find a designer.

Very often the best way to solve a problem is the most direct. We couldn't afford to advertise, so we issued a devastatingly simple press release to a number of newspapers and magazines: 'Wanted: 650 m.p.h. car designer.' This fabulous ruse was run all over the place, particularly in the *Daily Telegraph*, and brought a terrific response. We listed all the major companies who had been kind enough to help with *Thrust1*. For instance, Lucas had given us a switch and 12 feet of starter cable, and were listed as a major sponsor!

I was now working for GKN Mills, the parent company of GKN Floors, and as luck would have it I was sent abroad on business for six weeks. When I got back I found there had been some increasingly irate calls from a guy called John Ackroyd, who said, 'I applied for this job and haven't heard anything. What sort of organization is this?'

John and I arranged to meet the next day, and we immediately got on very well. Some very experienced and expensive people had applied, but when I explained that we were just at the starting point and had no money, they just went away. But Ackers was very keen to do it. The next stage was to give him the number of Ken Norris, the designer of Donald Campbell's *Bluebird K7* hydroplane and *CN7* car, and the godfather of British record-breaking. Ken had agreed to vet suitable applicants, and I asked Ackers to go and see him. The next morning I called Ken to tell him that I had given Ackers his number, only to find that Ackers was already there! It was confirmation of Ackers's enthusiasm, and I knew we'd found our man.

The complication was that I couldn't yet pay John, so when he was offered a job with Porsche in Germany I told him to take it. So he did, and he was very pleased because Porsche had this big library that he promptly raided for

My early sketches for Thrust2 were fairly primitive. Like Art Arfons I preferred a layout with the engine forming the length of the car, and two cockpits mounted either side.

information on land-speed record cars. I finally found sufficient money to pay him by March 1978, and when the crucial moment came for him to start, John, being John, just got straight on with it. The first thing he did was to change my rather naïve sketch into something meaningful. He, too, favoured Arfons's concept, but he cleaned it all up and then began drawing out the chassis, which would be a big tubular steel spaceframe.

By then we had leapt another hurdle. Shortly after the meeting with the RAF, David Benson from the *Daily Express* phoned. 'I was a great friend of Donald Campbell,' he said. 'I'd love to find out what you guys are doing.' We met and talked about it all. 'I think you guys have got what it takes,' he said. 'Would a stand at the Earl's Court Motorfair help?'

It certainly would. At a stroke we could put our story in front of people, and we might actually make some money out of it. The *Express* agreed to provide us with the stand space on the first floor of Earl's Court, and we went for the biggest we possibly could because of the length of the Avon engine – 1,000 square feet. George Myers designed the stand around a GKN scaffolding structure, but we had no idea who was going to pay for all the extras. We had the space, but we still had to build something on it, and we set out to do this to a very high standard. The bill for photography alone was 1,000 quid.

GKN Mills generously agreed to provide the structure, and we sold adverts alongside the stand to try to finance the rest. Companies such as Castrol, TI Group and Cadulac Chemicals came in, but it was tough selling ad space for a virtually non-existent project.

A guy called Jim Pople from Thames Television was a great believer in the project; he managed to get Thames and ITN to agree to film the stand as part of their Motorfair coverage, and after that companies started to pile in and buy panels at 200 quid a time. We needed every penny; the whole thing cost around £5,000. But it would be money well spent, I knew that. We had to get the message across. And we had only one shot.

I obtained a copy of a wonderful film by Tony Maylam called *The Fastest Man on Earth* from Cygnet Communications in Bushey, and we ran that non-stop on our stand cinema. We had an enormous amplifier, and we turned up the sound to such a level that we started getting complaints from the military band downstairs that they couldn't hear themselves play!

Everyone was going round this rather sombre Motorfair, and upstairs was all this roaring noise, explosions, screams and American voices. Out of sheer curiosity people just flooded up there – about 35,000 of them over the course of the show. We realized how terribly important it was to share our dream, and we had started a supporters' club as a way of encouraging members of the public to get involved with Project *Thrust*. At the Motorfair we sold something like 1,000 memberships at a pound each and probably generated about another £4,000 selling ad space, so we just about broke even; but much more important, the plan to spread the word had succeeded beyond our wildest dreams. The Motorfair also led directly to a long-standing relationship with Tube Investments. We had been contacted by Tony Newbold, director of publicity for TI Reynolds, famous for its 531 bicycle-frame tubing. He had made an appointment to come and see us at around four o'clock, but he turned up at midday with a posse of public relations people. I could see he was seriously interested, but there was a real danger of losing him. I needed to make our point strongly, so I said quickly, 'Come and have some lunch.' We took all these people out to lunch and had a good talk. Lunch cost 65 quid, and that was literally our last 65 quid. We were bust at that point. But Tony enjoyed his lunch, and he phoned me to say that they would build the frame for us. That was fantastic. We had an engine; now we were going to have a chassis. Things were really starting to move.

I knew that we had to raise public awareness of Project Thrust. When the Daily Express offered free space at the London Motorfair in October 1977, I grabbed the chance. It was one hell of a struggle, but our gamble paid off handsomely. As a direct result, Tube Investments agreed to build the Thrust2 spaceframe.

It was a hell of a commitment by TI, because they were doing this frame for a project that really had nothing else to it other than the jet engine and a whole lot of people saying, 'Yeah, we'll do it.'

They put a fellow called Ken Sprayson on to the project; he was a real ace, with vast experience building racing motorcycle frames. He got going straight away, but the chassis took three long months to build. People at TI began asking all sorts of questions about it: was the project really going to happen? Had they wasted time and money? Ken had to endure a lot of aggro, but eventually the chassis was finished, and the engine was test mounted. That was a great moment. We really were on our way.

John Ackroyd came from the Isle of Wight, and by taking him on as designer we were instantly able to plug into the island's incredible infrastructure of engineering skills and resources. He reasoned that what we needed were skilled people with low overheads, and to do that we could use all of his friends on the island as subcontractors. I realized very quickly that Ackers had access to the whole thing. So we set up shop in the decrepit but cheap Ranalagh Works in Fishbourne, on the banks of the Wootton Creek.

Frankly, it was an appalling situation for Ackers, because he was effectively on his own. He was working in the kitchen of a derelict house, and he stuck at it for ten solid months. It called for tremendous will-power to keep going under those circumstances. He didn't even have a telephone; he had to hoard his coins and use the public phone box. I don't know many people who would have stood that.

How do you find someone to design a 650 m.p.h. car? I simply advertised via a press release, and we were fantastically fortunate that John Ackroyd applied. Despite his amazing talent as a designer, John was prepared to work alone in spartan conditions on the Isle of Wight, because that was all we could afford. He always joked that his Hercules bicycle was his company car.

OTHER VOICES

JOHN ACKROYD

'There were certainly no mod cons down at Fishbourne. I used to tell my friends that my trusty old Hercules push-bike was my company car!

'If I wanted to get to the nearest pay phone I had to go by a devious route that took me across Wootton Creek. If I'd slipped it would have been a very wet walk. The nearest photocopier was a six-mile ride, and if I wanted drawings printed it was a fourteen-mile hike to East Cowes.

'They were interesting days, back then. I worked in that kitchen for the best part of a year, and in that time I hardly saw anybody else during the day. It got so that I began to look forward to Richard turning up with a potential sponsor in tow, just to have somebody to talk to. It was good to be able to ride from home to work each day, but sometimes, when I was sitting alone at the drawing board, I did wonder if I wasn't turning into some sort of nutter.'

By April 1978 we'd landed our first sponsors. Fulmen Batteries from Aldershot had come in with 1,000 quid, and Loctite came in with 5,000, so on the financial side things were moving quickly. But it wasn't until we got the frame and engine down to the island that I really started to appreciate the sheer scale of what needed to be done on the construction side. We'd got one guy, John, drawing away furiously, and another, Ron Benton, making parts. Ron was an absolute craftsman, who had been involved in almost every major project from the hovercraft to the *Queen Elizabeth II* Atlantic liner, and he was a real master of his art, but the reality was that it was going to take us a hundred years like this. Not only had we got to do the car, but we'd got to build up a whole workshop at the same time.

It was around spring 1979 that Eddie Elsom appeared. Eddie lived on the island and applied for the job as second draughtsman to help John, but he soon sussed that we didn't actually need

Early low-speed wind-tunnel tests at BAC Fitton had given us the confidence to go ahead with Thrust2, knowing that we might just have a chance to run for the world land-speed record.

By 1980 Thrust2 was taking definite shape in the Ranalagh Works at Fishbourne, on the Isle of Wight.

another draughtsman; what we needed was somebody to organize things. He was right, and he became our operations director. The first thing he did was to build a wall round the workshop, then install proper electrics. Before long we had much slicker-looking premises. Later on Gordon Flux came in as chief mechanic to make his own tremendous contribution.

We had set things up so that John could go out and spend what he needed on the project. He's a very sensible, practical bloke, and very tough on pricing. My job was to keep the cash coming in to fund him. It wasn't a cash-driven project, it was progress-driven.

I was in a hell of a situation now, because I couldn't get free from work and the project was growing every week. The fundamental problem was that every time I'd get some more money in it was gone. It went on the suspension, or on an electrical wiring system for the car, or whatever Gordon, Ron and co. needed to make or buy next. The project was simply eating money as the build proceeded. It was an absolute nightmare, because, of course, while I was trying to find money

I was still having to do my everyday job. I went to the GKN board twice for some financial support, but they just weren't interested. One of the reasons I'd joined GKN was because 60 per cent of their group revenue actually came from the automotive sector, and I felt they had to be interested. So much for the Trojan horse approach; it just wasn't going to happen.

Then, towards the end of 1979, we got Initial Services, the industrial towelling company, involved as a sponsor. That was really something, because they came in with £20,000. One of the first things that John had done was to build the seat, because it gave him a good feel for the size of the cockpit. *Tomorrow's World* had filmed the seat being moulded round me, and as a result somebody from Initial Services in Leeds rang up and said, 'We'd like to be a part of this. It sounds like a good thing.' I sent them some information, then heard nothing more. But they passed my response on to Tony Waring, at their head office in London's Gosling Road. Tony also thought it was a good idea, and from that moment on the deal got going.

This was simply terrific. For the first time we had some serious money. That November we thought we'd had another huge slice of luck. BP had apparently decided that it was going to sponsor a record attempt. There were two projects up for it: *Thrust*, and a bloke called John Terry, who claimed to have permission from Tonia Campbell to use the *Bluebird* name again on a record-breaking speedboat.

Suddenly we had an opportunity to snare a main sponsor, and to solve all our financial difficulties in one hit. John Terry got in first and was kind enough to call me shortly afterwards. 'Well done, Richard,' he said, 'you've got it.' I asked, 'What do you mean?' He said, 'We've been in and made our proposal, and we've been told no. They said they're going elsewhere, so I think you guys have got it.'

It seemed too good to be true.

5 BITING THE BULLETS

Shortly after my conversation with John Terry, I was invited to an expensive lunch at BP's headquarters in Victoria. I could feel terrific vibrations about the whole thing. We were talking about a chunk of money – £75,000 – and I came away from the lunch with a really warm feeling. This was it!

What happened afterwards was that for some reason or another the deal just wouldn't go. Later on I discovered that BP had started to shed people, and therefore decided that they couldn't go ahead after all. Meanwhile, I was absolutely frantic. I had given up all the other sponsorship prospects I'd embarked upon, because there is only so much effort you can put into it, particularly when you're doing a day job as well. I had concentrated exclusively on BP. Anything they wanted, I agreed to. I changed anything in our proposal to suit their requirements. 'Yes, of course we can accommodate you on this.'

I was racing round during lunch hours at GKN. I'd be in my car haring back to Victoria in order to deliver this, that and the other, giving it everything I'd got.

Early in the New Year BP said no. Well, actually they did the usual big company thing, which is to do nothing. It suddenly felt like they were playing with us. They'd been serious at first, but big company politics seemed to have got in the way. I was absolutely livid. I'd wasted months. We'd only got enough money left for three weeks' more production. In desperation I even borrowed money from Father, anything just to keep it going. It's amazing what you can do, but the chance of bringing in another major sponsor in the time remaining was almost nil.

I now had to take stock of the harsh reality of the situation, which was that we were going to run out of money. But though I didn't know how the hell we were going to keep going, I knew that somehow we had to. The problem with these projects is that if you stop you've lost it, because the people working with you will then say, 'I've got to go. I'm sorry, but I can't be a hostage to fortune.' Once those people start going then all the learning goes, and with it all the momentum. It's terribly hard to get it back.

It was disaster time, so in February I got hold of all the sponsors and asked them to come to a major meeting at the Horseguards Hotel in London, where I managed to cadge a room. I sat them all down and took them through where we'd got to and how we were getting on.

I said, 'There you are, that's the situation. Now we've really got through the worst, we've got the suspension done, we've almost got the car together and we're going to run it in May. Somehow we've just got to bridge this gap between now and May.'

I told them that the cash requirement was £40,000. There was an appalling silence.

And then they all walked out!

It was absolutely awful. Probably the nicest of them all was the director from Fulmen who said, 'Richard, I can't support anything like this, we're only a tiny battery company. But we gave you a thousand pounds to get started, so here's another five hundred. That's it.'

There I was, with Loctite, Initial Services, TI, the whole lot having apparently walked out or else given very good reasons why they couldn't help. It was disasterville.

A few days later I was asked to go and see Tony Waring. A team from Initial Services had visited the Isle of Wight without me being down there, to see for themselves how things were going and to make up their own minds what to do next. Now I handed Tony the books. 'Everything is here,' I said, 'you can check any figure you like.' He smiled. 'No, I'm not going to do that. I'm just going to let you know that we are doubling up now.' And he handed over a cheque for £20,000.

That was simply fantastic. It requires an enormous amount of guts for a sponsor to do that. It's not the amount of money, it's the commitment. It's the personal courage, something that's so often sadly missing. It was remarkable. Thanks to Tony Waring and his colleague Richard Chisnell the project marched on with a renewed surge of enthusiasm. Subsequently we were able to renew our relationships with Loctite and TI, too.

Not all of our deals worked out so well, as I'd discovered with British Airways. When we were starting the project, and when Tube Investments had just agreed to go ahead, British Airways had said they were interested in taking part. We'd come to some agreement, and we had British Airways logos on the first artworks and rough models of *Thrust2*, which created quite a stir on *Tomorrow's World*. We even had somebody senior calling from BA's Manchester office saying they didn't like seeing the model with the BA name on it.

I'd met two guys from British Airways publicity and they were very keen on the project. They could see that it fitted British Airways ideally. 'We'd really like to do this,' they said, 'but we've got a big problem because the shape of the tail fins of *Thrust2* basically won't fit our logo, and to change our logo we'd have to get board approval.'

So I said, 'You'll never get that. Why not change our tail fins?'

I rang John Ackroyd and said, 'Why don't we change the tail fins to a Boeing 747 tail fin?' and explained why, and John replied, 'Yes, we can do that, it's no problem.' So we agreed to change the shape of the two fins to accommodate the BA logo.

I told the British Airways guys, who then said, 'We have another major problem in that we can't actually give you any money. But what we can do is to refund British Airways tickets to a certain level.'

I was still working for GKN, so I persuaded all the senior staff in all the major GKN offices to fly British Airways. The way we set up the system, their secretaries would collect the used tickets from the directors and send them to me. British Airways would then reimburse *Thrust* on the used tickets. We had literally sacks of them. Nobody at GKN could believe that we could convert used tickets into cash, but it worked brilliantly.

That was a crucial stage of the project, and probably generated the best part of £5–6,000, which in those early days was a lot of money for us. We had Fulmen as the first sponsor, then Loctite, and then the British Airways deal. At this stage our involvement with Initial Services was still in the future.

Unfortunately, British Airways were always afraid of any publicity knock-on if anything happened to the car. There was corporate concern over the risk factor, and they eventually took a 'no risk' decision shortly after a brief association with the 1,000-kilometre sports car race that was staged annually at Brands Hatch in the late 1970s. This would lead to them withdrawing from the project.

When we came to the end of the contract I called the guys at British Airways and said, 'Look, I can get you plenty more tickets. I'm getting lots of GKN people to fly BA, so you're getting a direct benefit. And now it's spreading to other companies.' They'd had good publicity, too, because the model had been shown on *Tomorrow's World* with the logo on the tail fins. But when I turned up to renegotiate the contract the guys had gone; there'd been some sort of putsch overnight. I found myself upstairs with the manager. I'd just sat down when he said, 'Well, it's the end of the dangerous ones, Richard.'

There were photos all round the wall of him shaking hands with famous conductors, and he continued, 'I just wanted to tell you that that's the end of it, we're not going to do anything dangerous now. You've done jolly well, we've had great publicity. A very good deal and a very good return. But I'm sorry, from now on we're going to sponsor orchestras.'

Suddenly all the pictures clicked. I was really pissed off, because we'd worked seriously hard at this and the long-term idea had always been to bring in British Airways as a major sponsor. But this guy obviously liked orchestras, and that was that. I was so angry that I waggled my finger at him and said, 'You've got to give me ten days!' He just looked at me and said, 'But why, Richard? I'm turning you down. It's the end. Why do you want ten days?' I said, 'Because it'll take me that time to get an orchestra together!'

I'm afraid the British Airways fiasco just typified our problem. Sponsorships are often not properly established in the culture of a company. They're actually terribly important. They generate enormous publicity and they tell you what the company is about. There are so many messages that they can broadcast. So when people just disregard them I feel it's desperately unprofessional. But if you want to pursue this sort of career, you soon learn that such blinkered rejection is simply a hard fact of life.

John kept saying to me, 'Go on, just leave GKN.' And I would say, 'I can't do that, John, there isn't enough money to support us all.'

Things were approaching crunch point. As early as March 1980 I'd used up all my holiday for the year, and I was stealing days off. Desperation set in, because plans to run *Thrust2* for the first time were racing ahead and I would obviously need a lot of time off work. GKN Mills in Ealing had always been amazingly tolerant of my speed activities. There was one classic moment when I was using the phone in the office, trying to do this crucial deal on which the whole project depended. I'd been trying to reach the director concerned for days; now I was speaking to him and he was actually listening. I was trying to close the deal, and in walked Bill Orwin, the GKN Mills managing director. I couldn't just put the phone down. I couldn't do anything. I had to continue to get the deal through because it was so vitally important.

Bill walked over to the window and put his hands in his pockets and looked out, and eventually I closed the deal and put the phone down. I was red-faced, incredibly embarrassed. Bill said, 'How's it going, then?'

I stammered, 'Well, Bill, we're about to introduce steel scaffolding into Brunei, and the big job in Hong Kong looks as if it's going. The Russians want our steel stand system for the Moscow Olympics.'

He just gave a big smile. 'No, no, no, Richard. Not that crap! The car, the car! How's the project going?'

Despite such terrific encouragement, I knew the time was soon coming to do the decent thing. In May 1980 I wrote to Roy Roberts, who had just become GKN Group managing director. I told him the car was nearly ready to run; I was terribly sorry that I couldn't give him my contractual notice, but I simply had to go and drive it. I finished by saying that I hoped he wouldn't sue me for breaking our contract, and though I was grateful for everything I did think it was an awful shame that GKN wouldn't support the project financially. I slung the letter in the postbox, thinking all the time, What am I doing? But then it was gone, and it was too late to change my mind.

I got home and told Sally what I'd done, and she just said, 'Yes, that was the right thing to do.' It was a great relief, because by that time we had a young daughter to care for. Miranda had been born in 1979, and many spouses would have said I was utterly crazy to quit my job, if they had been capable of speech at all. But from the project's point of view it was the right thing to do, even though it seemed one hell of a gamble for a family man to throw in his job for a car that hadn't turned a wheel.

The funny thing is that I actually forgot about the letter. At the time I had so many problems, on so many fronts, I just fired it off and forgot about it. Instead I concentrated on organizing a static engine test at RAF Coningsby, scheduled for early July, and completing the final arrangements for the runs, which were scheduled to take place at the end of the month at Leconfield, just north of Humberside. It had been an active airbase, but was now an Army training centre run by Colonel Pat Reger. I'd been chasing all over the country trying to find somewhere to drive *Thrust2*. We wanted somewhere that had a nice long runway in case the brakes failed, and plenty of width and space. Operational bases such as RAF Fairford, where we had crashed *Thrust1*, didn't mind the odd weekend thing, but said no to the idea of a whole week or two of running. A dragstrip such as Santa Pod didn't offer us the sort of space we wanted. Nobody else was at all helpful. 'Christ, you can't run that thing on our runways,' was a typical response. But Reger was terrific. 'Bring it up,' he said. 'We'll have a lot of fun with it.'

In the middle of all this planning an extraordinary thing happened. I hadn't yet left GKN and there seemed to be a real *frisson* there as the letter I'd forgotten about went through the system. All sorts of things were happening, but I didn't seem to be part of them. Then suddenly there was a letter from Roy Roberts on my desk. It was addressed to me, but it had been opened. GKN was a very political organization in those days!

'Dear Richard,' it read, 'this is a fantastic achievement to get your car built and I think GKN should support it. I have reached agreement with your board that you will have eighteen months' paid leave of absence. Please make sure the GKN logo is on the car. Good luck to you and best wishes, Roy Roberts.'

That day I left GKN in twenty minutes. I never even cleared my desk.

Up at Leconfield, I now began to drive *Thrust2* for the first time. It was a tremendous shock. I had to battle with the car itself, within my limitations and the limitations of the venue and the unrealistic expectations of those around me.

By 1980 we had a partially completed car that could be used in demonstration runs at airfields up and down the country. After a shaky start, I found these 260-m.p.h. runs exhilarating.

We had quite a few military guys helping in the team, and they seemed to expect an enormous performance straight away. I seriously disappointed them. I was trundling along at what I initially thought was 70 m.p.h., but turned out to be 50 m.p.h. Everybody was getting too worked up and too excited, but with jet-powered cars you've got to start very, very slowly, and that is exactly what I was doing. Before long I was haring up the track at 180 m.p.h., but this continued to disappoint those who said, 'Come on, Richard, do two hundred!'

What we wanted more than anything was peace and quiet. We needed to get away from the media, the outside world, everything. We just wanted to do our own thing and learn about our new car. We were a commercial concern, we had to run this car, day in, day out. We had to develop it ourselves and get to grips with it.

We did all of that, but the trouble was that I found Leconfield seriously difficult and disorientating. There was a major intersection with traffic lights halfway down the runway, and for some reason we couldn't switch the traffic lights off. That didn't help. There was also a huge hump in the middle, and as you went up to it you couldn't see what was on the other side. I was driving blind at 180 m.p.h., and that, too, felt most uncomfortable. We were also bottoming the car and damaging its suspension on the runway.

Gradually we got faster and faster, and then we started using the afterburner. This is a device at the back end of the engine that injects neat fuel into the stream of exhaust gas. By igniting the unburned oxygen – a process known as reheat – it boosts the power significantly. We were learning, but continuing to pace ourselves. With a jet engine it's very easy to misjudge the amount of power you are using. The worst thing you can do is jump into a new vehicle and go too fast.

Off the track we lived very comfortably in the mess at Leconfield, where the food was marvellous. The Army does things like that very well. There was also a wonderful sort of culture there. The Padre was known affectionately as the Rectum, and Colonel Reger was known as the Ayatollah. It was a great life, and they were so kind, tolerant and understanding. That side of it was just brilliant. Which made it doubly disappointing that we didn't go very well in the car. We managed to edge up to a shade under 190 m.p.h. or so, but I was pretty timid with the afterburner. Frankly I was scared of the thing. I was worried about that hump in the middle of the runway, the traffic lights and all the rest of it. I just couldn't seem to get my act together.

Ackers wasn't very supportive. Like many of the others he was expecting greater things, and he went back to the Isle of Wight a bit disheartened. It was understandable. I'd sold all of these guys on this dream, and I'd failed to deliver the goods. They had every right to voice their disappointment. All you can really do in that sort of situation is to believe in yourself completely. You just have to say, 'Look, we are going to do this. Just keep with it, and we'll do this together.'

The plan after Leconfield was to keep running the car in its current unfinished form, without bodywork. The next thing on the schedule was our first public exhibition run at HMS Daedalus in Lee-on-the-Solent. I wasn't particularly looking forward to it, but we did a demonstration run for the press in the morning, even though it had been pouring with rain. Eventually it dried out in the afternoon, when we were due to run again. And suddenly everything came together. I cracked off down the runway at 200 m.p.h., and the thing just suddenly clicked. It was like shooting, when you suddenly come to the point where you get your eye in. I don't know whether it was that Daedalus had a better runway, without distractions, or whether I had thought things through a lot better. Whatever it was, I was profoundly relieved.

After that we spent the whole summer going round air shows. We went down to Cornwall, back up to Humberside, on to Teesside, all over the country. We were pretty good at performing by the end of it. I felt ready to move on to the next stage, which was to attack the British land-speed record at RAF Greenham Common. Since the *Thrust1* days this had been raised to 191.64 m.p.h. by Robert Horne, chairman of Hornes outfitters, in a Ferrari 512M racing sportscar.

We had quite a difficult time at Greenham, because we were pushing the car absolutely to its limits on the short runway. The aircraft tyres Dunlop had provided were not supposed to be used at more than 240 m.p.h. I was braking very hard from more than 250 m.p.h., and finishing up twelve feet from the end

In September 1980 we took Thrust2 to RAF Farnborough. A series of highly successful timed runs culminated in a new British Flying Mile record of 248.87 m.p.h.

of the runway. It was really stretching the car, and it was really stretching me, but we were now working very well together. I was having an absolute ball.

Official record attempts are based on the average speed of two runs in opposite directions over the measured mile or the kilometre, with both runs undertaken within the hour. To be ratified as an international record the runs must be timed by the relevant national authority as recognized by the Fédération internationale du sport automobile, the sport's governing body. In this case we were attempting a national record, so the RAC Motor Sports Association was the sanctioning body in charge of the timekeeping. Over the weekend of 24 and 25 September 1980, we claimed six new British records, the most satisfying being the Flying Mile at a speed of 248.87 m.p.h. We didn't dare use the reheat, except for initial acceleration, and I kept getting ticked off for exceeding the 240 m.p.h. rating of the Dunlops, but we were pretty chuffed with the way our four-ton monster performed. I now felt completely comfortable with *Thrust2*.

We'd spent about £105,000 to get to this stage. Our financial requirement had multiplied by about 300 per cent per annum. The first year we spent £7,000, the second £20,000, and so far in the third about £78,000. But we'd broken several records, and in doing so we had established ourselves. We no longer lacked credibility. We had done a good job, and we had proved our ability and commitment. What we had to do now was to forge on with the completion of *Thrust2*.

Along the way Ackers made a highly significant discovery. We had gone back to British Aerospace for help with our transonic wind-tunnel test programme, and initially their technicians hadn't been particularly complimentary about the bodyshell shape Ackers had come up with. I think they felt it was far too bricklike to possess the sort of characteristics such a car would need if it was to get up to transonic speeds of 600 or so m.p.h., which is what we initially envisaged. They thought that both the frontal area and the drag coefficient would be far too high. At the start of the project we had tested a tenth-scale wooden model, with promising results. But it was when we moved on to the transonic testing of a twentieth-scale model, which had to be machined from solid aluminium, that the surprise came.

'We don't know what the hell it is you've done with this shape of yours,' the British Aerospace guys told John, 'but our test results suggest *Thrust2* has a maximum speed of around six hundred and fifty m.p.h.'

Suddenly, *Thrust2* was no longer the interim stage to a pukka land-speed-record contender. It was a genuine challenger in its own right.

6 DRAMA AND DISILLUSIONMENT

An attempt on the land-speed record was going to cost us around £120,000. As I sought that sort of money, more would be needed to complete *Thrust2* to the necessary standard. We'd run with only minimal bodywork at Greenham Common; now we had to create the aluminium bodywork capable of withstanding speeds of up to 650 m.p.h. At the same time we had to keep a growing organization going. The mountain became ever harder to climb.

The more you develop this sort of vehicle, the slower becomes the progress you can show to current and prospective sponsors, and the more your overheads rise because you need to employ more people. By the end of 1980 we'd spent the best part of £300,000; now we were looking for a similar amount just for 1981.

After Greenham Common I did something very unpopular, but ultimately it was to mean the difference between success and failure. I insisted that we fitted a Rolls-Royce Avon 302 engine which we'd acquired on the back of our success. This time we paid around 4,000 quid for the engine.

It all went back to a meeting I'd had years before with Donald Campbell's chief mechanic, the late Leo Villa. 'Always make sure that you have a lot more power than you think you will ever need, just in case,' Leo counselled. The 302 was a later model than the 210, and had 17,000 pounds of thrust – over 2,000 pounds more than the 210 – but fitting it meant a great deal of work as many of the engine systems had to be changed.

We were then faced with an enormous programme, modifying the car and bringing in expert panel wheelers, such as Brian Ball, to join Ron Benton in making the aluminium body. Ron did most of the work from the front wheels back, but Brian used all his craftsmanship, learned from years working at British Aerospace, and wheeled the very complex double-curvature panels at the front.

At the same time Westland moulded the glass-fibre intake nacelle – the structure at the front of the engine – for us, and there was a drama when it didn't fit the first time. It had to go back, and there was a huge row that dragged on. But the day finally came when we had a finished car. We rolled *Thrust2* out of the Ranalagh Works and took it for a static engine test to RAF Wattisham in Suffolk.

We were all terribly proud of what we'd created, the first credible British land-speed-record contender since *Bluebird* had first been rolled out of Motor Panels twenty-one years earlier. But as usual when we were feeling good about something, harsh reality threatened to spoil the mood. We had to find £100,000 in a month, or else we weren't going out to Bonneville.

Somehow we made it. The *Daily Mail* came up with Trust Securities. We launched *Thrust2* on 8 September in Birmingham's Metropole Hotel, and literally in the week before we were due to leave for America I clinched a deal for £40,000 with Fabergé.

In the 1930s Bonneville had taken over from Daytona Beach as the spiritual home of record-breaking. It had the experienced infrastructure, it was the logical place to go. But, for us, it would be a shambles.

As they had been at Leconfield, expectations were very high. But I'd made the crucial mistake of trying both to run the project and drive the car. The two were absolutely incompatible. There should be somebody in overall control, making the major decisions in consultation with the technical director. Reporting to him must be the guy driving the car, not the other way round.

In Sir Malcolm Campbell's day it was different, because he paid for everything, called the shots and drove. But in our case you had people who were unpaid and took part on their own terms. If it wasn't properly structured, and we weren't, then it didn't work. At times it would be a relief just to get into the car!

Things got worse when I came to drive *Thrust2* down the salt for the first time. I had dreamed of this moment for much of my life, particularly during the last few years. The reality was an utter nightmare.

The important difference was that *Thrust2* was too fast for rubber tyres: we were using undeveloped solid aluminium wheels. Ackers called it cart-wheel technology.

We had decided not to use the afterburner. Ackers said, 'Right, what we want is for you to hold the car on the brakes, and when the wheels start to slide we want a steady hundred-m.p.h. drive down the track.' I tried to give him that, but the car just slithered off course to the right at 80 m.p.h. It was absolutely awful.

In the cockpit the steering felt dead, at slow speed the entire car seemed to yaw around the rear wheels. I felt uncomfortable and unsafe. At Greenham I had felt confident and successful. Suddenly all that had evaporated.

We persevered, and gradually worked up to 175 m.p.h. – below the speed I had achieved initially at Leconfield – but again the car just veered right and ran miles across the salt. We got up to 250 m.p.h. and the same thing happened.

By the middle of 1981 we had completed Thrust2 to record-breaking standard, clothing the spaceframe chassis in a smooth aluminium bodyshell. Full of hope and optimism, we took it to the hallowed ground of the Bonneville Salt Flats in Utah, intent on breaking Gary Gabelich's record.

I had an engine with a huge amount of throttle lag, because that's how turbojets behave. They are nothing like a normal car's piston engine, where the throttle response is usually instant. You apply throttle and for a moment nothing happens, then suddenly, as the turbine spools up, all hell breaks loose. I had a fair amount of experience of the car by now and had been quite happy banging the Avon straight into afterburner on airfield runways across Britain, where we'd gone up to 260 m.p.h. time and again. Then, of course, we'd been using rubber tyres, which provide a better grip on tarmac. But driving *Thrust2* on its aluminium wheels across salt was like trying to ride a bicycle without tyres across a frozen pond. It felt terrible!

I was being very gentle, treating the car as if the cockpit was full of eggs. I just didn't know whether this was going to get worse, or whether it was a phase I was going to be able to drive through.

Ackers came for a run with me; this time it went better and we hit 400 m.p.h. But after that run everything was as bad as it had been before. Of course, a lot of the guys in the crew were scratching their heads and pointing their fingers at me. Some of them even said that the only time I had the guts to drive *Thrust2* in a straight line was when John was aboard! As if it wasn't bad enough in the cockpit, I was having to put up with this kind of crap as well. We had gone out to Bonneville full of hope and expectation, and now the whole thing seemed to be falling apart.

I had been no different from anyone else. I'd thought I was going to get in the car and go. Record, here we come! But as soon as I started driving it I knew how bad things were. I'd been the one telling everybody back in England that it was going to be all right, and now I knew it wasn't.

I could understand how the crew felt, but I couldn't communicate with them. I'd been busy all the time, until now, chasing the money. The guys on the island had their heads down building the car. We hadn't settled down as a team yet.

This dramatic photograph reveals the beautiful, almost lunar quality of the Bonneville landscape.

On its solid aluminium wheels Thrust2 proved a nightmare to hold on course at 200 m.p.h., let alone the 630 m.p.h. for which we were aiming. The setback came as a terrible shock to a team expecting great things.

We didn't have that mutual trust that shared experience breeds, despite our air-show runs. It boiled down to two things: either the driver was no good, or the car was no good. There were more of them than there was of me, and naturally they didn't like the idea of me saying that we hadn't got the car right.

Record attempts are strange things. You invest so much time, emotion and effort into making a vehicle, and just doing that is a terrific achievement because it's so bloody difficult. Then, if you're lucky, you get out to a desert. At Bonneville we had to invest thousands of dollars having the track prepared. The way the salt 'grows' means you have to regularly smooth the course by scraping away the growth and the pressure ridges with a heavy drag towed behind a truck. It's all painstaking work, and it adds to the pressure of expectation. I soon discovered that if I hit the ruts the metal wheels had dug on a previous run, it was like hitting railway lines at Clapham Junction at 250 m.p.h. There was no point in telling people that the first man to try metal wheels, a rancher called Slick Gardner, who had bought and modified Arfons's old *Green Monster*, had struggled in precisely the same manner. When people expect excellence and don't get it, they can lose their sense of perspective. I could understand that, too, because I was like the Pied

Piper who'd led them all out there in search of an increasingly elusive dream.

From now on we realized that we'd have to prepare a new track for every run. That added to an already formidable workload, because there were so many other problems. We had minor technical hitches, then one night a storm very nearly blew our garage tent away. Only the team turning out at dead of night saved it.

Tension permeated the camp as we crept forwards slowly. We'd tried some minor suspension modifications, and on 10 October I went down the course at about 400 m.p.h. and the car felt a little bit better. This time we'd decided to try our first turnaround, because eventually the regulations would allow us only an hour between runs as we worked up to record speeds. Everything went wrong. The fuel bowser broke its propshaft, so we had difficulty refuelling. Then I found myself being towed by our accountant, who was trying to be helpful but hadn't towed *Thrust2* before. All through this Fred Karno act, Dave Petrali, the chief USAC timekeeper, was counting away the minutes. It was shambolic.

Somehow we got away in the nick of time. I was so angry that I just thought, Stuff it! I reverted to Greenham Common mode. For the first time at Bonneville I used the afterburner, and I used it to the maximum. And we just *went*!

Because I hadn't used the afterburner until this moment, there'd come to be a standing joke within the camp: 'Reheat is a myth.' Well, now it wasn't. I banged it in from the start, and miraculously stability came with the extra power. Nobody had twigged that. Certainly I hadn't. In the cockpit I felt happy for the first time. We were really motoring. We got up to a peak around 500 m.p.h. – the fastest we'd ever gone – as we approached the measured mile, but the car had been so hammered on the rough surface that a battery connection worked loose. We actually decelerated into the mile as we lost power, which was terribly disappointing, but we managed 447.029 m.p.h. through the kilometre. That gave us an average of 418.118 m.p.h., which meant that we were the fastest-ever British car and driver. At last we'd made a breakthrough.

Suddenly I was everyone's friend again, which felt good, but I was more concerned that we should capitalize on our discovery and press on. That night we dined in the Stateline Casino in Wendover – the closest town to the salt flats – and as the evening wore on it started to pour with rain. By the morning the flats were flooded by a couple of inches, and that was that. No sooner had we got going than we'd been washed out. It was an agonizing repeat of what Donald Campbell had gone through so often.

We were already on the knife edge financially after four or five weeks at

Bonneville, and now we had to get back home as fast as possible. Almost as soon as I landed at Heathrow I was summoned by Mr Fabergé, Hugh Wickes, who said, 'Look, Richard, you promised us gold and you only brought us back bronze.'

I said to him, 'Hugh, if you'd been out there and seen exactly what the hell we've been through I think you would be a bit more understanding.'

Later we got the sponsors together and explained what had happened, but nobody seemed to have any money for a fresh attempt in 1982. It was another uncomfortable period. Fortunately we got some very good objective press which was understanding of our problems, and this helped us to put the real message across to the sponsors.

We'd spent our last £1,000 before we set off to Bonneville insuring the desert against flooding at 75 to one. We put in a claim for £75,000, which would provide a good start for the following year's planned campaign. I told the sponsors about this, and their response was not to give us any more money.

There was an American rocket-powered dragster for sale, and I thought we should buy it. *Thrust2* would be out of commission being rebuilt, so we couldn't

John Ackroyd and me with Thrust2 at Bonneville in 1981.

No sooner had we made the vital discovery that the car needed to run with full afterburner to maximize its stability, and raced up to 500 m.p.h. without trouble, than the rain came to the salt flats. Overnight, our painstakingly prepared course was flooded, leaving us no option but to return home.

have run it until the following summer, and anyway, as we were to find out, every time you run a land-speed-record car on an airfield runway you take one hell of a risk. But we could have run this other car at air shows and on drag strips and made some money, while also keeping me from atrophying as a driver. But everybody was against the idea, so that one didn't work.

As for the insurance situation, we were completely naïve. We put in our claim and said, 'Look, the BBC has shown the desert on television, all flooded. Please can we have our seventy-five thousand pounds?' And they said no. We asked why and they said, 'You haven't made a record attempt.'

They said they would appoint an assessor, 'A fair-minded individual of enormous experience, who will make a judgement.' 'Who pays him?' I asked. 'We do,' was the answer.

It was quite clear they weren't going to pay up. As far as they were concerned it had been a failure. They didn't seem to care if we went bust. So we invited the director of the insurance brokers to a meeting, and I said, 'Look, you've got to understand that we want to go ahead with this project. I have called a press conference here at GKN House in ten days' time. I've sent out the invitations.'

'What are you going to say about the insurance?' he asked. 'That's very simple,' I said. 'If you're going to pay up, then we'll praise your insurance company and say how grateful we are. If you're not going to pay up then we shall explain our very severe difficulties, how expensive all this is, and I am personally going to hand out copies of your policy to the media.'

'You wouldn't do that!' he said. Those were his very words. And I told him, 'Yes we will.'

We didn't know until the morning of the press conference which way it would go. The director of the insurance company turned up with £75,000 in a special leather wallet. Photos were duly taken, and the *Thrust* project lurched on.

Another good move was Ackers's idea that Ken Norris should come aboard to run the project on the desert. That made very good sense, because I could be relieved of all the hassle. Ken is absolutely brilliant, and he's a very sensible, practical, humble person. He is a very good communicator, and is never frightened of saying what he thinks, but never once did he talk about Donald Campbell or any of his past work with him. This allowed us to learn about record-breaking ourselves, without constant reference to precedent, which was terribly important, because that's how team progress is made. Ken was part of that process and he guided us, but he never tried to lay down the law. He was truly one of us.

Things were finally coming along very nicely. We refurbished the car and tidied up a few things on it, made a few minor changes. And the sponsors were back with us.

I always felt it was important to involve the sponsors. We were a dynamic project, and they had to be part of it. They were all on twelve-month contracts, with an option to carry on, and we held regular monthly meetings to keep them informed of progress. The meetings were fairly lengthy and boring. But what they did do was to get the sponsors to act as a family. John used to moan like hell, because he had to come up from the Isle of Wight and lose a whole day, just for a twenty-minute presentation. But the sponsors had to get a feel for it. I've talked to a lot of other people about multi-sponsor projects, and the usual idea is that you keep the sponsors at bay. Sponsors should pay, then stay out of the way. It's our business how we spend your money. But I thought it was very important we share the accounts with them, so that they knew exactly what was happening and that there was no funny business, no money being salted away. It paid off well. Gradually we became a team.

As June 1982 approached we were ready to go to Bonneville again, as soon as the weather conditions there allowed. But we had a shakedown run to make at Greenham Common first.

We had no way of knowing it as we arrived there on 15 June, but the following day very nearly saw Project *Thrust* come to a catastrophic and terminal halt.

Dark clouds over a flooded Bonneville.

7 CRISES AT GREENHAM AND BONNEVILLE

It was a beautiful day when we arrived at Greenham Common. Really we just needed to shake down *Thrust2*, and I wanted to familiarize myself again with it before we went to Bonneville.

After we'd come back from Bonneville in 1981, I had taken up flying at Ken's suggestion. I knew I had to develop. I couldn't just sit around for a year without driving. The idea of buying the rocket dragster had been turned down, so then I suggested that a season of motor racing in two-seater Sports 2000s would be a good way to keep developing. The sponsors weren't keen on that either, but then Ken came up with the idea of flying. I loved it, though the need to keep looking for funding for the attempt was so intense it was very difficult to find the time to get my licence. I'd drive 80 miles down to the airfield, do four hours' flying before driving back again, and all the time I was in the air my mind would still be going round and round. I'd be thinking, Christ, I haven't done that. Oh Jesus, that deal's going to collapse. Not the best way to learn to fly!

I never went back to GKN. By the middle of 1982 I was thirty-six years old, with a wife, two young daughters (Genevieve was born in 1981) and a new pilot's licence, and I was a full-time member of a project dedicated to achieving a goal as soon as possible that, in its very moment of triumph, would put me out of business. To an outsider it might seem an extraordinary situation in which to place oneself so willingly, and many people have asked me whether I ever thought about the future in those days. But the answer, of course, is that you just can't worry about such things. I've always been a confident, optimistic type of person anyway; in this game you have to be. You just have to take the view that tomorrow will look after itself.

Once you have a project a long way down the line, once you believe the organization is capable of doing what it has set out to do, and provided you have no nagging doubts about people's abilities, then it's just a matter of pushing on and doing it. That's how I felt then about Project *Thrust* as we gathered at Greenham Common.

The first day was wonderful. We'd given a number of people 260-m.p.h. rides, among them were Paddy Hine and Henry Lewis, Initial Services' key director. They both absolutely loved it. I'll always remember Paddy sitting on the grass with his son, watching the runs. I went over to him and said, 'Well, Paddy, the next slot's yours. We're getting ready to go in about a quarter of an hour or so. What do you think?' There was a split second's hesitation, and then, 'Good, let's go!'

Afterwards he said, 'Even though I used to fly Lightnings, I've never experienced anything like that in my life.'

Henry said, 'Gosh, think what I'm going to tell them at the golf club: I've just been driven at two hundred and sixty m.p.h.'

The idea of the second cockpit worked brilliantly. You could take the most unlikely people, strap them in and hurtle them down the runway in this great big car. It was a perfect way of giving them a whole new insight into what we were trying to do. That summer day at Greenham was one of those times when you catch yourself laughing inside, and you know you've got life going just the way you want. They don't come very often.

The following day was one of the worst of my life. A day when just about everything went wrong.

Record cars use parachutes as their primary braking system to avoid the problems of heat and friction in trying to slow a car from speeds in excess of 200 m.p.h. Parachutes create high aerodynamic drag and thus are an excellent means of slowing cars rapidly from very high speeds; you can then use the normal brakes from 200 m.p.h. downwards. That day at Greenham we decided not to use our good parachutes, the three-chute cluster known affectionately as the 'triple-ripple', or the high-speed chutes. We wanted to save these for Bonneville. Instead we decided to use older chutes, from either a Lightning or a Phantom. There was a problem with one of them that prevented us from running until the afternoon, but then we did one run without any problems.

'As far as I'm concerned, the car is ready,' said Ackers. 'Let's pack her up.' But I wanted to get one more run in. Ackers reluctantly agreed, and we lined the car up at the west end of the course. Mike Barrett, who, ironically, was the team member in charge of the parachutes, jumped into the passenger seat. When things went wrong he and I were to get the ride of our lives.

Perhaps I'd become a little cocky. It was quite late in the afternoon, and we were only supposed to do 200 m.p.h., but by mistake I kept the throttle on a fraction too long. For a moment I just lost attention. I missed seeing the red Jaguar Firechase, which was my visual braking point. The next thing I knew was that

Anxious firemen cover Thrust2 with foam after I crashed the car during a test run at Greenham Common. Note damage over the right wheel arch.

smoke had started coming from the front wheels. I thought, Christ! What in God's name is that? It must be a puncture. But we're stable. It can't be.

It turned out later that the smoke from the tyres was where they'd expanded with the centrifugal load of excessive speed. We were now doing 300 m.p.h. instead of 200, and the tyres were fouling the bodywork. I wasn't supposed to exceed 240 m.p.h. on them at the best of times. Now, because we weren't running with the body cowls, I could see the smoke pouring off them.

I worked all that out a lot later, though, because right then I had my hands full of a jet car running out of control. The end of the runway was coming up very fast – and beyond it was a damned great quarry.

I thought I'd got the engine shut down straight away. I waited that split second while I tried to detect whether we had a puncture, then fired the braking parachute. It opened and collapsed. I jumped on the brakes so hard that they locked up. Should I put the second parachute out and turn left off the runway with it out? Or should I turn left off the runway before I tried the second chute? There was no time to think, I just reacted on instinct and actually got that bit absolutely right. I steered *Thrust2* off the runway first and the left-hand wheels apexed a corner perfectly at about 200 m.p.h. As soon as we got onto the grass I put out the second chute.

What I hadn't done, which was unforgivable, was to walk the course before the runs. What I thought was flat grass leading to a large concrete pan on which I could brake hard was actually rough and bumpy, and, worse still, it had zillions of gallons of jet fuel stored beneath it. We ploughed into this grass, and clouds of muck and stones went flying into the engine intake.

The front tyres had shredded when I'd locked up the wheels for 4,000 feet, and I just managed to stop before we ran out of space. But even as Mike and I clambered out to survey the damage, I knew we were in deep trouble.

The team were absolutely mortified. They were all saying to themselves, 'Well, we always knew Noble wasn't any good, and now he's proved it.' My immediate thought was that we had to get the car repaired, and Richard Aston of Loctite was one of the few people to keep promising me that we would. But others weren't so ready to offer comfort. Most of the team, I suspect, felt I'd just demonstrated the Peter Principle, where you can reach your maximum level of efficiency, and then get tipped over the top by promotion. I had reached beyond my level of competence.

Ackers was very angry. All the team members were. It was stupid driver error, totally my fault. All the love and affection and everything that had gone into building this car had been seriously damaged. The whole organization went into shock for about a week. Ackers just disappeared down to Cornwall.

A week later we had a meeting at Ken Norris's aviation business at Hurn Airport, sort of neutral territory. It was seriously tough. John had worked out exactly what he thought had happened in the accident, which was actually quite different to what I thought, and I'm not sure he got it right. What seemed to have happened was that we'd peaked at 300 m.p.h., and then basically I didn't get the engine shut down fully. I only got it down to idle, but there was residual thrust against the brakes, which had taken an enormous amount of energy. The bodywork at the front was badly damaged, but even worse was the engine damage, where it had ingested half of Greenham Common's stones and grass.

This meeting was a very solemn affair, and everybody said what they thought. All I could say was, 'Look, I'm very sorry. It was my fault. I've put an awful lot of effort into this and I want to carry on. I do think I can do this, but I can't do it without you guys. So what do we do?'

People were saying, 'Richard, it was your fault, you weren't disciplined enough. We were all worried this was going to happen sooner or later, and now it has and it's an awful lesson to us all.'

Of course, *Thrust2* had no telemetry, so we had no data to analyse after each run. While we were out at Bonneville in 1981, I'd had nothing to back up my observations about the car's erratic behaviour. The only telemetry was between John and I, and communication between us had become increasingly difficult at that stage. I would say, 'Look, John, I can't feel the steering.' And he would reply, 'What, no feedback? You must be getting feedback!' As the problem continued there was one school of thought that the car couldn't possibly be wrong, and therefore it must be the driver. My defensive position was, 'I'm doing my best. The car just isn't behaving as it should do.' Some of the team didn't want to hear that. Once I started using the afterburner those problems had receded, but now my mistake at Greenham had brought them all flooding back.

I think that Ackers in particular wanted me to stand down as the driver. No alternative was actually mooted at that time, but Ackers and some of the others would probably have been happier that way. It was definitely not comfortable where I was sitting, but at the end of the meeting everybody agreed to keep together and to keep going with me as the driver.

Considering the initial acrimony, we came out of that meeting amazingly strong. Ken chaired it, and he handled the situation impartially and brilliantly. I was reminded how his superb diplomacy had kept Campbell's project together during the black days at Lake Eyre. As a result the organization came back together vowing to bloody well get this thing right.

As part of the discipline procedure I had to go out and get my IMC-instruments-only-flying rating, which meant hours and hours of flying blind in cloud, and I had to get it done by a certain date. It was a sort of credibility test, but unlike my RCB test at Westbury all those years earlier, it was one I was desperate to pass. I did, but it was bloody difficult because this was all on top of more crises over money.

The accident set us back twelve weeks, which was the time it took the team to rebuild the front of the car, and the true effects were not to become apparent until we left again for America. But we came out of the Greenham disaster a very much tougher and more professional organization. It was quite clear that we were never, ever going to let such a thing happen again.

It was interesting how the organization changed. Mike Barrett became the leader in the workshop, whereas up until then John had been leading things. Now here was a different voice, of the man who had the most right to criticize because he'd actually been there in the accident with me. Mike is a natural leader, and the way he pulled things together was very encouraging.

We had whipped the engine out on the night of the accident. Our Avon expert, John Watkins, wanted it sent straight up to RAF Binbrook. 'I've never seen one so badly fodded,' he said, using the RAF term for foreign-object damage, 'and I'd like to be able to show it to the people here.' I thought, Oh my God, it's going to cost us 200 quid to send the Avon up, and we haven't got 200 quid for that sort of thing. I was rattling through the logic of it all. But I also realized that we were going to need every bit of help we could get. Of course the engine must go up. This was no time to lose friends. As things turned out, that was one of the best snap decisions I've ever made.

I got a letter out to the sponsors explaining what had happened. The response was not good. Many just said, 'Look, we gave you a lot of help and you've just gone and thrown it all away. Why the hell should we go through all that again?' It was quite understandable, and it was perfectly clear that the whole thing was going to be seriously difficult.

A crisis was brewing on the engine front. I had started negotiations with the Ministry of Defence to buy an ex-Rolls-Royce test bed Avon 302, which wasn't a particularly good one but the only one available. Nobody was at all helpful. Rolls-Royce had said they would rebuild our old engine, but at a cost of £80,000. We certainly didn't have that.

I had reckoned without John Watkins, the man we called One Take because whenever he was being filmed he always got it right first time. One night I had a call from him. 'How are you getting on then, Richard?' he asked, and I told him we were in awful trouble. 'Well,' he said, 'we've had a look at that engine of yours, and a right mess you made of it. What should we do with it now?'

I groaned. 'Oh God, John, it'll cost two hundred quid to send a truck up to collect it. We haven't got that. Can't you just dump it wherever you dump scrap?'

There was a brief silence, and what he said next just stunned me. 'Why would you want to do that when the entire RAF Binbrook engine bay has worked nights rebuilding your engine – and the Queen has paid for the parts?'

I couldn't say anything for a moment. John and his colleagues at RAF Binbrook had rebuilt our Avon to a better specification. One Take and his friends had solved our engine crisis. What a wonderful thing to happen.

Visible here and in the picture opposite are the 'dancing diamonds' in the supersonic airstream from the engine as it runs in full afterburner during tie-down tests.

By August we had *Thrust2* ready to roll again, and I did some very timid 100 m.p.h. runs down the runway at Bournemouth. It was like walking on eggshells. But everything went OK.

While all the dramas had been going on, Eddie Elsom had solved another problem. You have to pay the American Bureau of Land Management for time on Bonneville, and this needs to be booked in advance because, believe it or not, Bonneville can be quite a popular place. There is only a limited period each year when it's available and when the conditions are right for record-breaking – in the late summer, when the desert has dried out completely. Don Vesco, one of the legends of Bonneville history, was planning to attack the motorcycle-speed record, and had already booked the flats for the period we wanted. Ed negotiated with him, and Don very sportingly offered to share the time he had booked with us. So in the middle of September 1982 I boarded a flight from Heathrow, bound once more for a date with the glaring white salt.

When we'd started *Thrust2* we didn't have the money to do anything but take a lot of blind decisions, and with these projects you are always terrified that in those early stages you have taken one that will, unknown to you at the time, ultimately prevent you from getting your record. But I shared Ackers's confidence that we'd got most of our technical decisions right first time. He had now incorporated new six-inch-wide front wheels in place of the four-inch units used previously, and made revisions to the offset and castor settings of the front suspension to give the steering more self-centring and better feel. All of this would make a huge difference, and after our problems we were raring to prove ourselves.

But another rude shock lay at the end of the flight.

It was raining as we arrived in Wendover. To our horror, we realized that the salt flats were not white, but grey-blue. They had flooded so badly overnight that we were actually able to go swimming there.

We had salvaged the project from the edge of extinction after all the drama of Greenham Common; we had somehow borrowed salt time from Don Vesco; we had shipped everything 6,000 miles; and now we had nowhere to run. It was a terrible feeling, much worse than 1981. This time it seemed that we were beaten even before we'd turned a wheel in anger.

We returned to Bonneville in September 1982, only to discover that the salt flats had again flooded overnight.

8 COUNTDOWN TO THE RECORD

One thing was crystal clear. We could not go home. It was out of the question even to consider it. We knew there was a body of resentment building up against us; they said that we'd got the shape of the car wrong, that we were wasting sponsors' money which might have been used for other motor-racing ventures. What had happened was that we'd been around too long. I began to understand the line I'd heard about Donald Campbell's last troubled attempt: a record-breaker is only good for a certain number of failures.

When you ask people to invest their dreams in yours, and then you don't deliver, things can fall apart pretty quickly. That's why all down the line it's so important to take the right decisions. I had to do that now.

It was 28 September, and I held an emergency meeting over dinner in the Stateline Casino in Wendover. Our number-one priority was to find a new venue, and find it fast. There were a few options, but we quickly whittled down the list. We weren't going to get into the famous Edwards Air Force Base, where the *Budweiser Rocket* had supposedly gone supersonic three years earlier. Muroc Dry Lake was too short. But during the Stateline discussions a British *Thrust* follower, Peter Moore, asked, 'Have you ever considered the Black Rock Desert up in Nevada?'

The Black Rock Desert had come up in conversation before. Eddie Elsom and I had earmarked it as a possible venue back in 1980. In fact, Eddie had actually rung a place there called Bruno's Country Club,

An intensive search of western America yielded two potential alternative sites. We chose the Black Rock Desert in Nevada, and relocated immediately to Gerlach, a small town on the edge of the desert, where Bruno's Country Club became our operational headquarters.

but it was a bit difficult to ask them, 'Is your desert any good for running jet cars?' Frankly, there had never been enough money in the kitty to do anything more than put these places on a list. Now we were absolutely desperate, and would have run anywhere.

'We need a minimum of eleven miles of flat area which is dry, accessible and devoid of any plant life,' Ken Norris explained, and Peter smiled. 'I've camped up at Black Rock, and I'd say it satisfies all those criteria. It's got to be worth a look.'

Immediately we formed two assessment parties. The next day Ackers and my brother Charles, our photographer, went up to Alvord Lake in Oregon. They would find it too wet and too remote. Peter and I went straight across to Black Rock, approaching it cross-country via the dirt road from Winnemucca that brings you out at the ghost town of Sulphur on the eastern side. As soon as we came across the railway line there, and I took my first look out across the massive yellow-brown mud flats known as playa, I knew that we'd struck gold.

The surface was flat, so we wouldn't have to drag the course to prepare it the way we'd done at Bonneville. All we would have to do was defod the surface, to pick up any foreign objects. If the car got loose, there were miles and miles of run-off area in which to dissipate the speed.

Peter and I went into the little town of Gerlach (population: 350), and there we met Bruno Selmi, who ran the local motel and the grandiosely named Country Club, which turned out to be a bar-cum-restaurant. We took all his rooms and then lost no time in getting everybody on the road, heading west from Utah to Nevada.

The relocation was accomplished in six days, which was quite incredible when you consider the logistics involved. It was a real tribute to the new-found strength of the organization, and to the assistance of Walt Ashton, the vice president of Gerlach School, who put his air taxi at our disposal. It wouldn't be the last time we leaned heavily on the kindness of the townsfolk.

We still had problems. Before we could run *Thrust2* on the desert we needed a permit from the Bureau of Land Management. A prolonged argument followed, with the *Thrust* team on the one side and an environmentalist lobby on the other. One moment we had a permit, the next it was taken back. In the meantime we were restricted to doing brief runs of 100–200 m.p.h. just to get a feel for the place.

We kept pleading our case. What really swung it round for us was when the people of Gerlach and the nearby town of Empire, which was of similar size, got a petition together. Two of Bruno's employees, Joanne Irazoki and Kathy Mito, presented it to Jim Santini, Nevada's Congressman in Washington DC. In turn he backed up the findings of his representative, Susan Linn. I was determined that we would do everything through the proper channels, but I was damned if we were ever going to let go of the Black Rock Desert once I'd seen how perfect it looked.

Finally everything was sorted out, and in a very short time we were operational. The greatest irony was that we actually left the desert in better condition than we found it, after all our painstaking hours of defodding. Among the souvenirs we collected in this task were the odd live rounds of ammunition left over from the days when the United States Air Force used the desert for strafing practice.

The desert lived up to many of our expectations. It was flat and smooth, and felt an awful lot safer than Bonneville. The surface was dusty, made up of lots of little polygons of caked mud. It had a hard surface, with a soft gooey underlayer that made it behave rather like a vast mattress. Ackers's calculations showed that *Thrust2* had a rougher ride on its trailer going out to the desert at 30 m.p.h. than it ever did while travelling under its own power at over 500 m.p.h. Black Rock's surface was also much more suited to metal wheels than Bonneville's. Our sole concern, apart from areas that were still a little damp, was that the dusty surface had greater drag than Bonneville's hard salt. We considered that a reasonable trade-off, given that the greater stability of the surface would enable us to use all of *Thrust2*'s power for the first time.

By sheer chance we had lucked in to the optimum record venue. What really tickled me was when our old friends the USAC timekeepers, Dave Petrali and Mac McGregor, arrived; they looked around and said, 'Jeez, what have you guys found yourselves here?'

The experience that we'd acquired of laying out a course at Bonneville the previous year stood us in good stead, and the modifications to *Thrust2*, allied to the new surface, made a huge difference to the car's stability. On 21 October we broke our British car and driver record with a speed of 463.683 m.p.h. through the mile and 468.972 in the kilometre. On 3 November we went over 500 m.p.h. for the first time with new marks of 575.489 m.p.h. and 575.652 m.p.h. respectively. The next day we went over 600 m.p.h., when *Thrust2* peaked at 615 m.p.h. on the way to setting another new British car and driver record of 590.551 m.p.h. in the mile and 590.843 in the kilometre.

It was clear that *Thrust2* was capable of taking Gary Gabelich's record of 622.407 m.p.h., but the weather was closing in. Winter was on its way, the course was still a little too damp, and therefore our rolling drag was too high. Wet

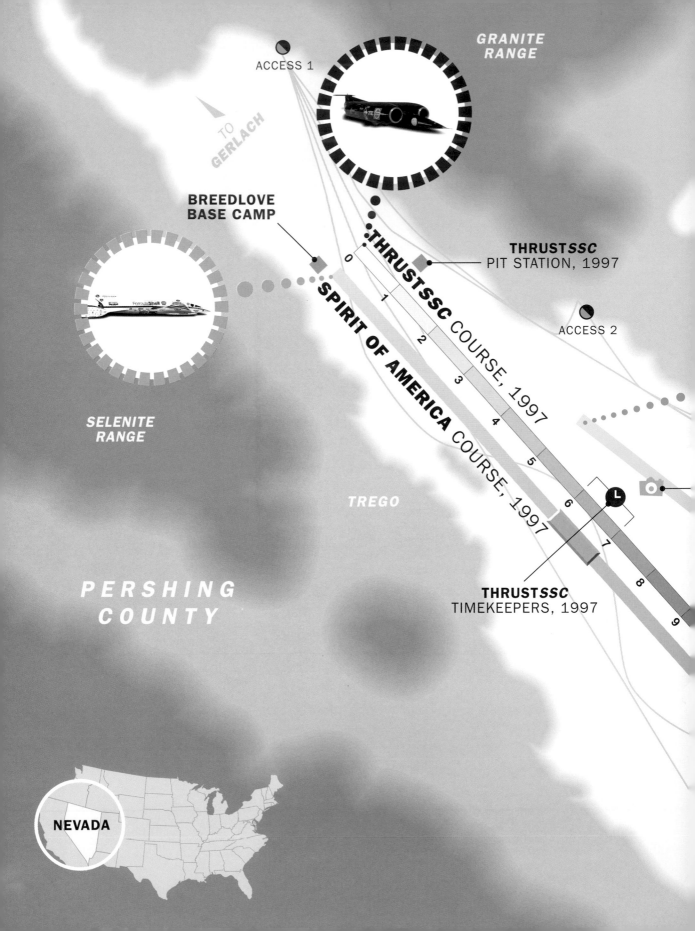

GRANITE
RANGE

ACCESS 1

TO
GERLACH

BREEDLOVE
BASE CAMP

THRUST*SSC*
PIT STATION, 1997

THRUST*SSC* COURSE, 1997

ACCESS 2

SPIRIT OF AMERICA COURSE, 1997

SELENITE
RANGE

0
1
2
3
4
5
6
7
8
9

TREGO

THRUST*SSC*
TIMEKEEPERS, 1997

PERSHING
COUNTY

NEVADA

BLACK
ROCK
D E S E R T
GERLACH, NEVADA, USA

HUALAPAI FLATS

W N S E

CALICO MOUNTAINS

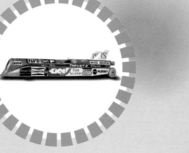

THRUST*SSC*
PRESS PEN, 1997

THRUST*2*
PRESS PEN, 1983

THRUST*2*
TIMEKEEPERS, 1983

NOBLES TRAIL

11
12
13

THRUST*2* COURSE, 1983

TO
BLACK ROCK
MOUNTAIN

Thrust2 on the Black Rock Desert in 1982.

patches meant that the course available to us was too short for record runs. We also had a major problem with the afterburner. *Thrust2* was down on power, and it would take us a year to figure out why.

The team had been under sustained pressure for a very long time, ever since the accident at Greenham in June. Ackers wanted us to stop, while John Watkins was all for carrying on. I, too, believed that we should stop, because we were so shattered that we were likely to make a mess of things from then on. But the most compelling reason to abandon the attempt was that we needed a huge surge in ambient temperature to dry the desert properly, and we just weren't going to get it. A day later it started snowing, so that really was it. We said goodbye to the wonderful people of Gerlach and promised to come back the following year.

I knew that 1983 would be our last shot, but we approached this final hurdle in a very much brighter frame of mind. We had already proved that *Thrust2* could perform in the right conditions. Eleven sponsors – Castrol, Champion, Fabergé, GKN, IMI Norgren Enots, Initial Services, Kluber, Loctite, Plessey, Trimite and

Trust Securities – stayed with us for the final push, though they all made it clear there was no prospect of continuing beyond 1983. In March we settled our insurance claim against the snow, which had finally forced us to abandon the 1982 record attempt.

Ackers tidied the car up a little more and, after we'd fought and won another battle with the conservationists over the BLM permit, we were back in Gerlach by the end of August 1983. We ran *Thrust2* for the first time that year on 16 September, and it felt terrific. Unfavourable weather conditions then held us up for a few days, but as the wind helped to dry out a small sump on one part of the course we put the downtime to good use. My brother Andrew and Mike Barrett devised a ridiculous little escapade that had locals either falling about with laughter, as we were, or else scratching their heads in total perplexity. At sixty-six, Ron Benton was filmed becoming the fastest man ever to cross the earth sitting on a portable toilet. It was the Keystone Cops meets 1930s record-breaker George

As we filled a moment of downtime, our British sense of humour dumbfounded some of our American friends when veteran team member Ron Benton was officially timed as the fastest man on earth sitting upon a portable toilet.

Eyston. As the triumphant Ron emerged victorious from his portaloo, he was greeted by Andrew and Mike saluting him with a fanfare of sink-plunger trumpets. Ron was in his element, hamming it up, a toilet-paper scarf adding a raffish air to his flying helmet and goggles. It really was hysterically funny. Morale was soaring.

Television presenter Rob Widdows asked him why he had done it. 'It's like a mountain, you see,' Ron replied. 'Because it's there.'

'What does a man with your ambition want to achieve next?' Rob asked.

'Well, you know,' Ron said, 'I want to break the sound barrier.'

Days later we upped our British car and driver mark to 606.469 m.p.h. That was actually six m.p.h. faster than Craig Breedlove's old record for jet-powered cars, as opposed to Gabelich's rocket-propelled *Blue Flame*, but we missed the one per cent improvement required to claim a new class record by a fraction.

It seems that I may actually have released the parachute a fraction too soon on that run, so we felt we could have gone faster still. But Ackers, Ken and I were worried that we seemed to be reaching a performance plateau, as we started to edge into territory uncharted by any other jet car. The build-up of drag as we reached the transonic region might be hurting us. The speed of sound varies according to temperature: the higher the altitude and the temperature, the faster the sound barrier. Until this moment we'd been running early in the day, when the air was cold and dense, which meant that drag was higher but the engine produced greater power. Now we opted to seek the hottest part of the day, so that the speed of sound, and therefore the start of the transonic drag region, were high enough up the speed range not to cause us so much of a problem.

We hit 617 m.p.h. through the mile on our next run, but again we sought excuses for a relatively disappointing performance. Our peak and average speeds were getting uncomfortably close, whereas I should still have been accelerating as I left the timing traps. The afterburner wasn't quite right yet, and we thought the engine would benefit from some subtle tweaking for Black Rock's altitude. The problem was that John 'One Take' Watkins was still tied up back at RAF Binbrook, where they were 'painting the coal' in preparation for a royal visit.

The following day Gary Gabelich was in town to watch the car in action for the first time. To the outside world it appeared to go well enough, but an improvement to 607.903 m.p.h. for the sole run of the day was not what we had in mind.

I don't think Gary really thought very much of *Thrust2*, but he was decent enough to keep such views private. When he said, 'Nice run, Richard,' I was

As John Ackroyd rightly observed, when we weren't actually running Thrust2 all of our time was spent maintaining it. We based the car at Cecil Courtney's garage in Gerlach, where the weather was usually kind enough to allow us to work without shelter.

probably a little brusque. 'Not really, Gary,' I snapped. 'We can do a hell of a lot better than that.' I think he secretly thought we'd reached our peak and that his record of 622 m.p.h. was safe.

Perhaps it was, because we were having engine trouble. The Avon had lost its flame during the run. The jet-pipe temperature had suddenly shot up, forcing us to abort a scheduled return run. The flame-out could have been the result of surge, where a turbojet ingests too much air until it vomits it back out of the intake. At the sort of speeds *Thrust2* had been attaining, that might have resulted in serious internal damage. Just as it seemed we had been climbing the mountain, we had slithered into another technical crevasse.

The RAF sportingly agreed to liberate One Take, but once he arrived he found the situation difficult because his experience was limited to Avon installations in Lightnings. Now that we were into development stuff, he needed Rolls-Royce's help.

I knew if I appealed direct to the Rolls board the chances were that we would be turned down. They saw what we were doing as an unofficial installation of one of their engines, over which they had no control. Therefore we had to put them in a position where they simply had to do something. The way we did it was to give an exclusive story about the problem to our old friend John Griffiths from the *Financial Times*; in return he would obtain for us the private fax number of the Rolls-Royce chairman, Sir William Duncan.

'It's very simple,' I wrote to Sir William, 'we can get this record, but the problem is that the engine has let us down. It's probably only a settings problem that can be fixed relatively easily, but we can't keep running up and down the desert at 617 m.p.h. If you decide not to help I quite understand, but then we will have to come home.'

The next morning our prehistoric sofa-sized Plessey fax had spewed out the response from a seriously angry Rolls-Royce board. I suspect Sir William had read

After our experience of Thrust2 at Black Rock in 1982, it was clear that the car was capable of smashing Gary Gabelich's record of 622 m.p.h.

his *FT* on the way into work, then arrived at his office and discovered our fax. The gist of his message was, 'Who the hell do you think you are? How dare you put the Rolls-Royce board in this position?' However, the letter closed by effectively saying, 'By the way, we're sending Mr George Webb from Atlanta to sort you out.'

George, a cheery Lancastrian, quickly told us the engine hadn't surged, and that we would have known all about it if it had. He crawled up the jet pipe and discovered none of the metal spatter that would have indicated internal trouble. 'I think what you had was a simple flame-out,' he summarized, to our intense relief.

As he went right through the system he discovered that the reheat linkage, which was part of the car rather than part of the engine, had been connected wrongly. This meant that since 1982 we hadn't been using the fourth and final section of the reheat. We took the car down to Reno airport, and George gave the Avon a compressor wash just to clean things out. We were back in business, and suddenly *Thrust2* had a new spring in its step, with a hell of a lot more thrust available.

On 29 September 1983 we achieved 622.837 m.p.h. in one direction, bang on Gabelich's record. But once again I couldn't make the mandatory return run. This time I couldn't start the engine, because there had been a serious fuel surge when I deployed the parachutes at the end of the previous run. Again it seemed we had reached the point where its rate of acceleration had flattened out. Things were so desperate that we even resorted to the old four-inch Bonneville front wheels to reduce drag, but they just brought back all the old instability problems.

Now the sponsors were getting restless. The contracts with them ran only until 30 September. They had agreed to continue contributing for a short period on a pro-rata basis if the project over-ran that date, but some of them were losing faith. We were back on the knife edge.

Fortunately Ackers and Ken had some other tricks to play. We fitted small deflectors on the underside of the car, ahead of the front wheels, to smooth the airflow, and the underside was painstakingly polished to a mirror finish. The

The front wheels had been widened since our first dramas at Bonneville in 1981, and proved perfectly suited to Black Rock's surface.

Preparing the car for a high-speed run was always a painstaking affair as everything was checked and double-checked.

Bad day at Black Rock. I thought we had damaged our engine, after it flamed out during a run at 622 m.p.h. The expressions of Glynne Bowsher, Ken Norris, John Ackroyd, Gordon Flux and John Watkins reveal their anxiety as we begin preliminary checks.

paintwork, too, was rubbed down. We did anything we could think of to reduce drag. Mike Hearn suggested fitting an automatic timer to balance fuel flows and prevent the fuel-surge problem. Then Ackers proposed one other crucial change.

Up until then *Thrust2* had been run with zero rake; the front of the car had the same ride height as the back. In this form it generated 6,360 pounds of downforce on the front wheels during the 623 m.p.h. run, 5,760 pounds of that being static weight. The difference was aerodynamically induced. Now, after extremely precise calculations, John and Ken raised the front ride height a fraction higher than the back. It was literally a fraction, seventeen hundredths of a degree, but this would reduce the amount of downforce that was tending to make the front wheels plough and increasing our rolling drag.

What this meant in real terms was that at 450 m.p.h. *Thrust2* would have a maximum downforce on the front wheels of 1,200 pounds, moving to zero at 600 m.p.h. At a peak of 650 m.p.h. there would be 2,040 pounds of positive lift on the front end. This, however, would be countered by the 5,760 pounds of static weight of the engine.

I was concerned about all this, because always in the back of my mind was the fear of the car flying. *Thrust2* had a totally flat underside, which would make it fly like a transonic kite. I knew that Breedlove's *Spirit of America – Sonic 1* had lifted its front wheels at 600 m.p.h. Ackers patiently explained it all, pointing out that there would still be 3,720 pounds of static weight from the engine acting on the front end.

Initially our runs were made in the cool dawn, when the air was dense and the engine therefore developed its greatest power, but as the speeds increased we began to run later in the day. When the setting sun cast its long shadows, the desert was a breathtakingly beautiful place.

OTHER VOICES

CRAIG BREEDLOVE

'When I first went up to visit Richard at Gerlach, when he was running the car, I spoke to Ken Norris and said, "Do you mind me asking what kind of ground loadings you're experiencing?" because I observed the track and it looked as if it was really pushing in, especially as Black Rock is a fairly soft surface. He said it was thirteen thousand pounds. Then I asked where the main weight distribution was on the car and he said that it was mostly on the front. I said, "Oh God, you've got so much rolling drag you can't possibly get the car through the record!"

'Ken said they sort of suspected the same thing and had talked to Richard about it, but that he was a bit unnerved about pointing the car up. I told Ken I understood that and, of course, with the flat bottom it was a very touchy thing to do. But nevertheless, when we ran *Sonic 1*, not by design but what the car did, it had zero weight on the front end at that speed. I told Ken that somewhere between zero and six thousand three hundred was a world-speed record.

'That was when he asked me to go talk to Richard about pointing it up, with all my experience. So I went to talk to Richard and he agreed after that, and the adjustment, if I remember, was about point zero two degrees. Maybe less. It was really a little bit, a small change to make, and it put the car through the record.

'Years later, Richard called me when they were doing the wind-tunnel analysis for the new car, and said, "Craig, you son of a gun, you almost got me killed!" I said, "Whaddya mean?" He said, "Well, we took a look at *Thrust2*, and, at the rate the lift was increasing, if I'd gone another seven or eight m.p.h. faster I'd have been going up at fifty gs!"

'"See Richard," I said, "there is a God!" Sometimes these things are pretty close.'

Days after the engine drama Thrust2 was given a clean bill of health, and we were ready for the final push to the top of the mountain.

I remained decidedly uncomfortable about this. It had all started because Breedlove was there the same day that Gabelich turned up, and Craig had said we were carrying far too much load on the front end. This bugged John and he decided he wanted to lighten up the front. I went along with it; what else could one do? But I was concerned that the weight would come off very quickly. What happens is that you get a servo effect. If you increase the angle of attack, the result is that the nose will lift a little bit more, and it only needs to lift a fraction too much before the wind acts on a very flat and very large underside and suddenly you are flying. I hadn't forgotten the sight of Donald Campbell's somersault on Coniston. We had no means of knowing what our critical angle was, and we had no idea what was happening to the airflow beneath *Thrust2*. The system we had for measuring loads on the front suspension was relatively crude, so to an extent I felt we were second guessing.

Whenever the element of danger arose, I could rationalize it by saying that the worst part of land-speed record-breaking is driving the car on an airfield runway. If you come off the runway then you're on the grass, as we were at Greenham, with all its associated stability problems. If it's going wrong at 500 m.p.h. on a desert, it's OK, you just let it run off course for a few miles.

Speed is also relative. Doing 260 m.p.h. on a runway seems a lot faster than 500 m.p.h. on a desert, because the desert is much more open.

The more experienced you get, the slower it all becomes. With *Thrust2* I reached the point where, after the savage parachute deceleration that got us down to about 400 m.p.h., I was desperately bored. All I wanted to do was to pop the lid, get out and run alongside. Then it would hit me: Christ, I'm still doing 380 m.p.h.!

It's funny, but the kick when *Thrust2* decelerated down to about 400 m.p.h. was far greater than anything Andy Green would experience with *ThrustSSC*, even though he had a far more powerful and faster car. That was because we had relatively big chutes and a very light car, which was aerodynamically very draggy. Our deceleration was peaking at around 5 or 6g, which means I temporarily multiplied my normal weight five or six times.

Once we'd solved our instability problems at Bonneville there was only one really bad point with *Thrust2*, and that was the awful last stage right up at 650 m.p.h., where I'd come out of the measured mile and then had to go through a quite complicated shutdown procedure on the engine before I could start to slow down. To get maximum thrust we were deliberately overspeeding and overtemping the Avon, so we had to get the temperature down again to stabilize it before shutting it off. This meant dropping the engine from well over 104 per cent to 93 per cent, and then counting to three before I shut it down. At these moments the car felt awfully unstable.

Ackers had it absolutely right. *Thrust2* was only really stable, as we discovered early on at Bonneville, under savage acceleration or savage deceleration. Cruising along at top speed was dodgy. Accelerating hard was all fine and dandy. It went reasonably straight, and, though I had to work quite hard at the wheel, the steering ratio was twenty-five to one, so I needed to move the wheel 40 degrees or so. I'd go through the measured distance, then, coming out the other end, I'd get this awful feeling: I'm slowing down the engine now, we're building up the drag in the front end, the car feels as if it's going to snap sideways. It never did, but it always felt as if it was about to. There was this period of uncertainty at the point when I couldn't yet have the chute out because I had to decelerate and restabilize the engine.

I prepare to drive Thrust2 for the last time.

When I did put the chute out there was another terrifying moment: it felt as if the world had tipped over and I was plunging headlong down a mineshaft. But this would be followed by the lovely feeling, Fine, the chute is out and holding us straight, that's the end of it, we're OK, we're safe. After that the rest was boring.

High winds kept us in Gerlach for the first three days of October. We all knew that if and when the weather window opened it would do so only momentarily. We had to be ready.

On 3 October, within sight of the finishing tape, Fabergé decided not to continue with more funding. Two other sponsors, Kluber and Trust Securities, also decided not to provide further funds. But Castrol, Champion, GKN, Initial Services, Loctite, Plessey and Trimite put £20,000 into the kitty, enough for one final week's running. This was a profound relief, because we could all feel that things were building up to the big climax. We called them the Magnificent Seven, and they were. They kept the faith when it mattered most.

Our first run, heading south, yielded a speed of 624 m.p.h., a fraction over Gabelich's record... But the draggy surface of the starting point at the northern end of the desert compromised our acceleration badly... We hadn't gone fast enough yet to beat Gabelich by the mandatory one per cent.

The fourth day of October brought a beautiful dawn. Many people told me later that they'd woken with an uncanny feeling of certainty that the record would fall that day. I felt no such thing. For me, it was just another day on the desert.

We were all ready for action by the afternoon as the temperature sidled up nicely into the low seventies. But then there was yet one more nerve-stretching moment at 2.45 p.m. when a fuse in the ignition failed. I began to fret as our electrician, Gordon Biles, made a desperate run to the south for a replacement. Of all the minutes in our nine-year crusade, these felt the longest as I waited, strapped into the sweltering cockpit.

Then it finally happened. The first run yielded the fastest speed yet, 624.241 m.p.h. I thought we could have done a lot better than that, but the north end was so dusty and draggy that it badly hurt our initial acceleration – 624 m.p.h. was actually a very good result in those circumstances, but it was still a big disappointment.

With practised efficiency the crew turned *Thrust2* round and sent me on my way again, this time from the firmer southern end, which promised superior initial acceleration and therefore higher speeds. And this time the promise of *Thrust2* was finally realized. That second run was astonishing.

As I slowed at the north end I remember seeing Mike Hearn, an old friend from the earliest ICI days, alongside me in the Jaguar Firechase, waving. And hearing Dave Petrali giving the speed through the mile: 642.971 m.p.h. My God, I thought, that's bloody fast! I think I swore, too, out of sheer relief, because I knew the struggle was finally over. Nine years' graft, and now surely we had got it!

We had pushed ahead of Gary Gabelich, and set a new world land-speed record with an average speed through the measured mile of 633.468 m.p.h.

Our peak speed had been just over the 650 m.p.h. target John had always set. I'd had no sensation of the front end lifting, though I suspect that you wouldn't until the thing had reached the point of no return, and by then it would be too late. It was only years later that I would come to realize how lucky we had been.

We were so elated that we rather foolishly tried another southward run, to try to capitalize on the significantly greater speed of the second run in order to boost our average. It was an anticlimax. The light was going, I was tired and struggling to keep my concentration levels up, and we were back at the draggy north end for the start. The result was slower than our first run, but it didn't matter.

Under the setting sun I was hoisted aloft on the shoulders of the men who had worked so long and so faithfully, and the champagne flowed. As the shadows

The return run was much quicker, at 642 m.p.h. My God, I thought, that's bloody fast!

lengthened over the desert Sally and I hugged each other. 'Thank God, it's over,' she said. We leaned on the car as friends stood round chatting, and Mimi and Genny waved the Union Jack. It was one of those wonderful, fleeting moments of contentment. When a television reporter asked me why I'd ever become involved with the land-speed record, I told him I had done so, 'For Britain, and for the hell of it.'

The euphoria wore off quite quickly, within hours, and was replaced by a feeling of immense sadness, because the team would now have to disband.

Immediately afterwards we were still trying to stop people driving on the desert because we had laid out our course and didn't want it spoiled, though, of course, it didn't matter any more. We all felt unable to cope with the situation.

Success can be very sad, actually, once you've got over the initial elation. You realize that the whole excitement of such projects is everybody working, communicating and travelling together, and fighting against the odds. Then suddenly it's all over, and it can never be savoured again.

I loved the fight to build *Thrust2*, and I loved driving it. I was absolutely on top of things by 1983; I had conquered the car. We were both on the top of our form. We had our day in the Nevada sun, and *Thrust2* wasn't going any faster.

It was incredibly satisfying, yet the result was bitter-sweet.

Record-breaking is an intensely selfish business, for all the importance of teamwork. *Thrust2* was like a great big metal mistress to which each of us was enslaved. Looking back now, the person who I think really came out of the whole *Thrust* saga best was Sally.

Thrust1's accident at Fairford in 1977 was far worse for her than it was for me.

When the car went into the roll, we think the engine probably flamed out. So she could see these great clouds of white smoke. She was with a group of people on the wrong side of the crash fencing, and they couldn't get through. I was probably shutting down an engine that had already flamed out, but the shock and anxiety can't have been easy on her.

She didn't try to stop me carrying on after the Fairford incident, as many wives most certainly would have done. She thought that we would never actually make it to the *Thrust2* stage, and that the thing would fizzle out somewhere along the line.

Of course, we did carry on. Yet she never tried to stop me, though her resolve must sorely have been tested over the years. When we started *Thrust2* we played the film *The Fastest Man on Earth* so often that some people on the project were word perfect on the script: half of it seemed to be taken up with footage of record cars tumbling to destruction, or of speedboats flipping over. Then there were our own dramas at Bonneville, when *Thrust2* wouldn't run straight; the crash at Greenham Common; a few parachute malfunctions at Black Rock; not to mention a husband engaged in a constant battle against disappointment and rejection from people who didn't want to share in what he was trying to do. I've no doubt I was hard to live with at times.

I'd never really realized what Sally had been through until I'd stopped driving. It was only when I started watching *ThrustSSC* hurtling back and forth on the Black Rock Desert that I began to appreciate fully what she'd had to endure.

I think she's fantastic; I don't know anybody else who could ever have put up with it all.

As Mimi and Genny played on the desert, and the sun began to sink slowly from the sky, Sally and I at last had a rare moment of tranquillity in which to savour the end of the long struggle for the land-speed record.

9 AHEAD IN THE CLOUDS

After we returned with the land-speed record there were a number of ceremonies and awards: receptions in Reno; a press conference in London; the British Racing Drivers' Club's annual dinner, where I received the John Cobb Trophy and a special BRDC Gold Star; and later, the RAC's Sir Malcolm Campbell and Diamond Jubilee Trophies and the Segrave Trophy.

There was one memorable evening when GKN hosted a dinner for us all. I asked each team member in turn to stand and say a few words about what the project had meant to them. Some were a little embarrassed to be in the spotlight, but I felt it was important that each individual's role should be identified.

We were also invited to take part in the Lord Mayor's Show. It was quite fun being driven with the car on a long trailer round the streets of London, and we received a terrific reception. I got a fair amount of stick from some team members because I refused to wear my black driving suit; instead I wore the same baggy blue Initial overalls which they all had. I was told that even if I didn't want to stand out, the crowd wanted me to. But I felt very deeply that Project *Thrust* was a team thing, and that we had all done it together. I didn't want to stand out, and I'm afraid that I didn't care if the crowd would rather that I had. This was not about Richard Noble. As soon as you start identifying yourself as being different, then you're saying, 'This is my record.' It wasn't.

Public acclaim has never been important to me. It's important to the sponsors, and you have to do some things in order to raise the funding, but I hate that on a personal level. I don't mind getting up and speaking; I've made my living often enough from that. But it just seems to me that one person searching for public acclaim devalues the whole project. When you are a close team, you know that so much is dependent on the skills and input of the people you worked alongside – people like John Ackroyd, or Glynne Bowsher, who was responsible for the brakes, and who was to play a much larger role in the *SSC* project. Without their knowledge, experience and ability, it wouldn't have happened. As far as I was concerned, I found the money, and I just happened to be the guy in the cockpit.

Some time after we set the new land-speed record with *Thrust2*, I got a call from Stan Barrett, the American stuntman who, late in 1979, had been in the hot seat of the *Budweiser Rocket*, one of the most controversial vehicles in land-speed history. He complained bitterly to me that I had the record yet he had nothing, though he claimed to have been the first man back then to drive a car faster than sound.

I wasn't there, so I can't judge. The *Budweiser Rocket* had a hydrogen peroxide rocket engine with 13,000 pounds of thrust, augmented by a 6,000-pound Sidewinder missile. On 17 December it was tracked on a course at Edwards Air Force Base by a hand-panned United States Air Force radar dish which appeared insufficiently uncalibrated for this application. The *Budweiser Rocket* did not run through a mile in either direction within 60 minutes, but once over a distance of 52.8 feet. They recorded a speed through the trap of 660 m.p.h. This did not satisfy Budweiser, which refused to loosen the purse strings on a bonus payment, but later the peak speed before the timing trap was announced as 739.666 m.p.h., and no less a figure than Brigadier General Chuck Yeager was called in to add weight to the team's claims to have gone supersonic. After noting that the rear wheels had been airborne at the time, Yeager concluded that the car had indeed broken the sound barrier because this indicated an established shock wave beneath the vehicle. They claimed to have reached Mach 1.01 for under a second.

Neither Craig Breedlove nor the late Gary Gabelich, record-breakers both, gave the Budweiser claims the slightest credence.

The whole operation was cloaked in secrecy. The truth of it was that the *Budweiser Rocket* team decided to do things entirely their own way with complete indifference to the rules and regulations laid down by sport's governing bodies. I was always determined that we would do it absolutely by the book, so that when we succeeded there could be no doubt whatsoever in the eyes of the world.

I sometimes think the most important part of any major project is knowing what you're going to do when it has reached its natural conclusion. I suppose I have always had this restlessness that makes me want to keep pushing on to new horizons. I just can't bear sitting down and looking backwards. I always need to have my head full of plans for the future.

In Formula One there is always the next race, or the next World Championship. It's a never-ending cycle. One week's anticlimax is next week's exhilaration. But one-off projects such as *Thrust* are very different.

It is desperately important to move on once you've succeeded at something like that. You reach a sort of crossroads, where you can either go off and be some sort of media star on the back of it, which again has a finite life, or else you quickly get back into doing something else that motivates you. You have to hit the ground running and push on hard. I was one of the lucky ones, because within a month of breaking the record I was working on something new.

My plan was to build a new light aircraft. I loved flying, but I could never understand why the costs were so excessive. In the summer of 1983 I met Bruce Giddings, an intuitive engineer who had designed and built a microlight, and had taught himself to fly. Through him I met some guys who were struggling with a plane project called the Sheriff, a twin-engined design. It was 60 per cent built, but they'd run out of money. One of them was a very talented designer, James Morton, the other, Nick Sibley, was a brilliant aerodynamicist. They were stuck, and we decided to join forces.

My first inclination was to do an aerobatic single- or twin-seater, but we eventually decided that the market for that would be too small. Then Nick made the observation that most single-engined aircraft had about four pounds of airframe weight per pound of engine. He suggested that we could use modern technology and materials to produce a smaller, lighter and more cost-efficient two-seater trainer. But it would have to feature a new lightweight modern engine. It all began to look very attractive, a really worthwhile challenge. Could we turn established aviation thinking around?

The next move was to talk to Champion, our old *Thrust2* sponsor. I said, 'Right, you do spark plugs. Who's doing engines?' They gave us a list, and one was Lotus, who had what looked like a wonderful 80-horsepower four-stroke unit. But we were seriously misled by somebody senior there, who told us quite categorically that it had run for twenty hours. An hour later, when I rang a guy on the test bed, he said, 'Not bloody likely, Richard, it's still in bits . . .'.

The other name on the list was Hewland, world famous for its racing gearboxes. Nick and Bruce got on like a house on fire with Mike Hewland, who is a very creative designer. He'd made a two-cylinder, 500-cubic-centimetre engine for microlight use. It had been well developed, and the relationship between Mike, Nick and Bruce gelled so fast that at the end of their first meeting Mike let them take one of the engines away for evaluation. Quite extraordinary!

The engine seemed reliable and did what Hewland said it would do, so Bruce, James and Nick started designing the ARV Super2 around it. ARV stood for air recreation vehicle; Super2 because it was a two-stroke engine and was a two-seater, designed for the private flying and flying club market that had been dominated for so long by the American Cessna and Piper marques.

Things happened really fast, and shortly after our success in breaking the world land-speed record I joined the project full time. We soon met the inevitable problems trying to finance the thing. We got a merchant bank involved initially, then realized the solution had to be via business expansion scheme private investors, who would get tax relief on their investment. I soon found out, however, that the City had a legally enforced monopoly on capital investment, which meant that I couldn't just meet somebody in the street and hand over a document inviting him to buy shares in our exciting project. This

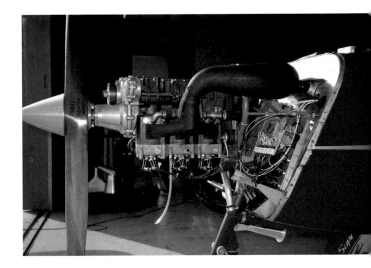

The most important thing once any project finishes is knowing what to go on to next. The key to my next move was this remarkable two-stroke engine designed by Mike Hewland.

could be punishable with a prison sentence. I had to go via the City, expensive solicitors and accountants, long form and short form reports and all the hoopla which appears to be a device to perpetuate the monopoly. That was the reality in the ARV days.

I believed that if you wanted to put a company together you should be able to put an ad in a national newspaper to explain that so much capital is needed and the offer price per share. People should be free to join and take their risks. But it didn't work like that. It was known as protecting the investor, and you then got involved with solicitors and merchant bankers, Uncle Tom Cobbley and all, at huge, huge cost. For instance, in those days just to set up ARV as a public limited company we'd have had to spend something like 100,000 quid. That money should have gone into the design team or the build! You can't spend it on lawyers and all these expensive people.

The Hewland engine formed the basis for the ARV Super2, a new light aircraft with which we challenged the American monopoly of the market.

The fundamental problem with the City, I found, was dealing with people who don't understand. They've seldom done it themselves. Anybody can be a wheeler-dealer. Mike Hewland got it right. He said, 'Anybody can take money from one pocket and put it in another pocket and take a fifteen per cent commission. Any fool can do that!' But not anybody can build an aero engine, not anybody can build a supersonic car. That's where the skill is, that's where the value is. The money is purely incidental. You need to free up the system, and so long as it's clogged you'll get a Cockerell struggling with his hovercraft or the clockwork radio designer having to get his product built in South Africa.

I also saw the other side of monopoly, where the City institutions made outrageous demands like a 40 per cent return on capital. 'Hang on, how are we going to deliver you forty per cent?' The answer was, 'Oh well, that's your problem. Forty per cent is the market rate if you want our capital.' I went to Castrol's chief executive and asked, 'What's your return on capital?' and he said, 'About nineteen per cent.' So how was I supposed to do 40 per cent with a new company building aeroplanes?

It was a proud day when I flew an ARV Super2 into Heathrow. Christopher Tugendhat, chairman of the Civil Aviation Authority, and I posed with it beneath Concorde.

Where did the figure of 40 per cent come from? The banks had lost so much money through poor investments that they needed twice the performance from their surviving investments to balance their books. So what businesses do they end up investing in? Property development, importers and boutiques! The real value, which lies in manufacturing, is lost.

In 1986, the Financial Services Act was passed, which would free up the whole system. But it was too late for ARV, which was shackled to the old system.

Despite all this we pushed on. We set up production on the Isle of Wight, where I knew that engineering skills were available inexpensively. The first flight came in 1985, and eventually we got the Super2 certificated in 1986. To celebrate we flew three of them into Heathrow, which was terrific. I've got a picture of one under the nose of a Concorde.

Then the sales started. We had over 2,000

enquiries from all over the world. We got a huge amount of very good publicity, and everybody who flew a Super2 spoke extremely highly of it. The airframe was built to a very high standard. It was all properly corrosion proofed and its handling was absolutely brilliant. The forward-swept wing meant the stall characteristics were very benign, while the visibility was remarkable. The handling was outstanding, and it was very safe. It was a very clever design and it looked fantastic.

The weak point was perceived to be the two-stroke engine. I soon came to realize that there was enormous prejudice against two-strokes in the aviation world. Pilots are a very conservative lot, particularly private pilots who don't fly very much. Then there were the flying clubs. A lot of them had ex-service chief flying instructors, and they tend to control the training side of it. They know the ubiquitous Cessna and Piper planes backwards, and many of these people didn't like the idea of a making a change. The general view was, 'Yeah, fine, let us know when the aeroplane has been around for two or three years and we might consider it.' There was no urge to change. They were all too comfortable, even though we believed there was a 20 per cent difference in operation costs.

Some of them were worried that we couldn't match Cessna's long-established service infrastructure. But on the Isle of Wight we were knocking out parts at a hell of a rate. At one stage we had parts in stock for sixty-six aircraft. I'd like to think there were more ARV parts in England right then than there were Cessna!

The downside also focused on the reliability of the Hewland engine. We had a problem with the break-up of little-end roller bearings, which caused misfires. We had to put all the aeroplanes down on the ground to get that one sorted out.

Next there was a torsional vibration problem on the propshaft, which caused failures. Under certain circumstances seals in the crankshaft would work loose so the engine would idle only at a very low r.p.m., and this would hammer and destroy the propshaft. The problem was that some flying clubs didn't realize that you had to treat the engine in a different way to the usual American one.

The rot started off in Shoreham, where there were three ARVs. One day a student started up his engine and the propeller didn't go round. We had a team racing round fixing them with replacement gearboxes, but eventually, in August 1987, we had to put all of the aeroplanes on the ground again while we cured the problem. The whole workforce, 127 people, had to be laid off. That was just terrible. I remember having to ring the sales team in Southend, where they thought they'd got two aeroplane sales, and telling them to leave the planes on the ground and come back by train. The humiliation was just terrible. It all started to collapse after that.

The sad thing was that Mike's engine was brilliant, and the fix wasn't all that difficult. Hewland very quickly came out with the D version of the engine, which solved the technical problems – although it was hard to convince people of this.

By then, though, our other problems had taken root. We weren't selling aeroplanes fast enough to keep pace with cashflow requirements. We also had a political split because of general unhappiness about the City involvement. To add to the difficulties, I think the bankers saw me as the *éminence grise* who'd got them into all this in the first place. They just wanted to be shot of it. They didn't intend to put any more serious funding in – just when real financial courage was needed – and we had nowhere else to go.

We had a company with what I thought – and still think – was a really brilliant little aeroplane. But the people working for us were very tired and probably emotionally bruised after all the ups and downs, and we just couldn't rise to that final push. I think the guys on the Isle of Wight felt uncomfortable with the City people, and they probably saw me as one of them – which was deeply ironic, because in my opinion the City is partly to blame for the problems we have in industry in this country, and for the fact that manufacturing in the UK now accounts for less than 20 per cent of gross domestic product.

I don't know whether the City in turn saw me as part of the Isle of Wight mob, but they did get very disenchanted with me. I was in a category of my own!

Midway through 1986 things had come to a head and I'd been asked by the bankers to stand down as chief executive. In my place they appointed a chap called Tom Carroll, who had experience of production after working at Shorts, the Belfast aeroplane manufacturers. I can't say my relationship with him was particularly good, but he certainly knew his production. I moved over to become marketing director.

I suppose all of us encounter failure in our lives, but the ARV thing for me was seriously bad. It was a terrible time on a personal level. I'd started this company, and then I had to move aside to satisfy the bankers. It was easy to see conspiracy at every turn.

The big problem with an aircraft company is the learning curve. You can control the price of the components of the aircraft, but the trick is in controlling the number of man-hours that go into actually building it. Normally you work to an 85 per cent learning curve, which means that if aircraft number one takes a hundred hours, the next one will take eighty-five, and so on. It's only when you

Still a distinctive shape in the sky, the Super2 is a lovely plane to fly.

get down to aircraft number sixty or seventy that the company actually starts to make a profit. We went into production too early, as a result of financial pressure from the banks. As it was, we reached aircraft number thirty-five, which was one hell of an achievement.

In hindsight we should have fought our way out of the doubts about the engine by producing a record-breaking version of the Super2, and then flown it to Australia or somewhere similar to prove its reliability.

I still think that, had the bankers been a little bit braver and given us a chance to get back into production, it could have worked. The market was there and, with hindsight, there were no more competitive aircraft certificated until much later in the 1990s.

It's very interesting that the French Government, for example, will help similar projects in France by offering to finance the production of enough aircraft to get the manufacturer down the learning curve. At one stage I went to the Department of Trade and Industry, who agreed that what we were doing was very interesting. They had a wonderful scheme; they would buy three of your products and put them into the market place and then you could find out how good they were. Terrific. That would have been enormously valuable, but I simply couldn't get them to do it in our case. Eventually I just gave up trying to persuade them. I was wasting my time.

Things went from bad to worse following a board meeting with the bankers in London on 29 October 1987. They didn't want my complete resignation, because it suited them to keep my name on the board, but they now wanted me to step down as marketing director. They wanted me to relinquish an active role altogether. I decided to remain as a shareholding director, because I felt responsible for all the private investors. Somebody ought to be on the board to look after them. But it was quite clear the thing was going downhill fast. There was going to be no more meaningful working capital from the banks. ARV seemed to be in a kind of terminal decline.

That was the day the hurricanes hit England, and I felt as if there was something equally destructive blowing through my own life. The one bright part at that dark time was that Sally was pregnant with our son, Jack.

I felt very bad about the whole ARV situation, particularly laying off the workforce. It wasn't something I was used to doing, and it certainly wasn't something I wanted to do. My own very strong belief was that together we should have brought this damn thing off and won through.

As intended, I remained a director without taking any further part in the running of the company. I tidied my desk, gave back everything that belonged to the company – the models and everything – and walked away. That was one of the most difficult things I've ever had to do in my life, and I was extremely upset about it. It was also upsetting the way some of the people concerned behaved. I thought we'd had a real understanding, but I was wrong. It was an absolute low point. We'd created this wonderful aeroplane, we'd got it certificated and had fought all the battles, and now my part in it was over.

ARV finally went into administration in May 1988. It was horrible to see the firm go under. It was eventually sold to the financial director, Chris Wald, and later to Aviation Scotland.

I'm still terribly proud of it. The ARV Super2 was a lovely little aeroplane. In January 1998 I bought Super2 number twelve, which is my pride and joy. Sometimes I just go and look at it in the Farnborough hangar, and I think, God, we created that! Whenever I fly it I still think, Hell, it really flies well. It's absolutely super!

10 MAKING WAVES

A month after the collapse of my role in ARV the next project presented itself. After *Thrust2* I had begun lunchtime and after-dinner speaking as a means of bringing in day-to-day income. One or two engagements a month really helped. But now an old friend, Adrian Hamilton, came back into my life. An expert in the sale of classic cars, and a familiar figure in classic motorsport circles, he was the son of the late Duncan Hamilton, one of those colourful and legendary figures of motor-racing lore, who had twice won the Le Mans 24-Hours endurance race for Jaguar in the 1950s.

Adrian wanted to build a boat that would set a new record for the fastest crossing of the Atlantic Ocean. Richard Branson had captured the record in 1986 with an average speed of 36.62 knots, but only by refuelling en route. Adrian thought it would be more in keeping with the traditions of the Blue Riband and the Hales Trophy, the titles awarded to the fastest liners in the inter-war years, if we could set a new record without refuelling. Before long I was beginning to see that this could be something quite spectacular.

Adrian had come to an agreement with well-known marine architect Don Shead, a great friend of his, who took the sensible, long-term view that such a project would undoubtedly be a stimulus for his business and his already significant reputation. The other key figure was businessman Ted Toleman, a very well-known figure in powerboat racing and motor racing. He owned the Cougar boatyard with Clive Curtis, and had

After land and air, it was time to try water in 1988, when a friend persuaded me to become involved in an attempt to set a new record for crossing the Atlantic without refuelling. The result was Atlantic Sprinter, seen here in an artist's impression.

been involved with Richard Branson's *Virgin Atlantic Challenger* projects. This well-qualified team asked me to go out and find the backing for it all. The vessel was going to be known as *Atlantic Sprinter*. Don came up with a design for the hull, and the project gradually began to advance in late 1988.

The engine had to be very thermally efficient, to minimize the amount of fuel that was burned. We looked mostly at industrial gas turbines or big diesels. But then I met an absolutely brilliant guy called John Scott-Scott, the project manager for Rolls-Royce on the Hotol hypersonic space-plane engine. He became interested in what we were doing, and then one day he made a simple but very clever suggestion: 'If we can get hold of a Rolls-Royce RB211 Lockheed Tristar engine, we can take the fan off, replace it with a coupling, drive forward to a gearbox, and then drive back to the propellers. This will give us the power and the efficiency of a thirty-five-thousand-horsepower diesel.'

Rolls-Royce liked the idea, and by sheer good fortune it appeared that an engine was going to be made available, an RB211-22B which had just been refurbished for a museum. This was fantastic news, particularly after the problems we'd had getting Rolls-Royce interested in *Thrust2*. I don't know what made the difference. Perhaps it was the success we'd enjoyed with the land-speed record. I wasn't too interested in analysing the reasons why; I was just grateful that the company seemed so interested.

The project all depended on one phone call from Rolls-Royce, on one man at the Derby headquarters making a decision.

I sat at my desk at home for twelve days, waiting for this guy to phone. It was one of those situations where you simply dare not move away in case he calls and you aren't there to take it immediately. All I could do was be patient, because there was simply no way that I dared apply pressure on him to make up his mind. At last he phoned, and said that in principle he thought it was going to be all right. The men at Derby were so enthusiastic that the engine was relabelled with my name.

But then, a few days later, came the blow. The Rolls-Royce board and its lawyers had vetoed the idea. They felt they didn't want the RB211 name used in conjunction with a boat that might fail. If the engine failed in circumstances for which it had never been designed, it might dissuade the public from flying in aeroplanes powered by RB211 engines. It was too risky.

At that point we couldn't see a way forward. Early in 1989 I decided to take a couple of days' holiday, almost the first I'd had since the end of *Thrust2*. While I was away I got a call from a bloke I'd met who specialized in aircraft parts.

'Richard,' he said, 'you're looking for an RB211. Well, I know where there are four.'

I said, 'Yeah, I know, hanging on a wing at Heathrow.'

He laughed and said, 'No. Something very odd has happened. Four of them have turned up at a scrap dealer's near Wolverhampton.'

Sure enough, the guy there told me they had RB211s. I broke off the holiday, jumped in the car and drove straight up there to look them over. It seems Rolls had been clearing out the Hucknall site and had found these old engines, which had then been sold off for scrap.

Unfortunately, I couldn't get the money together quickly enough to secure the one engine that was suitable, which had fresh fan blades and was in good condition, and it was sold to a third party in Southend. But he was prepared to sell, and eventually we were able to raise the money for a deposit. We then had a month within which to test-run it, or face the choice of having either to forfeit the deposit or buy the engine untested.

Enormous problem. Where do you run a Rolls-Royce RB211 engine? Eventually we found a group at Cranfield that was prepared to help us. We built a huge steel test stand for the RB211, bolted it down to a concrete road, and connected the huge engine directly to the Cranfield fuel tank farm. In cold conditions on 21 January 1989, a Sunday, we managed to get it going. Of course, I'd been used to the jet engines in *Thrust1* and *Thrust2*, but this was something else. It was huge, nine feet in diameter, and there it was, lighting up, with great sheets of flame coming out of the exhaust. We ran it up to flight idle, but we couldn't take it any further up the power range as the slabs of the concrete road began to slide. The results as far as they went were exceptionally good – and on that basis we went ahead and purchased it.

In March we launched the *Atlantic Sprinter* project officially at the Mermaid Theatre, down by the River Thames in London. Up until then we'd been moving very fast, and the launch was designed to attract a major sponsor. It failed to do so.

We were somewhat flattened by this, then Shell stimulated some serious questions about the project. They said they were really interested, but that they needed a lot more information on the boat's performance. We weren't able to provide it, and I suspect that was where we began to lose them. We also had a lot of indecision within the team, and eventually John persuaded me that we needed to use far more advanced technology than we had been considering to date. At this point Don Shead dropped out, and then Ted had his own problems to resolve.

By now we had realized that the whole key was the Breguet Range Equation, named after Louis Breguet, the great French aviation pioneer. He had devised a formula which every aircraft designer uses today to determine the range of an aeroplane; it basically equates the range to propulsion efficiency of the engine, the efficiency of the overall airframe, weight, fuel load, etc. By applying the Breguet Range formula we discovered that we needed a very much more efficient hull form than had originally been proposed, bearing in mind the range of sea states that was known to exist on the projected route.

We were also lucky at this stage to secure an agreement with Ove Arup, the civil engineering company. There was a particularly brilliant guy there called Pat Dallard. He came up with a very original idea that would reduce the weight of the boat substantially. It was almost a monocoque structure, in which the bodyshell would itself provide the chassis, like a Formula One car. We could build the boat out of extruded aluminium planks. The huge Norwegian company Nordsk Hydro agreed to provide the aluminium.

We then came across a very clever Turkish designer called Erbil Serter. He'd been playing with boats all his life, and had come up with an interesting hull form. It was banana-shaped; the rear section ran at a different angle of incidence to the front. It had a big, fine bow to cut its way through the waves, and a deep V section, so it would be a semi-planing craft. It offered the prospect of excellent performance and significantly reduced overall resistance. The chines, the actual edges of the hull, were sharp, and they had a very special shape as they moved aft towards the transom. This created two horizontal vortices which provided the stability in roll; in other words, it was as if the boat went along riding at the stern on a couple of rolled carpets of water and air. Serter had been doing a lot of work on this, and soon we had produced a scale model together. We spent two exhausting days belting the model up and down the HSVA water tank in Hamburg, and the results were incredibly impressive.

We also put a 12-foot model in British Aerospace's Hatfield wind tunnel, and John Scott-Scott was flogging away with the figures. Gradually we were getting the feel of it, and by this time we were convinced it was going to work. The figures looked really good. On 350 tons of fuel and 30,000 shaft horsepower we could probably achieve a 60-knot Blue Riband record in sea state four.

Hydrodynamics designer Erbil Serter came up with a dramatic shape for Atlantic Sprinter's hull. Water-tank testing delivered highly promising results.

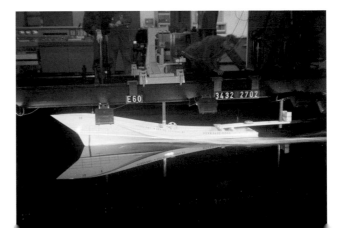

The primary propulsion was changed to a group of four surface-piercing propellers, which were to be made by industry doyen Phil Rolla, who was very keen to help.

This was all very important, because there was a lot of competition for the Atlantic crossing record. The Aga Khan was building a large boat, *Destriero*, which simply had conventional hull-form technology and three huge Allison engines totalling 70,000 shaft horsepower. It needed 700 tons of fuel to do the crossing, twice our projected

Our wind-tunnel testing suggested that Atlantic Sprinter could shatter the existing transatlantic record.

capacity. Fiat created their own boat, the *Azimut Challenger*, and in America, the late Tom Gentry built *Gentry Eagle*. We knew we were capable of going a lot quicker than all of them, ten knots or more faster on average, on half the fuel and half the power of the *Destriero*.

Later on we took all of our data and fed it into a flight simulator at RAE Bedford. We actually rode this boat at 60 knots. It felt very comfortable.

Towards the end of 1989, our first full year of *Atlantic Sprinter*, we found that the city of Newcastle, with its history of shipbuilding, was seriously interested in the project. Together we developed the concept of creating a construction hall for *Sprinter* in Gateshead, where the public could watch it being made. With a local sponsor we erected this hall. We had high hopes that a local sponsor would invest further once he saw how much progress we were making. A shipyard manager was lined up to build the boat. We were all set to start off at the Gateshead Garden Festival a little later in the year, and planned to rename *Sprinter* the *Spirit of Newcastle*.

Unfortunately, we failed to generate much interest from sponsors. But looking back at *Atlantic Sprinter*, it's important to remember what was happening back in the late 1980s. There was one hell of a lot of money being spent on sponsorship at that time. The recession was still in the future, and nobody believed it would ever really come. Things were going right up the hill, closing to the peak. Figures of £1 million or £2 million in sponsorship were really not uncommon, even outside Formula One. We were looking for £2 million, and we genuinely thought that we could get it.

Atlantic Sprinter's Gateshead build shed.

And now, literally as soon as this large construction hall had been built, the bottom fell out of the market. Our very large local sponsor had indicated that they wanted to come in, but now they had to withdraw.

Soon we were ducking and weaving every which way to survive. The problem with building this type of boat is that you can't just build it in small bits, the way that we would with *ThrustSSC*. We really had to go for it; there was no building a little bit here and a little bit there.

All we could do was retrench, but we were about £250,000 in the red. Fortunately the *Daily Express* and Scottish & Newcastle Breweries helped us out, which enabled us to clear some of the debt. We still had some sort of legal action impending every week, and it was a very difficult time. I was lucky to have Sally fighting alongside me, helping to keep me sane through this nightmare. It was a truly terrible period.

You really can't give up the moment things turn sour. Half the battle is in forcing yourself to keep going when others might be tempted to stop.

What had happened, effectively, was that *Atlantic Sprinter* had become a 1980s project that had dragged into the 1990s, and the recession made everything much more difficult. But we did keep fighting, and gradually we were able to work our way out of it and pay people off, one by one.

You don't realize the difficulties of these things until you actually do them, and I suppose the boat just didn't grab the public imagination in the way that we thought it would. What really brought this home was the Boat Show early in 1989. We had the engine on a stand as we'd done with the Rolls-Royce Avon engine intended for *Thrust2* at the London Motorfair twelve years earlier. We had a lot of HSVA footage showing just how Erbil's hull worked in our tank tests. And there we were, at the Boat Show at Earl's Court, the Mecca of the boat world, and when we talked to people they weren't interested. They just didn't want to know how this magic hull worked. It seems that many people buy boats without knowing too much about how they actually work.

I was very surprised by all this. I have to admit that at times I felt that perhaps I was out of my element. After all, I'd lived and dreamed the land-speed record for twenty-two years before I actually got down to doing anything about it. But I hadn't known much about boats before we started *Sprinter*. Then again, we were doing something that hadn't been done before. Nobody knew much about it, and because we possibly knew more than 'the others', no-one believed us.

During this dark period our real friends stuck by us. Nordsk Hydro were brilliant; they supplied us with extruded aluminium sections so we could test weld sections, and though we were insolvent, and so couldn't actually trade, we kept battling on behind the scenes.

In October 1990 I was able to forget about boats for a week, when I went back to Bonneville. In retrospect it was to prove to be one of those defining moments, though I didn't fully appreciate that at the time.

Salt Flat Films was making a movie about Art Arfons, who, though now in his sixties, was intending to have a go at our land-speed record in a tiny little car called *Green Monster No. 27*. Autocar commissioned me to write a piece about *Green Monster*, and it seemed like the sort of interlude I needed to clear my head.

To be honest, I felt a complete clot turning up at Bonneville without a car. I just felt desperately inadequate. But as it turned out, I had a ball. It really was great to meet Art, who is one of the real legends of land-speed record-breaking. I'd met Craig Breedlove and the late Gary Gabelich out at Black Rock with *Thrust2* in 1983, but I'd never met Art before. He was brilliant, putting his *Green Monsters* together with minimal budgets, and going out and winning the record three times in the 1960s during the game of Russian roulette that he played with Craig, who had been his main rival. And, of course, *Thrust2* was based on Art's 1960s *Green Monster*, so there was a degree of affinity there, too. I admire that man enormously. He didn't disappoint; he's a magic personality, a really great man.

One of the regular Bonneville hot-rod meets was going on while we were there, and Art was planning to run this new car of his along with all the other guys. While all this was going on Craig turned up, because he was also going to be part of this film on Art's life. The three of us had a good session in the evening for the film, where we talked about our projects and experiences.

It was while we were doing this that Craig took me on one side and said, 'Say, Richard, I've decided to build another car. It's twenty-five years since I last ran at Bonneville, but I've just come from purchasing two J79 8 series engines. I'm committed.' That was the first I'd heard of his plans, and right then I thought to myself, This is where we come in again.

The thing is, once you break a world record you virtually put yourself out of business. I'd wanted to keep going after *Thrust2* and build *Thrust3*, but we found that nobody seemed remotely interested in backing us to break our own record. Now Craig's surprise announcement had changed everything. As far as I was concerned, the next chapter in the land-speed history book was ready to be written: a contest between Britain and America. It was a fabulous concept, guaranteed to stir the old patriotic juices.

Craig had spoken of trying for 700 m.p.h., and I suddenly realized that a fabulous opportunity now lay ahead. He would be probing deep into the region of transonic airflow, but I wanted to go one stage further and create the world's first genuine supersonic car, capable of more than 750 m.p.h.

There was a fascinating counterpoint to this Anglo-American rivalry. Back in 1943 what was then the Ministry of Aircraft Production in Britain issued specification E (for Experimental) 24/43, which called for an aircraft with the capability to fly at 1000 m.p.h. This was an incredibly far-sighted specification at a time when special test Spitfires at Farnborough were scraping to Mach 0.9 in near-suicidal full-power dives, even more so given the paucity of knowledge of transonic, let alone supersonic aircraft aerodynamics.

Sir Stafford Cripps, the Minister for Aircraft Production, favoured the proposal from the small Miles Aircraft Company run by chairman and managing director F. G. Miles, who promptly accepted the challenge. Miles liaised with Ben Lockspeiser, the controller of Research and Development at the Ministry, RAE Farnborough and the National Physical Laboratory. Top-secret plans were laid down by his brother, George Miles, and designer Dennis Bancroft for an all-metal craft which looked like a bullet with razor-edged wings and an all-moving tailplane. The shape pre-dated that of Bell's X-1, which would ultimately be successful. The power unit would be the very first afterburning turbofan engine, designed and built by Frank Whittle's Power Jets company, where Whittle, predictably, had been an enthusiastic advocate of supersonic flight.

By February 1946 the design and construction of the M52 was 85 per cent complete. Then Lockspeiser, now a knight and the director general of Scientific Research at the Ministry of Aircraft Production, dropped a bombshell by informing a devastated F. G. Miles that the project had been axed, with immediate effect. A fleet of trucks turned up at Miles's with crates to collect the nearly complete airframe, jigs, tools and drawings. A few days later it was almost as if the M52 had never existed. Nobody will say where the M52 went – it may still be in the UK!

Just as the world's knowledge of Yeager's historic feat would be delayed by the spurious need for secrecy, so the Official Secrets Act in Britain kept taxpayers in the dark about the demise of the supersonic aircraft they didn't even know they had. It was September before Whitehall plucked up the nerve to make things public.

The decision to cancel was craven. Lockspeiser admitted in a letter to Miles that he did not believe that aircraft would fly at supersonic speed for many years, 'and perhaps not ever'. There certainly was little chance of it while he exercised control. He said he was worried about the dangers of manned supersonic test flights and also cited the poor state of the economy, but it seems he was simply a man who was in the wrong job.

Lockspeiser and his advisers, among them Sir Barnes Wallis (who in better days had designed the wartime 'Bouncing Bomb' that destroyed the Ruhr Dams, and the geodetic construction of the Wellington bomber, and who would go on to design the swing-wing aeroplane), were scandalously content to hand the lead over to the Americans. They must have been laughing all the way to Edwards Air Force Base. The Supersonic Committee cancelled the M52 in a meeting on 12 February. Extraordinarily, no minute of such an important meeting survives, and the reasons for the cancellation appear obscure. On 9 October 1948 a rocket test model of the M52 reached 930 m.p.h., or Mach 1.38.

The reason for the cancellation may have been due in some way to the Lend Lease situation under which British patents often found their way to America. John Scott-Scott more recently told me how horrified he was to learn that some of his classified engine patents had been found new owners in the US. Others hint at more murky political reasons for the sudden and unexplained cancellation of the M52, which centred on rival factions seeking to stymie Whittle's burgeoning jet-engine success.

In 1997, Dennis Bancroft, the M52's designer, came down to see us at Farnborough and spent a very happy day. He told us that Whittle had designed the first-ever afterburning engine, and that the M52 had been streets ahead of anything the Americans were doing at the time. Yet we gave it away! In a subsequent letter he said, 'Do you realize that if we'd actually been able to proceed with the Miles M52 at that time, Andy Green would not have been flying an old Tornado today?' Basically, the British aircraft industry would have jumped at least ten years further ahead.

Sir Roy Fedden, one of the country's leading aero-engine designers, was unequivocal in his condemnation when he said: 'No single act set back Britain's aircraft development quite so drastically as the Government's decision not to allow supersonic investigation.'

Half a century on, I felt that a British supersonic car might go some way towards making up the lost ground. We could be first to break the sound barrier on land, as we should have been in the air. But to do so, we had to beat Craig Breedlove.

Craig is one hell of an adversary. Speed is in his blood. In 1963 the urge to go fast had taken him to the top of the world, when his three-wheeled jet car *Spirit of America* achieved 407.45 m.p.h. at Bonneville. At a stroke he outdated fast cars such as the *Railton Special*, driven by my hero, John Cobb. Craig figured that if Malcolm and Donald Campbell could drive boats propelled by pure-thrust jet engines, he could do the same with a car. He was thus one of the first to usher in the new era of pure-thrust vehicles, which brought the explosion in speed from Donald Campbell's 403.1 m.p.h. in July 1964, in the wheel-driven *Bluebird*, to Craig's own record of 600.601 m.p.h. in the pure-thrust *Spirit of America – Sonic 1*, set in November 1965. Breedlove's two-year duel with rival Art Arfons in his Green Monster was undoubtedly one of the most exciting in land-speed record history.

At the end of one Bonneville run in his original *Spirit of America* tricycle in October 1964, Breedlove's parachutes had torn away, and when he used the brakes at close to 400 m.p.h. they melted. Unchecked, the *Spirit* chopped down a telegraph pole before vaulting a bank and nosediving into a brine lake. Craig was lucky, and managed to swim ashore. He stood on top of the bank waving his arms and laughing with relief. 'For my next trick,' he said, 'I'll set myself afire!'

Craig is a cool customer. That day he told me of his plans to go after our record, I knew that he was deadly serious. I suspected, too, that he would be able to attract the support of major corporate sponsors in America. I suppose there and then, out on the flats, I made a decision that he wasn't going to take our record without a real fight.

But at that precise moment, and for a while afterwards, there was nothing that I could do to move forward.

When I got back, the chance we had so desperately been waiting for with *Atlantic Sprinter* appeared on the horizon. A major German shipyard, Abeking and Rasmussen, who had already built a number of Erbil Serter's designs, suddenly took a shine to the *Sprinter* project. I was cautious, because I'd already been around a lot of British shipyards, armed with a report from the HSVA in Hamburg, trying to get people interested. HSVA is very well respected in the marine world, and here we had their independent report with all the data. But the people I spoke to wouldn't even look at it. Here was something revolutionary, and they wouldn't consider it.

'Look, Richard,' I heard time and again. 'We're just shipbuilders. We don't speculate, and we don't take risks.'

I went to Vosper's, which ironically had built John Cobb's *Crusader* back in 1951, and I was appalled to find that they'd laid off most of their workforce. Somebody had told me they had an awful lot of money in the bank, and I said to them, 'If you build this, it could give you guys an enormous leap forward over the competition.' They said no, the City bankers would never permit it, even if it allowed them to reinstate the workforce and take a giant step forward.

I found this attitude terribly disappointing, a throwback to the time when it all started to go wrong for Britain as an industrial force in the 1960s. Instead of aspiring to lead, so many of our captains of industry actually seemed to feel safer doing nothing about their present plight and nothing about their future. None of them was prepared to take any risks. The shipbuilding industry typified this. People said to me, 'Richard, it's up to the Government to take risks like this, and to fund them. It's not for us, we just build them.'

The project had now dragged through to 1991, but despite the problems I was still enthusiastic that we could turn the corner as I set off for Abeking and Rasmussen. I took out the passenger seat of Adrian's Ford Transit so that I could fit this huge 12-foot wind-tunnel model in, then drove out to Hamburg. We had a terrific meeting. Pat Dallard from Ove Arup had done an enormous amount of work on the structure; we had sections of test aluminium from Nordsk Hydro for Abeking and Rasmussen's people to test weld; Martin Francis down in the south of France had done all the drawings. The whole package was seriously impressive, and I really thought that we were going to get the deal. Abeking and Rasmussen held a meeting with their key people, which went on all day and into the next. They said that they liked the concept, the hull form and the method of building. They thought it was very interesting and they wanted to try it. They said they hadn't got much work on at that time, and, in direct contrast to Vosper's, they had retained their workforce.

But there were two non-technical weaknesses. Who was going to fund the gearbox? GEC wasn't interested in helping with that side of things, though they were interested in building it. That was a serious problem because it was going to cost over £200,000. The other thing was that Abeking and Rasmussen wanted to see Rolls-Royce back the engine side of it. I had to say to them, 'I'm very sorry, but it simply won't happen.'

That's the point where they didn't feel able to go any further forward. After three years of graft we were absolutely shattered, and we knew we'd reached the end. The *Atlantic Sprinter* project was over. In December 1991 it went into liquidation.

It's almost like a death in the family when something like that happens. These projects take an enormous amount of energy and enthusiasm to get off the ground, and sheer hard work to keep going, and losing them is simply devastating. All along you never believe they won't come off, despite all the troubles that you face, and you never give up because you always believe you have to win through no matter what.

It was terribly sad. I felt again that we had failed very badly. I was convinced that we had something very special – but industry and the public simply weren't interested.

Gary Gabelich used to say that when you get knocked down you just have to learn how to get right back up again, and by God he was right.

It was around this time that I met a chap called Ray Steward. The whole idea of a new car was burning away deeply in the background, but I was heavily in personal debt from the *Atlantic Sprinter* project, and somehow I had to earn some money. It was time to get a 'proper' job again. So Ray and I formed a company called Programme Funding, the plan being to fund television programmes. The idea was to use the television programme as an advertisement in an oblique way.

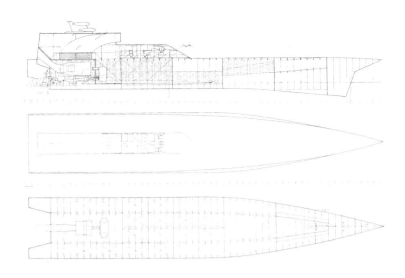

Atlantic Sprinter blueprints. I remain convinced that our concept was as feasible as it was exciting, but the sad truth is that Altantic Sprinter was an Eighties project that dragged too long into the Nineties.

It wasn't exactly product placement, it was much more a connection of the programme content with a manufacturer's product values. We would use a programme to raise commercial funds from the programme sponsors. A lot of people have very good ideas for television programmes, but have an awful time trying to raise the money.

We struggled away with this, but as I began to get to grips with the business I came to realize that what we were effectively doing was trying to elbow two groups of people aside: the broadcasters and the production companies. Our service was to provide the production funding that traditionally was sourced from the broadcasters.

I've been lucky in that I've never really had to wait too long for the next major project to come along. Ever since the *Thrust1* days I'd had the idea in the back of my mind for a third *Thrust* car, and that meeting with Breedlove back at Bonneville in October 1990 had given the scheme greater definition and impetus. But I hadn't been able to get going with a new land-speed-record attempt, partly because of *Atlantic Sprinter*, partly because of my practical need to earn a living, and partly because I knew I would require somebody with a very specialized knowledge of aerodynamics to help on the technical side.

As 1991 moved into 1992, and I neared my forty-sixth birthday, I didn't know that I was about to meet the man who would help me break through to the next stage in my life.

11 THE SUPERSONIC DREAM

Early in 1992 I was feeling absolutely miserable. Ray and I were pushing hard with Programme Funding, and had an office in London's Gloucester Place. We met a lot of people and had a lot of tough meetings, but I was commuting to town every day by train, and hating every minute of it. I just couldn't settle. I felt as if I'd gone back to the worst days of ICI and GKN, without the bonus of foreign travel. It was pure graft. I'm certainly not averse to graft itself – that was what had made *Thrust2* successful. But this existence was far less stimulating, and I felt very unhappy with what I was doing. After all the nervous energy and excitement of the *Thrust* years, ARV and *Atlantic Sprinter*, I felt that I'd gone backwards. I didn't want to believe that I had ended up back on the treadmill I had stepped off twenty years earlier. Life had to hold more than that.

The fundamental problem with my aspirations to create the world's first supersonic car was that I just couldn't get a grip. I had the idea, I wanted to do it, but I wanted to do it really well, so that it would be a spectacular success.

I suppose that at the back of all this I also felt on my mettle to prove myself again. We had been successful with *Thrust2*, but so far as the public was concerned that had been followed by two failures. To me, ARV was a partial success, because we'd gone quite some way down the line and created a viable aircraft; but the boat was a total failure.

So there I was, forty-six years old and feeling increasingly frustrated. I just didn't seem to be able to identify the way forward.

Ackers and I had always wanted to build another car, and we looked at several ways of doing it. But we were worried by a number of things. One was the question of what had actually happened to the airflow underneath the car. Frankly, the graph of the loadings on the front suspension of *Thrust2* was horrendous! We calculated that it could have gone about seven m.p.h. faster before the front end started lifting. John and I had kept talking, exchanging ideas and so on, but nothing seemed to gel. John had subsequently developed an interest in high-altitude balloons, and had gone off to pursue that.

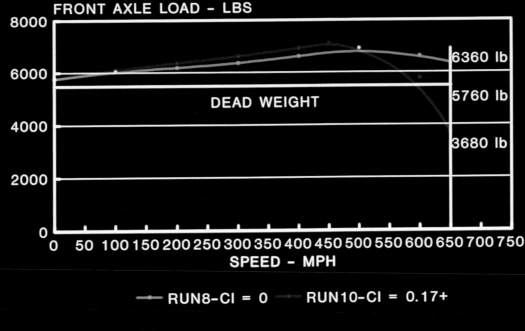

FRONT AXLE LOAD - LBS

DEAD WEIGHT

6360 lb

5760 lb

3680 lb

SPEED - MPH

⎯•⎯ RUN8-CI = 0   ⎯•⎯ RUN10-CI = 0.17+

CI = CAR INCIDENCE

During our initial research into a supersonic car, one of the first things we investigated was the airflow beneath Thrust2. John Ackroyd's original graph indicated that, had we gone 7 m.p.h. faster, front-end lift might have made the car fly.

Then things suddenly turned my way, completely by chance. It was just good fortune that Ron Ayers and I ever met. In some ways the whole *ThrustSSC* project owes its existence to traffic jams on the M27 motorway. It's ironic that something so slow should have led to something so fast.

On 14 July I went down to the Bournemouth Flying Club, at what was then still called Hurn Airport, just outside Bournemouth itself, to see Ken Norris. Ken, of course, had been team manager with *Thrust2* from 1982 onwards, and this was just a social visit. We had always kept in regular contact. The fellow that Ken was supposed to be seeing at ten in the morning had been held up in roadworks on the M27, so he was still with Ken when I bowled up at our scheduled eleven o'clock meeting. Ken introduced us. 'Richard,' he said, 'this is Ron Ayers. Ron is doing research into past land-speed-record contenders.'

Ron was retired, and since he lives at Claygate, close to the old Brooklands race track at Weybridge, he had taken to helping out at the Brooklands Museum. He had managed to get hold of data there relating to old record attempts, and had unearthed all sorts of nuggets: fascinating things, such as the fact that R. J. Mitchell, the designer of the Spitfire, had actually discussed the design of *Bluebird* with Sir Malcolm Campbell.

The three of us had an entertaining lunch together, over which Ron outlined his concern that all the land-speed-record cars appeared to have under-performed, given their technical specification and ultimate speed. 'It's got to be something to do with the wheels, not the aerodynamics,' was his summary. He suggested that the rolling resistance was always higher than anyone expected it to be, and he wanted to prepare a paper to that effect.

Ron is not the sort of man who tells you who he is and what he has done. He keeps himself to himself. Over lunch I gradually realized that he was extremely clever. He asked me all sorts of questions about record cars, and *Thrust2* in particular, that I would never have thought of.

I was intrigued, and asked if I could come and see him. So we got together again and that was where I learned more of this self-effacing man's remarkable background. He had been head of Operations Research and deputy head of Management Services for the British Aircraft Corporation Guided Weapons Division at Bristol, and he was the chief aerodynamicist on the Bloodhound 2 anti-aircraft missile. Ron was very interested in the fact that there always seemed to be a 4,000-pound thrust difference between the potential power of the Avon engine and the actual performance of *Thrust2*. Was all that power absorbed by the rolling resistance of the Black Rock Desert?

As I told him of my plans for a supersonic car, we agreed that before we could even consider such a thing we had to know exactly what had been happening with *Thrust2*. But once we had conducted those primary calculations, we then reached a stage where we really couldn't go any further without some funding for more research. So for the second time the project hung fire.

On the right is Ron Ayers, ThrustSSC aerodynamicist, and on the left is Glynne Bowsher, who designed the brakes for Thrust2, and then came into his own as the mechanical designer of ThrustSSC.

Later that year I was able to put another piece of the jigsaw together. After *Thrust2* we had formed the 633 Club, which comprised the team members who had worked on that project. Every year we'd meet as close to 4 October as possible. In 1992 our meeting took place down at Paul Ffoulkes-Halberd's Filching Manor Motor Museum. There were an awful lot of people milling around the tents, but at one stage I managed to grab Glynne Bowsher for a quiet word. Glynne, a displaced Welshman living in the Midlands, had designed the brakes and done the finite element analysis on the wheels of *Thrust2*, and was still working for Lucas.

'I can't tell you very much, Glynne,' I said, 'but it looks as if we've got to do a wheel about the diameter of *Thrust2*'s, but one that will rotate to about ten thousand revs a minute. Are you on?'

Glynne just looked at me for a moment. 'Are you telling me what I think you're telling me?' he asked. 'Yes,' I said. 'In that case,' he said, 'I shall start work tomorrow.'

Glynne began by doing an enormous amount of finite element analysis using Lucas's equipment, which they had generously given him permission to use for our purposes. He worked the most appalling hours. We all saw this new car as the last throw of the land-speed-record dice, so it had to be bloody brilliant. Glynne, like Ron, was prepared to invest his own time to ensure that it was.

Then, towards the middle of 1993, came the massive stroke of luck that really kick-started the *SSC* programme.

Castrol holds a meeting of its most senior worldwide directors every five years. The latest was due to take place in Palm Springs, California, between 7–11 June, and the fellow they'd lined up initially as the guest speaker had to drop out. I was asked, on the basis of our relationship back in the *Thrust2* days, if I would step in at late notice and do a presentation. I said, 'Yes, of course. I'd love to.'

I felt that perhaps some of the Castrol directors just didn't realize what a heritage they had. So Castrol International gave me access to their archives, and I dug out all these fascinating pictures and put a presentation together. It was really a history lesson: this is who you are and how the Castrol name was built up.

The founder of the company, Charles Cheers Wakefield, later Lord Wakefield, had supported the Alcock and Brown Atlantic crossing in 1919, and then, through sponsorship and patronage, had done a tremendous amount to support record attempts. He had wanted to use his resources and his skills to enhance the reputation of his country. As a result, record-breaking held the attention of the population during the inter-war years on a far greater scale than Grand Prix racing.

At the end of this presentation I just said, 'So this is what Castrol stands for. You guys have got to remember that you have one of the most valuable brands in the world, and every generation has to make its contribution to keep that reputation alive.'

I passionately believe that. You simply cannot live on past glories, whether as an individual, as a corporation, or as a country. You cannot rest on your laurels. In the 1950s Mercedes-Benz and Jaguar established phenomenal reputations on the racetrack, yet both allowed them to become diluted over the decades following their withdrawal from competition. Then each came back in the 1980s, and once again achieved success to inject fresh credibility into the marque.

After the presentation I went back to my table. I had deliberately refrained from alluding to our future aspirations. That would have been a cheap shot, and I was not there to make a sponsorship pitch. That was not the point at all. But as I sat down Jonathan Fry, the chief executive of Castrol International, leaned across and said, 'You're setting us up, Richard, aren't you?' And I had to reply, 'Yes!'

Dr Brian Ridgewell, Castrol International's marketing and technology director, was also at our table. 'In that case', he said, 'you'd better come to see us when we all get home.'

The new project had a name by now: *ThrustSSC*. The *Thrust* name was an obvious must, but I thought *Thrust3* seemed a bit unadventurous. *ThrustSSC*, meaning supersonic car, had a much sharper edge and told people immediately what it stood for.

I took Brian Ridgewell at his word and made a presentation on *ThrustSSC* at Burmah Castrol House down in Swindon shortly after our return. Right from the start I made our situation clear. 'There is something you must understand,' I told them. 'First of all we're dealing with something that is dangerous, something that is unknown, and we've got to do some very sensible research on this. I'm terrified of a situation where we might end up working on a project that we all believe in, but which, without the research, in practice turns out to be desperately iffy and which may even result in someone being hurt.'

They shared that view, and we had an extremely fruitful discussion afterwards. On 6 August I received a letter from Brian offering £40,000 to fund our research.

This was a fabulous boost. Ron, Glynne and I could obviously work in our own time. But now we had the wherewithal to push ahead with detailed research. It took enormous guts for Brian to make that sort of commitment to such an experimental project, especially since both Ron and I had firmly agreed that we would not go ahead with the build if our findings suggested that we could not do so within satisfactory parameters of safety. Not many corporate executives would have dared to take such a bold decision. Thanks to Brian, the *ThrustSSC* project was finally rolling.

Craig Breedlove was without question our strongest competitor, but we knew there were others who coveted a similar goal. Of the two most serious, we felt that one represented more of a short-term threat to *Thrust2*'s record; and that the other was definitely a contender in the race to Mach 1.

The former was an Australian drag racer, Rosco McGlashan. His *Aussie Invader II* was a *Thrust2*-type car, with the potential to break our old record, and take it up closer to 650 m.p.h. That seemed to be on the cards. But as I saw it, there was

As Ron and I developed our ideas for ThrustSSC, we knew that we were not alone in seeking to break our own record. Besides Craig Breedlove, the Australian Rosco McGlashan had created a Thrust2 lookalike called Aussie Invader II with which he sought speeds closer to 650 m.p.h.

a huge leap between the 1960s-shape cars – and both *Thrust2* and *Aussie Invader* fell into that category – and the supersonics.

Rosco is what they call in Australia a battler. He was trying to do this in a country with very little indigenous industry. He was literally just battling his way through. It took him ten years to produce his car, and he built most of it himself. *Aussie Invader II* was 26 feet long, with a SNECMA Atar turbojet engine, which made it more powerful than *Thrust2*, with roughly 1,000 extra pounds of thrust.

Simply getting the car built was a landmark achievement. Rosco had invested £60,000 of his own hard-won money, and also ingenuity, effort and commitment in equal measures. Given his scant resources for both research and construction, it was hardly surprising that *Aussie Invader* looked so much like *Thrust2*, with twin cockpits slung either side of the centrally mounted engine. The line of these cockpits was lower than *Thrust2*'s, however, and *Invader* had a single rear fin. The one-piece bodyshell was another departure, reminiscent of John Cobb's *Railton Special*, but was manufactured in carbon fibre and Kevlar. The wheels were solid aluminium, just like *Thrust2*'s, which was not surprising since they had been designed by the same man, John Ackroyd. Rosco once said to me, 'When I first approached John to help I expected him to say, "No way, mate," because we were opposition, but he couldn't have been more positive.'

The inevitable financial delays held Rosco back until December 1993. Then, as soon as he got to Lake Gairdner, a salt lake 400 miles north of Adelaide, he was devastated by a torrential thunderstorm. When he finally made his first runs, *Invader* demonstrated the same unnerving lack of directional stability as *Thrust2* had done at Bonneville. Rosco admitted, 'It was scary, mate, bloody scary.' I knew just what he meant! He then demonstrated his courage by reaching 475 m.p.h., using a keeled rear wheel in place of one of the front wheels to try to get better directional grip. The following March he went back, with redesigned wheels, sponsorship from Australia's Channel 7 television network and a new sense of purpose. After hitting 450 m.p.h. in one direction, a parachute failure sent him skimming through shallow water. *Invader*'s undertray was torn off, and to make things worse the timing lights hadn't registered a speed on the return run. Subsequently he fought off more disappointments, to raise the Australian record to 498.6 m.p.h. in the mile and 499.1 m.p.h. in the kilometre before his time on the salt expired. But now he and the world knew what we had suspected for months: the McLaren Formula One team had grandiose plans not just to build a land-speed-record contender, but to smash through the sound barrier.

*

As we progressed with our research programme word kept reaching us of an attempt on the supersonic record by McLaren. A whisper here, a suggestion there. Then one day Sally got a phone call from McLaren, saying, 'We want some land-speed-record film, could we have some?' When she told me I thought, God, I know what that means!

Not long afterwards we started getting a barrage of phone calls from our friends in the industry. 'Hey, did you know McLaren was here . . . ?' Everybody had apparently been sworn to silence, but people were ringing us up nevertheless and saying, 'You ought to know this, you ought to know that.' Then we knew for sure that McLaren was serious and that there was more to this than just a demand for a videotape.

It was all a great spur for us.

The McLaren situation was interesting because there is a crucial element to these projects. It's a bit like an artist. Van Gogh, for example, produced his best work when he was in deep trouble. When things are tough you are absolutely forced to make decisions that you wouldn't normally make.

Now as long as you have got a comfortable project, one where all the funding is in place and you aren't really having to think laterally, I don't think it will work. The decisions that generally are made are comfortable decisions. This was the situation with Donald Campbell and the *Bluebird CN7* car. Like McLaren, there was too much money swilling around. Campbell took comfortable and easy decisions. He opted for a gas-turbine-engined version of John Cobb's *Railton*, and it had a comfortable design and construction lead time. In fact it was too comfortable, because the design thinking began in 1956 and by the time *Bluebird* was finally ready, four years later, it was potentially outdated. Americans such as Dr Nathan Ostich and his *Flying Caduceus* were already experimenting with the straight-jet cars that would subsequently push the record well beyond *Bluebird*'s reach. If *Bluebird* had been ready in 1958, Campbell might well have got a more meaningful record.

McLaren were starting as a team, and a very successful one at that in Formula One. Their performance dipped slightly in the mid-1990s, possibly because projects such as *Maverick* were distracting, but their score of Grand Prix victories since the team entered Formula One in 1966 was second only to Ferrari, who had a sixteen-year head start. Their intended entry into record-breaking was the 1990s manifestation of Sunbeam's interest in the 1920s. But just taking people from a sport where drivers go round corners and transposing them into something supersonic might not have been as straightforward as some people expected.

Interestingly, the car they proposed was fairly traditional. The *Maverick* was going to be 46 feet long, weigh just under 7,000 pounds, and be powered by a 20,000-pound-thrust Rolls-Royce RB199 engine. I've seen sketches, and the *Maverick* was like the *Bluebird* rocket car that Donald Campbell wanted to build in 1966: a slim fuselage, with the front wheels close together and the rears outrigged. Where McLaren really broke fresh ground was that they planned to use carbon-fibre composites for the chassis structure. The designer, Dr Bob Bell, also intended to exploit McLaren's Formula One expertise to design a computer-controlled 'active' suspension, similar to the one Jerry Bliss would design for us.

With all their money I always felt that McLaren had only to pick up the telephone to get what they wanted. After all, they already had Rolls-Royce and British Aerospace involved, and I knew only too well how tough it was to capture the interest of the Rolls-Royce board.

In England, meanwhile, the McLaren Formula One team was also working in great secrecy on a supersonic car. Even now no photograph has ever been released of the stillborn contender, but this artist's impression is an accurate depiction of its tricycle shape.

The Castrol money was purely for the research programme, so none of it could come to us for personal expenses. But, of course, I still needed to earn a living. Ron was retired and had agreed to be self-financing at this stage, Glynne was still working at Lucas and said much the same thing, whereas I had a young family and all the responsibilities that entailed. I set up *SSC* Programme Ltd with both of them as shareholders, to reflect their enormous contribution, but in the meantime all three of us had to fund ourselves.

I reckoned I still had to work another year on Programme Funding, but I was worried because I really didn't think we were getting anywhere. Nobody would give us a chance. We would go and see a lot of people, but nothing happened as a result. My partner Ray had been the marketing director of the *Daily Express*, so he knew exactly what he was talking about. I seemed to be labelled as a cranky land-speed-record driver. At first, whatever we tried, we couldn't get it together.

Then we heard a most extraordinary story. Richard Creasey, son of the novelist John Creasey, one of the world's most prolific authors, was working for Central Television. His father had inspired him at some early stage by filling up their car with books and driving round the world. Richard was very taken with this, and it was something that he now wanted to recreate. He'd got all sorts of things going, and with money from Central and Meridian Television he had thoroughly researched a very clever idea. If he was quick about it there was a window of opportunity which would enable him to drive round the world from London to New York. He reasoned that you could literally drive through the Channel Tunnel, which at that stage was still under construction, before they put the rails down for the Eurostar trains. Then he found a machine called the Arktos, which enabled you to drive across the Bering Straits while they were frozen. This machine was also capable of climbing out of water onto ice. In theory, therefore, it was possible to drive from London to New York.

Being the influential chap that he is, and having managed to find the money to fund the research, he'd flown across Siberia in Russian helicopters to check out routes and arrangements. But now came the crunch. The television companies had no money to fund the actual event. Richard had given the responsibility for raising sponsorship to a couple of guys who had failed miserably. So all this research money had gone out of the door, and there seemed to be no prospect of making any sort of documentary to recoup the initial outlay.

Ray and I got to hear of this, and decided it was exactly what we wanted. I went to see the deputy chairman at Meridian. It was one of those all-or-nothing meetings, where somehow or other we had managed to barge our way in. He said, 'OK, I'm in seriously deep trouble. All this money has gone out and I haven't a hope in hell of financing this production. We're bloody angry about the whole thing. The sponsorship people we appointed have come back with nothing. Nobody wants to do it. I despair.'

I asked, 'Presumably this thing is going to get a lot of air time?' and he told us he could run anything up to eight hours of UK prime time. So we had a major sales point straight off. I said, 'Well, we can do it for you. How much do you want?'

'I need a million, really,' he told us. 'Eight hundred thousand pounds at the least.' So I said, 'We'll get you one and a half million within six weeks. How's that?'

There was this appalling silence. Eventually he nodded slowly. 'OK, have a go.'

We went like hell at it, and we managed to bring in Ford, for £1,500,000. It was simply astonishing. They would supply a team of Mondeo saloons and four-wheel-drive *Mavericks*.

We had rewritten Richard's idea so that it became a race between two teams. Richard had wanted to take a selection of celebrities with him, but we persuaded him it would be much more exciting as a race. 'Today the red team is ahead of the blue . . .' that sort of thing. That's what we sold Ford, but then the negotiations dragged on, and eventually it reverted to the original plan. But it got its television coverage, eight hours on mainstream ITV, and Ford was pleased because there were extraordinary shots of Mondeos battling with Arctic temperatures deep in Siberia, and coping well.

One of the celebrities was the former *Blue Peter* presenter and action man turned director Peter Duncan, who was approached at Sally's suggestion. I met him later while he was doing a play at the Regent's Park Open-Air Theatre, and asked him what it had been like. He just laughed and said, 'Absolutely appalling!'

They had a problem on the Bering Straits when the Arktos couldn't cope with slushy ice, because it clogged up the water jets and failed to provide enough grip for its caterpillar tracks. So they had to fly the cars across the straits. But they made it to New York, and duly arrived at the United Nations Building. It all got terrific publicity for Ford.

It was a great achievement, and that got Programme Funding going. But early in 1994, as soon as that project was over, I baled out. Ray is still running the company, very successfully, but I was always uncomfortable in the television environment, and we were now in a position to push ahead rapidly with the *ThrustSSC* project. I felt exhilarated again as I faced what would be the greatest challenge in my life.

12 ROCKETS AND RAILWAYS

Getting back full time into the land-speed-record business was like coming home. I'd been a fish out of water at Programme Funding, though the challenge was initially stimulating and ultimately successful.

The thing about all of these projects is that you never fully understand them until they are completed. The whole thing is speculative all the way down the line, and you've somehow got to dodge and duck your way through to come out the other end. But now I would be dodging and ducking in an environment that I knew well.

Right at the start, the first thing Ron and I had done was to get hold of all the data from *Thrust2*, and then try to recreate the car's performance mathematically on spreadsheets. We had done this separately. I did it the long-winded way and Ron was far more subtle. It had never been intended to be a research vehicle, so the amount of data that we had to work on was very limited. A lot of the wind-tunnel work, for example, had been done at Weybridge, where the transonic tunnel was designed for aircraft and couldn't simulate the movement of a vehicle over the ground. The figures we had gained there predicted that the downforce on the car would increase progressively as the speed built up, that there would be minimal Mach-number effect, and that we wouldn't have a problem with supersonic flow underneath. We could rely on it effectively sticking down harder and harder. The reverse proved to be the case.

It took us two and a half months before we believed that we knew what had happened to *Thrust2*. We had come up with an accurate estimate of what the thrust was and what the aerodynamic drag was, and from each stage we were therefore able to calculate the rolling resistance, and also the relationship between the rolling resistance and the speed. That was, of course, crucial.

We then started looking at other land-speed-record cars, and what we found confirmed Ron's view that the rolling resistance had been underestimated. Designers had put tremendous effort into streamlining the bodywork, when really they ought to have been paying similar attention to the wheels.

Because of the make-up of the Black Rock Desert, with its dusty playa, *Thrust2* had generated substantial drag at the wheels, and that's where the missing power had gone. We were able to quantify this, and to show that the problem increased with speed.

One thing led to another, and Ron and I then started looking at the usual problems of laying the car out, of deciding its basic design and where the engine, driver and systems would be positioned. We looked at early conceptual ideas Ackers and I had originally formulated for a third *Thrust* car. We both came to the conclusion that we had to look at something completely different, that the various ideas we'd been throwing around really weren't going to work. Ron started off with the cockpit right in the nose, a V-shaped butterfly tail and front-wheel steering. Then gradually the cockpit moved further aft and we got the T-shaped tail. As we did all this, we began to realize that we had to have a really enormous amount of power – far more than anybody had ever harnessed before in a car.

It may sound crazy, but power is a big safety factor in a record-breaking car, provided that you harness it properly. Had there been greater power available to *Thrust2*, we could probably have incorporated sufficient downforce to stabilize the front end, while still having the necessary push to overcome the resistance enough to move deeper into the transonic region.

Thrust2 had a number of problems. It was never designed to go any faster than 650 m.p.h., which was exactly the peak speed it achieved. Given the limited resources we had, it was frankly a bloody marvel. It was a great effort by John Ackroyd and the team, there's no doubt about that. But the problem was that in *Thrust2* we had a car with a big cross-sectional area, and in this game everything is about reducing cross-sectional area. *Thrust2* was powered by a turbojet engine, and the problem with turbojet engines is that, the faster you go, the more the thrust level actually decreases. What we needed now was another afterburning engine, but one that had an element of ram-jet, so it was half pure-jet and half ram-jet. Once we twigged that, we realized that, with the right intake design, we could have a vehicle whose engine power would *increase* the faster it went.

Around this time we reiterated our firm decision that we could not go ahead – really we *must* not go ahead – with any project if there was real doubt about the vehicle's effective ability to do the job safely. The stability was going to be even more important than the power.

We began to look intensely at the logic. Right, we need a lot of power. How are we going to get it?

We could use one engine, but that posed as many problems as it solved. If you were fortunate, as we were with *Thrust2*, you would have a really long engine. *Thrust*'s Avon was as long as the car, which meant we could get the centre of gravity near the front, so that 60 per cent of the overall weight was on the front axle. But this time we wanted a very long car, because the longer it was, the better would be its aerodynamic and directional stability. But that meant the engine would have to go further towards the back, because you cannot lengthen the engine jet pipe without affecting the engine performance. If you position the jet at the back, then the driver's got to go at

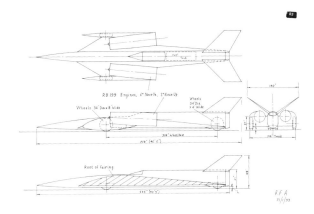

Ron Ayers's early drawings for ThrustSSC. Initially he inclined towards a long car with a butterfly tail, but eventually he came up with the T tail.

the front, so basically you end up with a Breedlove-type tricycle layout. Then you've got real problems. Basically you want the centre of gravity as far forward as possible to stop the front end lifting. But if you do that you need the front wheels wide apart. Imagine a loaded wheelbarrow with a single, central front wheel. Lift it, and it tips easily to either side. Now imagine a barrow with two front wheels, one on either side. It's much harder to tilt. The same principle holds good with a high-speed car. The tricycle layout makes a car unstable, liable to tumble if upset by a bump. The resistance to roll is much better if the front wheels are spread wide apart, with the centre of gravity forward.

This was where we took a crucial engineering decision. We would use two engines.

Ackers and I had looked at a twin-jet layout back in the early days, but this had closely paired front wheels, Breedlove-style. Ron and I now realized the advantage of using two engines, but with a different layout. If we put the front wheels wide apart, we could get the centre of gravity far forward and still have a long car.

We reasoned that everything is about reducing cross-sectional area, and the crucial part of that is net cross-sectional area. In other words, you take a cross-section of the car and you deduct from it the area of the filament of air that is going through the engines. So when you actually do your sums, you see that the thrust-per-unit-area is a hell of a sight greater for a twin-engine car. The improvement is about 20 per cent.

OTHER VOICES

RON AYERS

'The design problem is one of layout. Where do we put the engine, the driver and the fuel? Ideally the driver should be near the centre of the car to give him the best seat-of-pants feel for the vehicle's movements. He is also easier to protect if there is plenty of structure around him. The fuel tank should also be near the centre, so that fuel consumed during the run doesn't cause a substantial shift of centre of gravity. The engine has got to lie on the centre line, and being such a large item, it is bound to occupy the centre of the car. Clearly there are difficult problems reconciling these conflicting space requirements.

'Figure A shows the slender-body solution adopted by the early builders of the jet cars. The advantage is that the shape is very slender, so aerodynamic drag is low. The position of the fuel tank is not too bad, but the best thing that can be claimed for the cockpit position is that it gives the driver a good forward view. The most serious problem is one of stability. Where should the centre of gravity ideally be? For good roll stability it should be well aft, between the widely spaced rear wheels. But if this is achieved, the vertical fins (whether over the rear body or shrouding the rear wheels) will have small moment arms, so there will be inadequate yaw (horizontal) stability. Similarly, pitch (vertical) stability is lost if the weight is concentrated near the back. In practice a compromise is reached between these opposing requirements, which results in all stability characteristics being less than satisfactory. When *Spirit of America* rolled on its side in Autumn 1996, this inadequate stability was clearly demonstrated.

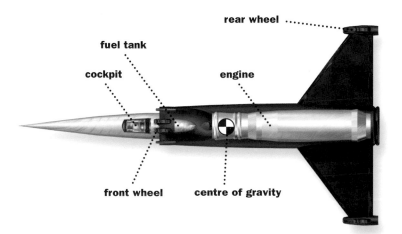

rear wheel

fuel tank

cockpit

engine

front wheel

centre of gravity

Figure A: this is the Breedlove-style tricycle favoured also by McLaren, with the front wheels on a narrow track, the rear wheels widely outrigged and the driver located ahead of the engine intakes.

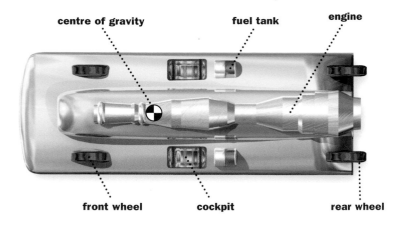

centre of gravity fuel tank engine

front wheel cockpit rear wheel

Figure B: this is the typical Green Monster, Thrust2, Aussie Invader layout, with the car measuring the full length of the engine, and cockpits mounted either side.

'Figure B shows the solution adopted for *Green Monster*, *Thrust2* and *Aussie Invader*. The driver is moved to one side of the engine, and is in a quite good position. However, for reasons of aerodynamic symmetry, a second cockpit must be placed on the other side. This shape proved to be very stable, but the large frontal area inhibited performance, and the bluff shape was totally unsuitable for transonic speeds.

'To drive at supersonic speeds, a slender shape is essential. We were also determined to achieve good static stability characteristics simultaneously in pitch, yaw and roll. Figure C shows how this can be done. With a two-engined layout, the centre of the car is made available for the driver and for the fuel. The centre of gravity is well forward, and well located between the widely spaced front wheels, so roll stability is achieved. The weight being well forward also gives a long moment arm for the fin and for the tailplane, so at the same time there is good weather-cock stability in yaw and in pitch. In order to control the potentially huge aerodynamic forces on the large planform, we incorporated an active suspension to adjust the pitch attitude.'

Figure C: the ThrustSSC concept, with a slim central fuselage and twin outrigged engines, wide-based front wheels and narrow rear track.

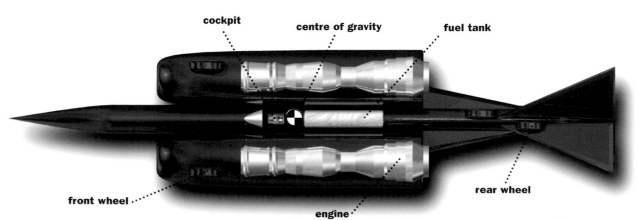

cockpit centre of gravity fuel tank

front wheel engine rear wheel

Now we were very excited. If we used two engines we could get the centre of gravity far forward, which is good and safe; we could get the front wheels widely spaced in the front nacelles, which improves resistance to roll; and we could have a nice long tail at the back, which makes it stable.

The thing was beginning to look not just possible, but probable. The big drawback was the planform area, the area of the car when viewed from above. Though the thrust per unit of cross-sectional area was going to sky-rocket up and the stability would be fine, the problem we were now facing was that we were going to have a huge flat area underneath the car.

At this stage I protested, 'Hang on, everybody who has ever mooted a supersonic car has been going the other way, trying to go for a slim, deep V-shaped hull. Our proposed shape is diametrically the wrong way round.'

'Yes, but let's just think of this,' said Ron. 'The truth is that nobody knows what the hell happens underneath these cars at speed. They make these V-section bodies in the hope that they are minimizing the interaction between the shock wave and the ground, but they are not fundamentally understanding or solving the problem. They are ducking the issue. I would rather tackle the fundamental problem of transonic ground effect, and base our design on knowledge rather than on ignorance. With our large flat undersurface the ground effect will dominate, so we *must* learn all about it.'

We had a concept that we both really liked, but it flew in the face of accepted practice. But since that practice had never been validated, there was only one acceptable course open to us. We would ignore the dogma and damn well find out for ourselves.

Ron and I knew that we had to be intensely careful with this project. The aerodynamics were the single most important factor, because of the high speeds that we envisaged and the massive forces that would come into play.

For an aircraft to stay aloft, it must generate aerodynamic lift force. This is achieved by having the wings at a modest nose-up attitude. With *ThrustSSC* our job was to ensure that it *never* took off. Although the relatively high weight of the car would be very helpful, it would not have been sufficient to keep the car on the ground if the aerodynamic forces weren't balanced. Potentially, these really were enormous.

If the nose lifted at supersonic speeds, *ThrustSSC* could leave the ground with an acceleration of some 30g. An excessively nose-up attitude of even half a degree would be enough to make this happen.

An excessively nose-down attitude was hardly any better, as we were to discover later on one run at 700 m.p.h. when the download on the wheels exceeded what the desert surface could support and the car became uncontrollable.

Bigger downloads would also crush the suspension. There was no alternative but to trim the car accurately at the correct attitude to keep the vertical aerodynamic forces within small tolerances. This was complicated by the fact that in going from subsonic to supersonic speeds, the forces would change so the car would need to be retrimmed.

We would solve this problem by measuring the force of the wheels on the desert, using strain gauges on the suspension, and using this information to programme the attitude of the car via computer-controlled active suspension. This would correct the nose-down attitude to accommodate the changing forces as the Mach number altered.

It can be difficult to envisage the sheer size of aerodynamic forces. But if Andy had been able – and misguided enough – to stick his head out into the airstream at *ThrustSSC*'s maximum speed, the wind force on his face would have been about three quarters of a ton.

The research stage was going to be absolutely crucial. Ron started off taking soundings from all sorts of people, particularly Ian McGregor and Professor Dennis Mabey. Both are very experienced aerodynamicists. Ian's speciality is the design of air intakes, and Dennis is an authority on unsteady flow and transonic aerodynamics. When they saw our proposals, they expressed grave concerns about the risks to the driver. As Ian succinctly put it, 'That's a very expensive way of killing someone.'

Although they continued to be concerned by the safety issue, they were also very constructive, and their many helpful suggestions made a fundamental contribution to the design of the car. They also agreed to continue acting as consultants and 'devil's advocates' to Ron during the research, design and operation of the car. It is impossible to overstate the importance of their contribution to the success of the project.

Our immediate problem was to find a method of getting aerodynamic data. It's not simply a matter of testing a model in a wind tunnel. That works well for aircraft, but to represent the airflow around a car you also have to represent the ground moving beneath the wheels. This is usually done by putting a belt, running as a continuous loop, beneath the scale model. Wind tunnels with such moving grounds exist for low-speed cars, such as Formula One cars, but for a supersonic car we would need a belt running at over 800 m.p.h., which is totally impracticable.

ThrustSSC model in a wind tunnel for low-speed stability trials. The woollen tufts attached to the bodywork give a visualization of the airflow.

Ron and I had talked all this through, and one immediate solution was to use computational fluid dynamics, CFD for short. CFD is an aerodynamic study on computer. By using high-speed computers you can simulate the airflow of fluid over a computer-generated model, and you can then distil the essential data.

A company called CDR, which was integrated with Swansea University, had developed a computer analysis programme called 'Flite' jointly with Imperial College. We asked Professor Ken Morgan there, 'If we do this, will you join us?' and he said yes. 'And if you join us, because we are possibly in a highly competitive situation, will you agree that no other car can use this system?' He said yes to that, too. We shook hands on the deal and got going. Soon we were getting all sorts of really interesting data.

Of course, it was expensive. You get some idea of the scale of this sort of thing when you realize that to do one CFD picture took several days of Swansea computer time. What happens is that the software programme breaks the air down into zillions of little elements, and each element has to satisfy six simultaneous equations with its next-door neighbours. The whole thing has to rattle itself through umpteen different iterations until it all settles down.

We were fortunate subsequently to make contact with Cray Research. They provided us with up to £200,000 worth of time on one of their C92 supercomputers, capable of five billion calculations a second. This was a tremendous bonus and enabled us to do calculations that had taken several days in several hours.

The problem with computational fluid dynamics is simply that it is computer generated. You get very credible pictures, but then you say, 'Hang on, can we really believe this? How can we prove this?' 'Flite' is used extensively by Rolls-Royce and British Aerospace and it's accurate to within 2 or 3 per cent. But it's designed for planes flying at 30,000 feet. How did we know that the same equations would apply to a car a few inches above the ground? The computer analysis certainly helped us to understand the flow under the car, and Ken and his colleague, Dr Oubay Hassan, were very confident in their methods. But safety was paramount. We had to find an experimental way to verify the CFD results.

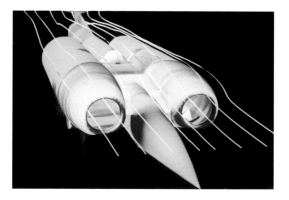

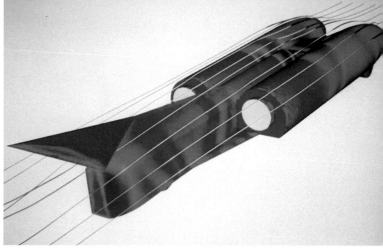

Computational fluid dynamics (CFD) provided a means whereby we could assess the likely performance of the ThrustSSC concept by using finite element analysis. This was a long process, but the results were encouraging.

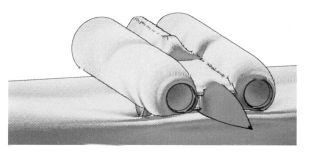

Even the slightest change in the rake of the car would affect the airflow beneath it. Here blue indicates high-pressure areas at the front of the car during transonic airflow, yellow slightly lower, green lower still and red the lowest pressure area. The green ahead of the front wheels indicates the build-up of a shock wave, while the green area behind the red zone between the wheels indicates a terminal shock wave.

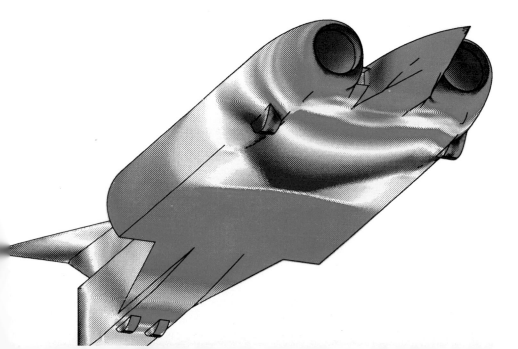

Ron and I had reasoned that if we couldn't run a model in a wind tunnel, in other words if we couldn't run the air around a static model situated over a moving floor, our only alternative would be a mobile model.

Years earlier somebody had told me about a rocket-railway system at Pendine in Wales, close to the famous sands on which Parry Thomas and Malcolm Campbell made their record attempts in the 1920s, and where our old *Thrust1* rival Barry Bowles had crashed the *Blonde Bombshell* in 1978. I mentioned this to Ron, and he felt it might be feasible to use it to do our testing. We had a wonderful meeting in London with Pendine's superintendent, Colonel Lowry. 'Our situation is that we're absolutely skint,' I explained. 'We've got this idea for a supersonic car, and we really think we can do it, but we desperately need to use your rocket track.' Colonel Lowry was terrific. 'We're really interested,' he said, 'and we'll help you in any way we can.'

The rocket railway is amazing. It comprises a laser-laid narrow-gauge railway track, just 1.6 kilometres long, and it's straight and horizontal to within 0.6 of a millimetre across that distance. Normally it's used for zapping bombs down the track into great concrete targets at three times the speed of sound. There are several such tracks dotted around the globe. America has four: Iggins runs to Mach 3; Sandio to Mach 6; Hollowman to Mach 9; and China Lake to Mach 3.3. Viscaross, in France, runs to Mach 3. Pendine would run to Mach 3.2, more than enough for us.

The sled gripped the outside edge of the rail, and Ron came up with the idea that we would fill the inside of the rails with a surface to represent the desert, build a model and instrument it with a strain-gauge balance and pressure sensors, and use the telemetry off the sled to get our readings. It was a lovely way of doing things, because not only would we get the readings at the critical speed that we were interested in, but we would also get the data on all the speeds either side of the range, both accelerating and decelerating. Because it all took place in the

1:25 scale model of ThrustSSC being built for rocket testing.

open, we wouldn't have the problems you have with a wind tunnel, where you can get shocks rebounding off the walls. We would film every step.

Despite Colonel Lowry's help this was all going to cost big bucks, and we knew that our £40,000 budget wouldn't go very far, so we simply had to go round and beg. By autumn 1993 we had our first composite model of *ThrustSSC* ready to run down there. It was made for us by James Morton and Simon Kingdon-Butcher, two old allies from ARV, who were now running their own company. James had hung on until the end at ARV, and then both had gone to work for Chip Ganassi, an American IndyCar racer who had set up a design and fabrication business down in Fontwell, using the remains of Mike Earle's defunct Onyx Formula One team. James and Simon had then bought Ganassi out, in partnership with John Biddlecombe, and changed the company name to G Force.

The model was attached to the front of a rocket-propelled sled on the long test track facility at the Proof and Experimental Establishment at Pendine in South Wales.

James had been in touch socially, and during the course of our conversation I happened to mention how Ron and I were planning to do these rocket-sled tests. 'Right,' he said immediately, 'we're going to make your models.'

One of the companies I went begging to was Kulite. Geoff Bancroft there liked the project, and produced miniature pressure sensors, which looked like teeth fillings with a couple of wires sticking out! They cost more than £500 each, and the model was festooned with them. We also needed a strain-gauge balance, which was worth something in the order of £25,000.

Our first model had seventeen channels of telemetry that recorded samples every hundredth of a second. We would then be able to run our film of each firing and measure the deflections of the model at precisely known speeds. The sled itself was equally fantastic. It was made of aluminium and carried the telemetric equipment on the top. It had eighteen two-inch rockets to accelerate it and four to decelerate it. It would go from zero to 850 m.p.h. in 0.8 of a second – that's Mach 1.1 and an acceleration rate of 50g!

When the rockets fired, our model could accelerate from rest to 820 m.p.h. in 0.8 of a second.

By filming the model's point of maximum speed, we were able to visualize what was happening to the model, not just at its maximum speed, but during acceleration and deceleration. Here at Mach 1.2, shock waves are visible over the nose, cockpit and tail.

The first time we put the sled and model down the track was absolutely amazing. It ran to Mach 1.08 straight away. You could see the shock waves clearly. None of us outsiders had ever seen anything remotely like it.

There was a very funny moment when a crew from *Tomorrow's World* was filming this. These guys had been everywhere and seen everything, and filmed it all. There was nothing scientific that was going to surprise them. Then this sled suddenly went shooting down the track at supersonic speed. It had one hell of an effect on you. It would go shooting past, then the retro rockets would fire to slow it all down, and finally it whammed into an arrester stop located across the rails, and then bounced back. The sheer violence of it all was astounding, and the crew became very quiet after that. There were awed comments such as, 'Was that really a supersonic bang?'

Other things weren't at all amusing. Our first G Force model came to a sticky end on only its second run. Halfway down the track it exploded. Ron reckoned the supersonic air stream had got into a seam and blown it open.

Fortunately, Geoff Bancroft took a deep breath and produced another set of sensors, and G Force built a new model in cast aluminium. James and his team worked extraordinarily fast to produce both models. We were trying desperately to keep the whole thing very quiet in case rivals got to hear of it. Suppliers were shouting at us, 'We can't do this in the time.' And we were shouting back, 'We've got to bloody do it. We've got to keep pushing on. Breedlove is ahead of us.'

While the aero tests were going on we needed to finalize the power unit. Initially we looked at the Rolls-Royce RB199 Tornado powerplant, which is a very fine engine, very light, with a good power-to-weight ratio. The

downside was that it would need a separate gearbox, so we would have quite a lot of installation problems; and it's a computer-driven engine, so you'd need to write the software. You could control your engine absolutely, and make it do exactly what you wanted, but there would be all that software to write, and then you'd need to develop it. What we really needed was a fit-and-forget engine.

There was another potential problem with the RB199. If you look at one of its turbine blades it's the most miraculous bit of engineering. Its air-cooling holes are about

We had a chilling reminder of the forces we were dealing with when our first model exploded at 820 m.p.h. and disintegrated.

the width of a human hair. My eyesight isn't what it was, and when somebody pointed out these cooling holes I couldn't see them! This was said to have caused problems during the Gulf War; what was happening was that desert dust was entering the engine during ground running, clogging up these cooling holes, and the dust was turning to glass with the heat. The melting point of the turbine blades was actually lower than the temperature of the gas stream, so consequently, as soon as those blades clogged up, they melted and you lost half of your turbine blades. We were worried about running on the Black Rock Desert, where we would have to do two runs within an hour, with large volumes of dust in the air.

The RB199 is also a very short engine. What you want with these supersonic vehicles is a really long, thin shape, and this becomes difficult when you're faced with an engine that is actually very short. While it's great to stick in the back of a Tornado, it just wouldn't work in a long nacelle like those we planned for *SSC*.

So we were a bit stumped. Subsequently I did the smart thing and went back to see our old friend Paddy Hine, who was now a very senior figure in British Aerospace.

An odd thing occurred during the research for this book, when David Tremayne produced the notes from our first-ever interview, which had taken place shortly after we first met in October 1977. We had gone all through the *Thrust1* saga and our hopes and plans for *Thrust2*, and I had outlined the intention that *Thrust2* should be a credible forerunner to *Thrust3*, which at that time we all envisaged as being the pukka land-speed-record car. And there, right at the end, he had managed to draw me out a little on my thoughts for the third car and I had said, '*Thrust3* will probably be a long car powered by two Rolls-Royce Spey engines.'

The extraordinary thing is that I had completely forgotten saying that. Now when Paddy said, 'Well, Richard, it's quite simple. You want the Spey,' my immediate reaction was, 'Oh God, not the Spey! That's 1960s technology. It's old and it's heavy.'

To which Paddy responded, 'But do you know about the supersonic Spey, the 205?' Of course I'd never heard of it. It transpired that this was a very expensive project undertaken by the Ministry of Defence to extend the turbine life, the hot-end life, or alternatively raise the power output, of the 202, the engine used to power the RAF squadrons of F4 Phantoms. They saw that the Phantom was going to remain in service for a long time and that they could improve its operational life by fitting single crystal-turbine blades. Paddy said the 205 was rated to 25,000 pounds of thrust.

By now he had my complete attention. One thing led to another, and eventually we managed to acquire two of the twelve 205s that were ever built, still in their Rolls-Royce wrappings.

This was later, however. In the meantime there was another key development. Rick Jones, a friend who had been highly successful at selling computer printers, put up the money, around £2,500, for two Spey 202s to get us started. Again, it was very cheap horsepower at around 22,000 pounds of thrust per engine. This was the depth of the recession and the Ministry of Defence couldn't give this stuff away, so we were able to get them at a very good price.

Rick was happy to remain a sleeping partner, and like Ron and Glynne he became a shareholder in the *SSC* Programme. His was the only capital that went into the project.

The Spey is a very complicated engine in comparison with the old Avon. While I was looking at some Spey 202s at RAF Wattisham I met John Rowles, an RAF sergeant who knew them inside out. When Wattisham closed down we bought a lot of Spey spares which went into John's garage for storage. It's always a comfortable feeling to know you've got something in reserve.

We went back to Pendine early in 1994 with our new model, and there were no further dramas. By the end of May we had completed all of our scheduled runs. It was now time to compare the readings from the rocket with the readings from the CFD. It was a nerve-racking time. If the results didn't match up, we wouldn't be able to believe either of them, so we'd be no further on.

Tube Investments sent two guys from its subsidiary, Dowty Aerospace, to go through the figures with Ron, and they agreed that he had done a fabulous job. Later that day, Ron came round.

'You remember what I said, that if the two sets of figures didn't match, I would have to go?' he began, and my heart started to sink. 'Well, I'd just like you to know that it's worked out. The biggest discrepancy over twenty-five separate stability cases is 4 per cent. It's absolutely astonishing. I can't believe our good fortune.'

He paused as I took all this in, and then I saw his face. Ron is not the kind of person to make this sort of comment lightly, but he said, 'I've never seen anything like this in my life. It's quite extraordinary to get results as good as this.'

Then he said, very quietly, 'Let's build it.'

13 THE WORLD'S FASTEST FORKLIFT

There was no time to lose. We were racing Craig Breedlove.

At first we knew little of his new car, except that he'd sold a sailboat to pay for the workshop in Rio Vista in which *Spirit of America – Sonic Arrow* was being built. Gradually we discovered that it would be 46 feet long, would weigh only four tons, and that Craig planned to sit right in the nose of its circular fuselage, just ahead of the front wheels and engine.

Craig Breedlove's Spirit of America – Sonic Arrow could scarcely have been more different from ThrustSSC. The fact that we adopted completely divergent technical philosophies merely added to the excitement of the duel between us.

Like Craig's original *Spirit* and Gabelich's *Blue Flame*, *Sonic Arrow* was as slim as a pencil. Its front wheels were positioned very close together and the rear wheels were outrigged and sheathed in streamlined spats. He would use the same sort of General Electric J79 afterburning turbojet as he had used in *Sonic 1*, but this time a more powerful 8 series with 22,000 pounds of thrust.

There were other unusual features to *Sonic Arrow*. It had three aluminium wheels at the front, each shod with filament-wound graphite 'tyres', which effectively followed the old Bonneville dictate of having rubber tyres pumped up almost solid. Where ThrustSSC would use carbon disc brakes to augment the parachute system, Breedlove did away with wheel brakes altogether. Instead he used a ski brake system mounted on the bottom of the car, which he said had proved effective in testing. He rather quaintly called it his Fred Flintstone brake!

Later I was shocked to hear that he'd done no wind-tunnel testing at all. 'It's just designed by eye,' he said, 'based on whatever experience I gained from the two previous cars. I eyed it and packaged it the way I thought it should be. We're going to have lots of sensors, and the plan essentially is to build the speed incrementally and evaluate the data. Once we get to seven hundred, we'll switch over to an unmanned test programme and put it through the sound barrier to confirm the design.'

CRAIG BREEDLOVE

'Generally my thinking hasn't changed all that much over the years. It's been refined as it's gone along, but it's the same basic concept. I didn't get very good results from the tunnel work that I did back in the 1960s, and that's primarily due to the lack of knowledge on how to do wind-tunnel work with cars. It's improved over the years, but with a Bonneville car there is still nothing available. We did consider the testing method that Richard Noble used, which has some validity, and that's using a rocket-sled facility. There is a company in Utah which has a test site like that, but it was relatively expensive to do.

'In the aircraft industry they have had experience since the turn of the century, probably starting with the Wright brothers. There's a history of designing a plane and doing the tunnel work and then building the plane and bringing it to fruition, and actually taking it to flight test and confirming what the tunnel told them. But as I've experienced it, the situation is different with a car. To take all of that data and rely on it as gospel truth has some dangers. If you get bad data it's worse than no data. In reality the car can confirm the testing procedure, but the testing procedure cannot confirm the car.'

Things were now moving very fast. G Force had agreed to construct *ThrustSSC* for us on almost a break-even basis. Part of the deal was that we had to fund the rebuilding of their assembly hall, which was a huge job but a fair return for their work on the car, and one which a local firm did for us in no time at all.

Once again Tube Investments agreed to supply tubing to our specification after their people had seen our research figures. Their then subsidiary, Accles & Pollock, produced all the special steel, and we started actually cutting metal for the spaceframe chassis late in August 1994.

A very old friend of mine, John Hill, had started importing Toshiba lap-tops into the UK, and he tried very hard to get Toshiba involved. They gave us help with equipment, but it was obvious they wouldn't contribute any funding. Much later John suggested I went to see Hugh Chappell at Taxan, which imports high-quality video monitors. We developed a great relationship, and Hugh put in around £50,000. Kidde-Graviner came in with finance in September, and they also agreed to do all the fire-extinguishing systems, plus such things as the cockpit water-mist fire-protection system.

Those early days seem quite clear, looking back, but from then on it was all a bit of a blur. It was one hell of a struggle to keep the project going. Our cash-flow requirement obviously varied according to how much work needed to be done or needed to be paid for, but I was generally having to find £50,000 from a new sponsor every month. That sort of money did not come easily, particularly in a country just creeping out of the worst recession since the 1930s.

G Force was tremendous during this time. They themselves were going through quite a difficult time, too, I think, as they tried to establish themselves not just as a manufacturer of racing-car components, but of complete racing cars, too. There was one stage when *ThrustSSC* was the major work that G Force had, so we were really supporting not just ourselves but them as well. It was a very tough period of mutual dependency.

Ron couldn't help but realize that I was having problems, and he suggested that we should approach the Department of Trade and Industry for help. I hated to rebuff his suggestion, but I had to tell him that I'd had the most terrible problems with the DTI. I'd been to see them on the ARV and *Atlantic Sprinter* projects, and I'd found out the hard way that all they were likely to say was how wonderful we were because we'd moved faster than they thought things could be done, which isn't saying much. It had happened to me during ARV, and they'd dragged it out until I had eventually challenged them, whereupon it became very clear that nothing was going to happen. It was almost as if we had become victims of our own speed and efficiency. Perhaps the DTI inspectors thought we were doing so well that we didn't need their help. I never did figure out what went on in their minds.

Ron kept on at me, and in the end I reluctantly agreed to go there with him. We took the project to them, in this great big marble palace where they live in Victoria, and explained what we were trying to do. They seemed very enthusiastic and interested. Afterwards, as we stood in the cold outside, I told Ron that I could see what was going to happen. 'We're going to be sucked into an enormous bureaucratic exercise. I can't waste time on it. I have to push on in the real world. You've run a company before, you know what's involved. I think the answer is that you should do this one.' He agreed.

Some time later, Ron was beavering away at home when an executive from the DTI rang him. From the questions he asked it became obvious that he had a large questionnaire in front of him and was working his way through it. At the end of it he simply said, 'Well, Mr Ayers, when are you going into production? And how many are you going to make each year?'

Ron couldn't believe it. He was very embarrassed and ducked the question, then tried to steer the conversation on to another subject. But that just started the DTI man on the cycle again, so he began to go through the questionnaire a second time. He came back to this unanswered box and persisted, 'You still haven't told me, Mr Ayers, when you are going to start production and how many of these cars you are going to make in year one.'

It was difficult to envisage a market for production supersonic cars, unless you worked for the DTI. At that point Ron saw what I'd meant and gave up. He simply put the phone down.

It was such a shame. I suspect the DTI doesn't want to bother with little people like us. They would rather put their money into safe projects like Airbus or Rolls-Royce or Jaguar, where there's a high chance of success and nobody risks getting bollocked for unconventional thinking. But we shouldn't have been led to believe there was any chance in the first place.

It's the crux of the problem in this country. I firmly believe that our wealth is in manufacturing, not in the service industries where it's just a case of doing each other's washing. The real wealth is in making things, and that's what we've always been good at. As a country we are incredibly talented, despite Margaret Thatcher destroying our manufacturing infrastructure and leaving us in a situation where manufacturing is now less than 20 per cent of our gross domestic product. That's terribly low in comparison with countries such as Germany. The evidence of this

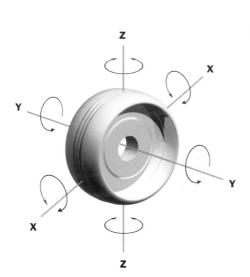

Glynne Bowsher's solid aluminium wheels were a masterpiece. By considering one spinning at 8,000 r.p.m. as a gyroscope, then attempting to introduce a directional turning moment, he calculated that ThrustSSC was in danger of suffering a significant lifting moment in the direction of the car. The only solution was to fix the front wheels, and take the controversial route of rear-wheel steering.

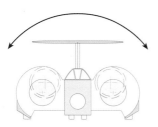

can be seen as German industry is now driving major industrial and financial acquisitions and partnerships.

Fortunately, I was surrounded by bold thinkers with the *ThrustSSC* programme. Glynne Bowsher is an amazing fellow, a very gifted engineer with an enormous amount of experience. He had played a funny sort of role in the *Thrust2* project. I couldn't say that I knew him very well then, because he's a pretty retiring sort of bloke. He would always be doing the brakes or whatever, and his technical reports on the project for Lucas were superb: very concise. Glynne was Glynne, but you overlooked his qualities at your peril.

After I'd asked him to do the wheels, he came up with a brilliant means of creating a bigger and wider wheel that would rotate faster, but on which he was able to reduce the stress by a third. Glynne had designed the brakes as well; he told me later that he'd designed these within a year of the record as an improvement of his *Thrust2* brakes – he'd simply been waiting for a vehicle to attach them to.

We'd made an important discovery when we were running *Thrust2*. John Ackroyd had got it absolutely right; virtually all of your time on the desert is spent on maintenance or driving. In order to maximize your driving time, you've got to be able to maintain the car easily – strip it down and be able to get at it to make changes – because, at best, you've probably got only a forty-day programme before the desert becomes unusable due to winter rain. With *Thrust2* we often spent long hours in Bruno's garage, and if we made late decisions, which we often did, we lost even more running time.

We knew the vehicle had to be much stiffer and much stronger than *Thrust2*; if we opted for monocoque construction we would end up like an aeroplane with

RON AYERS

'How do you start designing a vehicle that is totally unique? Here are the characteristics of the problem that faced us:

1. By travelling supersonically on land we would be exploring a region where no-one had ventured, where even the problems could only be guessed at, so there were no known solutions.

2. As the aerodynamic forces involved were so enormous, any accident was likely to be fatal.

3. The project would always be underfunded, short of people and time.

4. There would be only one chance. The final car was also the first prototype. The first lines drawn on paper could well be the ones that are made. The very first assumptions and decisions, if incorrect, could put the project on the wrong track and there would be no chance of starting again.'

'Problem: how do you make those crucial first decisions when so much is uncertain?

'First, every decision had to be a robust one. That meant it couldn't be invalidated by subsequent decisions.

'Second, we could only use technology we were very confident with. This militated against using the very latest technology in some cases.

'Third, although direct experience of supersonic travel on land did not exist, we consulted widely, with aviation and automobile experts in industry, universities and research establishments. Experience with *Thrust2* was invaluable, particularly in pinpointing practical and environmental problems that might otherwise be overlooked.

'Fourth, where possible we left room for adjustment or change, so we could incorporate knowledge acquired subsequently. Nothing was "hard wired". One reason for using a steel chassis was that it could be modified if necessary.

'Fifth, we didn't try too hard to integrate the systems. If we needed to change one of them, we didn't want to be forced to change them all.

'Sixth, our choice of a twin-engined car made the design massively overpowered. Thus weight was not a critical factor.

'The design resulting from such an approach must necessarily be "sub-optimum". A second attempt, incorporating the lessons learned, would undoubtedly be better. But the design was proved in practice, and there was little about the basic concept that would need to be changed.'

little hatches everywhere. So instead we decided to go for a steel spinal spaceframe down the middle, with the engines mounted on either side. Then we could easily mount the front suspension and the rear wheels, the rear fin and the tailplane. We could feed a lot of the loads through this structure.

This prompted the question: 'What's the weight penalty?' By this time we had a meaningful spreadsheet on the performance of the car, and we found to our surprise that the weight didn't seem to make all that much difference. The car's performance was going to be such that a few hundred pounds extra wasn't going to matter.

We knew we were looking at enormous aerodynamic forces: a dynamic load of three-quarters of a ton on every square foot of the car's bodywork. The spaceframe would cost us weight, but in exchange we would gain the ability to strip our car down really easily, to get at everything simply, and make any modifications quickly. It was a deal well worth doing. We decided to use steel for the frame, while the engine nacelles and nose moulding would be carbon-fibre composite, and the remainder a mix of carbon, aluminium, stainless steel and titanium.

Initially we hadn't actually done anything about the chassis frame as such, however. But at the end of our discussion about the structure Glynne had said, 'Well, I'm going to design the frame. Is that all right?' So I said, 'Yes, please.' Glynne just took over this task, and before long we had the frame designed and stressed. The project was really beginning to come together.

I think Glynne's ability was probably overlooked during the *Thrust2* project. He joined at a latish stage, when he was asked to design the brakes on behalf of Lucas. I think he might have fancied getting more involved, but John Ackroyd had the project tightly managed, so nothing much happened. Now Glynne was really racking up the hours. He even got very seriously ill at one stage, simply because he was working for Lucas by day and then he'd go home and start work on *SSC*. During the two-year research phase he was working a steady eighteen-hour day, seven days a week. He was doing all this for us on his own time, because at that stage there was no way we could afford to pay him. It was the same with Ron. In the preliminary stages both were effectively self-funding, and they were giving enormous amounts of time to the project.

It's a credit to Ron that the basic shape of *SSC* changed very little from his first concept; we modified the tail fin at one stage to avoid heat damage from the engines, and Ackers later suggested a few minor changes, but that was about it. It was the same with Glynne, who did just about all of the frame and all of the

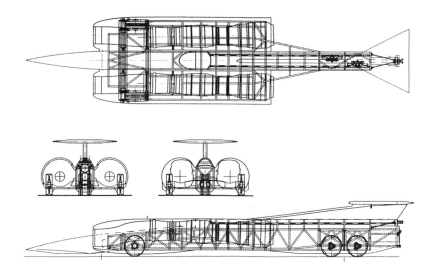

This diagram shows how Glynne's chassis structure fitted in beneath ThrustSSC's exterior.

suspension: the only other major change was to ditch the plan to use torsion bars in the front suspension in favour of gas struts, at the suggestion of Jeremy Bliss, who joined us later to do *ThrustSSC*'s systems. I believe that change was absolutely crucial, because I don't think that the car as originally designed would have performed as well on the hard surface we were to encounter on the Al Jafr Desert, but Glynne points out that since the torsion-bar system was never actually tried, and was more sophisticated than generally realized, that is a moot point.

One of my regrets from these early days of the project is that things didn't work out better with John Ackroyd. After *Thrust2* he'd said to me, 'Richard, I don't ever want to work as hard as that again.' His attitude was understandable; *Thrust2* had taken an enormous amount out of him. More than anyone he had been at the centre of it all, under huge pressure for six years.

After *Thrust2* he went to work very successfully on Richard Branson's balloon projects. I think he wanted to be sure that whoever he worked for had reasonable resources, so that he could really devote himself, knowing that the project would be properly funded. This again was entirely understandable. Ackers is a dyed-in-the-wool project man. You look back at the old days in the kitchen at the Ranalagh Works down on the Isle of Wight, when he never wavered, even when we were uncertain where the next tranche of funding was coming from, and you can appreciate what a massive contribution he made. Creative people like Ackers can probably do that once, but, having established himself as the foremost land-speed designer, it was entirely reasonable that he should have different expectations for subsequent projects.

When we started the *ThrustSSC* project we were very keen to get him involved as designer. He was the logical bloke. But he didn't seem to want to meet Ron, or

JOHN ACKROYD

'I did some work for Richard on *SSC* in 1995, on things like the chassis and the cockpit, but really all the main work was done. Ron had done the concept and Glynne had done the chassis well before I arrived, so there wasn't a key role for me to play. Anything I did, any competent engineer could have done.

'Then the global balloon project spooled up again, so I went off on that. I'd become very hooked on balloons, and, in any case, I'm not really sure you can do two record projects. Certainly I couldn't have done another one the way we did *Thrust2*. I think you're only ever capable of putting everything into one if you run it the way the *Thrust2* project had to be run. But this way everything worked out really well.

'I was working on balloons with Thunder & Colt in Reno when I happened to read about Craig going up to Black Rock in the *Reno Gazette*, so I went up there just for a chat. That led to helping him out in 1996 and 1997, and that was fine. To be honest, I'm not sure I would have wanted the responsibility of one of those projects all over again, whereas this way I could be there without that. For me, it was the best of both worlds. I think maybe the new blood Richard had was a good thing, and I'm very happy they succeeded. They didn't need me to achieve what they did. I was just very pleased to see it when it happened. I would never have forgiven myself if I'd missed it.'

to get involved. He was also talking to the *Spirit of America* project and had helped Rosco McGlashan in Australia, and both sides were aware of that. He was very torn between balloons and cars, but eventually he came to work for us for a while in 1995, principally on the cockpit, and during that time he made a number of changes to the frame.

For some reason John and Glynne didn't hit it off, mostly because they had different ways of working, and when you get two engineers talking about the same thing you're always going to get arguments. And both are probably right. But I suspect that John saw Glynne in the role he felt he himself should be in, and, of course, this time it wasn't his; there was no question of it being his. It was Glynne's by right this time round; he'd earned it through all the hard work he'd put in over the previous two and a half years.

John and I had a funny sort of relationship this time round, and it was clear he wasn't going to settle. I think in the end he thought we'd designed the whole thing wrong, and he went back to his balloon projects early in 1995. He later popped up again helping Craig Breedlove between ballooning seasons. We still talk and we're still good friends, and I will always admire what he did with *Thrust2*. It was just that this time things didn't work out.

Back in 1992 I'd had an indication of Glynne's lateral thinking when he had rung me with a bombshell.

'Look, Richard,' he said, 'I'm basically happy about the spaceframe design, but I've come up against a snag now that I'm working on the front suspension. The problem is in sandwiching the front wheels between the air intakes and the external body shape. Neither of these are structural, and therefore I'm having difficulty hanging the wheels. I've schemed a suspension that will do this, but you're not going to like it.

'The more fundamental problem we've got is that we simply haven't got room for the wheels to actually steer. If you want to drive it round a track, or whatever, we just can't do it. Now we can increase the diameter of the nacelles, but if we do that the overall drag is going to go up enormously.'

'So what's the answer?' I asked, alarmed.

And that's when he hit me with it: 'To me, Richard, the only answer is rear-wheel steering.'

I was momentarily lost for words, and then I just said, 'For God's sake, Glynne, we'll never persuade people that it's viable. I mean, the only rear-wheel-steering vehicles that everyone knows are out-of-control airport trolleys and supermarket trolleys, dumper trucks and forklifts. And you're talking about a supersonic car that steers by the rear wheels. It just can't be done.'

Months later I was clearing out a pile of junk and came across the visitors' book from the original *Thrust2* Motorfair stand back in 1977. Somebody had written a comment: 'Why aren't you using rear-wheel steering?' At the time I'd simply thought, That guy must be a nut! Now here was Glynne Bowsher, who had done such a cracking job on the wheels, the chassis frame and the brakes, suggesting the same thing. How could I let him down gently?

'Glynne,' I said, 'we're going way outside credibility. We can't convince people. I'm not convinced.'

Anyway, I agreed to think about it. And the more I did, the more logical it seemed. I thought, Hang on a moment, we've got a bloody great fin at the back, so provided the rear-wheel steering works you could use it as a sort of trimmer, and, of course, the fin would always straighten the car.

GLYNNE BOWSHER

'Richard told me I was crazy. But it was the only solution. He was very sceptical initially, and said a few rude things down the phone. He basically said that you just can't do that, but I told him we had no option. I couldn't see any other way round it. The other option was to have somebody else do the design; that was always there. I would still have done the wheels and the brakes, if nothing else. I wasn't that worried.

'But within the constraints of what Ron was trying to achieve, and the mechanical and physical difficulties of the wheel itself, I couldn't see that there was an alternative. My feeling was that anybody else looking at the problem would have had the same difficulties to solve and may well have ended up down the same road.

'The two big air intakes took up most of the room where all the support structure for suspension and steering would be. But it was far more than just a question of space. Because of the weight of the car, there were problems with bearings, problems with brakes and the gyroscopic couple. Those wheels were heavy and wide and were going to rotate at over eight thousand revs per minute. If they are steered, then they're in effect large gyroscopes, and a gyroscopic force couple will develop, depending on the steering input, which will affect the car in roll. At maximum speed it's possible to speculate a steering input which will try to lift one side of the car and bury the other. Steered rear-wheels, with their lower mass and inertia, would be much less of a problem. The adoption of rear-wheeled steering solved all the problems of mounting and running the front wheels.'

Ron, Glynne and I had a meeting to discuss it further, and we all agreed that the potential benefits were so great that we had to give it a run somehow. So we searched around and we found a wonderful chap called David Crolla, who was the professor of vehicle dynamics at Leeds University. 'Look, David, this is going to ruin your reputation,' I said to him, 'but would you like to take a look at it?'

It took a month or so before David came back with his report, which basically said that, provided we did this and this and this, it would work. 'But predominantly, one of the key things is that there must be absolutely no slack anywhere in the linkage,' he advised. We were heartened by this, Glynne most of all, of course, but we were back to computer figures again. Just as with our computational fluid dynamics, we had to find an experimental way of backing them up. Ron and I kept asking, 'Supposing we build this car and it's an absolute brute to drive, supposing you've got to keep working at it all the time? If you've got to think about steering it all the time, it's never going to work.' It was hard enough to steer *Thrust2*, but this thing promised to be something else again.

We were desperately short of money by now, but Glynne was determined to prove his concept. His brother-in-law had abandoned a BMC Mini in a field, and the two of them rescued it from oblivion. It had a 1300cc engine, so it had more power than normal. They set about converting it to rear-wheel steering. Glynne locked the front wheels in the straight-ahead position, and then, because we needed the same wheelbase-to-track ratio as the *SSC*, he built a spaceframe out the back, which incorporated two steering wheels set in the same 'tandem offset' arrangement as the full-size jet car. In fact, the wheel plan of the Mini was a true-scale version of that of *ThrustSSC*. With great trepidation we took it along to the Motor Industry Research Association's Leicester test track. When we turned up there with this alarming contraption, the PR manager, Keith Read, took one look and asked, 'Richard, what the hell are you doing?'

We started driving it on the straight, and initially it was all over the place. This appeared to confirm my worst suspicions. Then I started throwing it around, and I found that it never got away from me. With rear-wheel steering, instead of making an immediate turn as soon as the steering-wheel is turned, as in a conventional car, there is a short delay while the rear wheels reposition the rear of the car; only then do you start to turn. I soon got the hang of it.

Then we discovered there was a slight bit of slack in the linkage, so we tightened that up. From that moment on it was absolute magic! I could hare down the straights at 90 m.p.h., hands off, absolutely straight. I'd go into the curves at the end straight, and I'd lean into the curve and hold the car at around 40 m.p.h., and then I would drive right the way round the banking with my hands off the wheel. If I swerved, it remained controllable.

We were all absolutely delighted about this. It was actually quite safe, and quite fun. We had a lot of helpers, so we started letting other people drive it. Many of them telephoned me at home afterwards to say, 'You know, it's really interesting having driven the rear-wheel-steer Mini and then driven home in my ordinary car; do you know, I prefer the rear-wheel steer on the straight. It feels more stable.'

The trials with the Mini had proved that rear-wheel steering could be very accurate. It was going to work fine. I told Glynne he was a bloody genius.

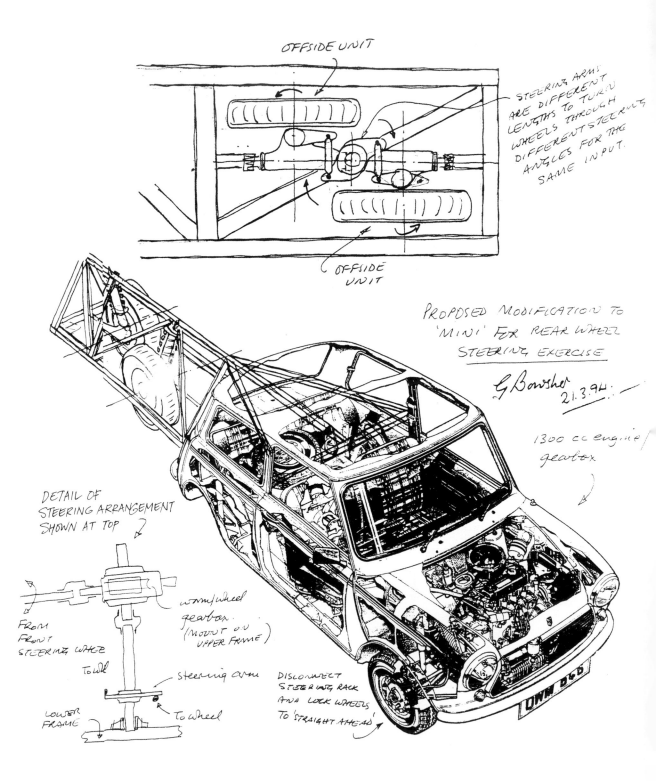

OFFSIDE UNIT

STEERING ARMS ARE DIFFERENT LENGTHS TO TURN WHEELS THROUGH DIFFERENT STEERING ANGLES FOR THE SAME INPUT.

OFFSIDE UNIT

PROPOSED MODIFICATION TO 'MINI' FOR REAR WHEEL STEERING EXERCISE

G Bowsher 21.3.94.

1300 cc engine/ gearbox

DETAIL OF STEERING ARRANGEMENT SHOWN AT TOP

worm/wheel gearbox. (MOUNT ON UPPER FRAME)

FROM FRONT STEERING WHEEL TO WELL

steering arm

To Wheel

LOWER FRAME

DISCONNECT STEERING RACK AND LOCK WHEELS TO 'STRAIGHT AHEAD'

We were now ready to tell this amazing story to the media, and we chose the headquarters of the Society of Motor Manufacturers and Traders, off Belgrave Square, to launch the *ThrustSSC* project early in June 1994. It was a fitting choice, for this was where we had held the triumphant post-*Thrust2*-record briefing. We filled their lawns in Halkin Street with Rolls-Royce Spey turbofan engines and the strange rear-wheel-steer Mini; inside, the DERA Pendine team exhibited the rocket test model on mock-up rails. The press conference was well attended, and everyone appeared enthusiastic. The extraordinary thing was that nobody asked if we had enough money. The truth was that we had only about £1,000 in the bank. Everything had the big Castrol brand over it, so I suppose they assumed that Castrol would be paying for it. Certainly no company came forward and said, 'OK, chaps, we're going to fund the whole thing,' which is what I'd hoped was going to happen.

Our little team had completed its basic aerodynamic research, designed the fundamentals of the car and had sourced its power units, and we were preparing to build what some people were calling, tongue-in-cheek, the world's fastest forklift truck.

Now we needed to find the right man to drive it.

Glynne developed this rear-wheel-steering Mini as a means of convincing sceptics – myself included – that this approach was practical for ThrustSSC.

14 THE RIGHT STUFF

I'd driven *Thrust1*, and I'd taken *Thrust2* to the land-speed record. To many it seemed entirely logical that I should drive *ThrustSSC*. I now made one of the hardest decisions of my career: to step down and let somebody else drive the car.

It was a very painful decision. I hated doing it, but it was the only sensible solution to a difficult problem. Looked at dispassionately, there was simply no alternative, and I realized this sooner than most. In order to get *ThrustSSC* operational as soon as practicably possible we had to go through one hell of a build operation. If we didn't, Craig Breedlove would beat us. I knew that managing it and finding the funding was going to be a tremendous undertaking on its own.

I knew, too, that Sally was not at all happy about the idea of my having another go, for a number of personal reasons. All these considerations pointed to one conclusion: we had to find somebody else. It required someone who was used to dealing with high speeds, who had the ability to process an enormous amount of information under stress and extreme pressure: possibly a pilot or a race-car driver.

With *Thrust2* we had hit on that devastatingly simple expedient of advertising for the designer of a 650 m.p.h. car. The outcome was the highly successful relationship with John Ackroyd. This time, I decided to do something even more straightforward. At the press launch I just let it be known that I was not going to be the driver, and left it up to the potential candidates to get in touch with us. After all, if they couldn't figure out how to do that, there probably wasn't going to be much point in aspiring to travel a mile in less than five seconds.

But how do you go about selecting a driver for an 850 m.p.h. car? What characteristics and qualities would you seek?

In the past drivers tended to select themselves, since they invariably initiated the projects that took them to the record. Castrol's stars of the 1920s and 1930s, Sir Henry Segrave, Sir Malcolm Campbell and George Eyston, were each the prime movers behind their respective efforts, as were Craig Breedlove and Art Arfons. Gary Gabelich was the last man to break that mould, for the former trainee astronaut was selected to drive Reaction Dynamics' *Blue Flame* only after the intended pilot, Chuck Suba, was killed while drag racing, and Craig Breedlove had subsequently turned down the drive.

PROFESSOR ROGER GREEN

'There are two ways of selecting somebody. For a regular job you can go out and find a few people who are doing the job already, give them a few tests. But obviously that's hard to do with land-speed record-holders so we had to adopt a different approach and decide, really, what characteristics were required in a driver for a world land-speed-record attempt. The most obvious thing to do, which leapt to mind, was to give them all a sanity test and take the ones who failed. But one Richard Noble is obviously quite enough already.

'We decided to take a slightly more studied approach, and that was to say, what does this person really have to do? The answer was that he had to do two things. He had to be able to drive and control the car, and he had to be able to get on with the rest of the team. Because one of the things that Richard made perfectly clear to us at the outset was that there is a very important team element to this sort of thing. It's the teaminess which enables the whole thing, and without that it won't work. There was no room for prima donnas or people who wanted to feel they were more special than anybody else. So that was a very important consideration for us.

'The favoured sixteen were invited to the Centre for Human Sciences at Farnborough, and the first step was to talk with them all and explain precisely what the project was all about before they were subjected to little batteries of tests to determine their basic personality and intelligence.

'And the reason for giving them an intelligence test was that (a) it's easy to do, and (b) we didn't want anybody who was bonkers, and the personality test would, to some extent at least, determine that. The reason for having somebody bright was that this person wasn't just going to sit in the car and go. He would have to be a development and test driver as well, and somebody who could come back and say, "This is what I think is going on," who could do a bit of analysis of a problem, contribute to the technical output of the rest of the team, was going to be an obvious asset. Plainly someone who was very dominant or very stupid was not the sort of person we wanted.

'We whittled the sixteen down to eight quite easily. And those eight, as it turned out, were all pilots of one sort or another. They then came back again to the Centre for Human Sciences, where we kept them for the best part of two working days and both nights. One of the things we had identified was that people get tired in the desert, tempers can get frayed, so we set out to aggravate them a little bit. We hadn't told them they were going to stay awake all night, and we hadn't told them we were going to put them in our heat chambers, but that's what we did. They stayed awake all night in a hot environment. Before they went into it they did a batch of tests, and we did some more tests the next day. The most important was a test to see how well they could control things, because, first and foremost, when he got into the car this person was going to be controlling it and keeping it straight. We wanted someone who was going to be very good at catching changes in the control dynamics of something, and adapting to them. The better ones were phenomenally good at it, better than we could conceivably have imagined. From the intelligence tests as well, they were amazingly good. They could have romped into MENSA. They were very bright, very stable and very good at controlling things.'

We were looking for excellence in all aspects of the programme, so we needed to be completely objective in the selection process. The driver would have to win his place through open competition. At this point I was very fortunate to make the acquaintance of the late Professor Roger Green at the DERA Centre of Human Sciences at Farnborough. A balding, cheerful fellow with a robust sense of humour, he jumped at the challenge. I explained to him that we weren't looking for a Richard Noble clone; we were looking for someone better than Richard Noble.

Of the thirty potential drivers who made contact with us, we were able immediately to whittle it down to sixteen on the basis of relevant experience. Those sixteen were invited to the centre to undertake a series of tests. All sixteen of them were either drag racers or pilots, which seemed like quite a good start.

The two stages of the selection process were fascinating to observe. Roger's assessments narrowed down the list to five remaining candidates: Tornado pilots Dick Downs, Andrew Green and Bernie Smith; Airtours MD83 First Officer Steve Warren-Smith and BA747 First Officer David Ramsden.

Making the decision not to drive ThrustSSC was one of the hardest things I've ever had to do. After an exhaustive selection procedure we whittled our list of prospective drivers down from thirty to five. From left to right: Steve Warren-Smith, Bernie Smith, David Ramsden, Dick Downs and Andy Green. In December 1994 we arranged an important test for them at the Chris Birkbeck Rally School at Brotton on the north-east coast.

ANDY GREEN

'My girlfriend, Jayne Millington, read an article about *ThrustSSC* in the *Sunday Telegraph* and said nothing about it. Then, when I read it, I looked at the six cars that were pictured. Admittedly the rendering of *ThrustSSC* wasn't great, but it seemed the least likely of them to succeed. It seemed the wrong way to go. Breedlove looked as if he had exactly the right design. If I'd sat down and drawn a land-speed-record car, that's what it would have looked like.

'It was only when I got to the bottom of the article that there were these ridiculous claims of going supersonic. I thought that technically it might be possible, but intuitively, surely not. It said Richard wasn't going to drive the car, but it was very understated. I didn't feel, Wow! I can do that job. But I thought, Hang on, it's a twin Spey-engined vehicle. I know about them and their dynamics and the problems of just getting used to jet engines. I thought to myself, Who on earth would you find to drive a jet-powered supersonic car? What sort of qualifications would they need?

'The more I thought about it, the more I thought the qualifications were likely to be those of a jet pilot rather than those of a racing driver. I suddenly thought, OK, if they are a jet pilot's qualifications, who is going to be better qualified to drive that car than me? Absolutely nobody. Right, it's got to be my job then. But I wondered if Richard was serious.

'I called his agent, expecting him to say it was a joke. Was I a test pilot? I told him no. He didn't say no outright, but he said that almost certainly I wouldn't have the right experience. What I didn't realize then was that he was saying that to everybody, working on the assumption that anybody who'd be turned down by a simple no probably wasn't the guy they were looking for. I sent him my CV anyway, and a week later they asked me for a full one. I won't say I made stuff up, but I made it look good, and later it appeared in the press and embarrassed me enormously.

'At Farnborough for the first batch of tests, all these guys kept walking through the door: Dick Downs, who'd joined the RAF on the same day as me, guys who'd instructed me and who I'd been trying to catch up for the last ten years. It wasn't overawing, but it was competition that deserved an enormous amount of respect.

'When Richard broke the land-speed record I'd just finished university and I was starting officer training with the Royal Air Force. I was at that impressionable age, joining as a pilot, having desperately wanted to be one. And I thought what Richard had achieved was just incredible, another level beyond.

'When I heard he was intending to breakthrough the sound barrier, I knew it would be the last great challenge in land-speed record-breaking. Once it was done the next big number would be a thousand m.p.h., but that's all it would be, a number. The speed of sound at ground level would be something else, and there would be nothing else like it.

'The challenge was irresistible. Who knew what would happen to the shock waves that were generated? Would they bounce back and pitch up the car's nose? Would they prove to be of destructive magnitude?

'I believed that it was very important for a British driver to be the first to go through the sound barrier. The land-speed record is one of the few things that Britain has done really, really well, and we'd held it for longer than every other nation put together. The supersonic record was the ultimate land-speed record. And second, it might just be one of the last ever records. Once you'd gone supersonic, it was going to be very difficult for somebody else to build a car to go even faster - I mean significantly faster - and it was going to be difficult to get the funding because it would have to be a complex, very expensive car.

'So we were really at the pinnacle of land-speed record-breaking, almost a hundred years after the first record was set. We were close to the ultimate record. And because we've been so successful in the last ninety-nine years, I really wanted the British team to succeed, and I wanted to be the first one to actually do it.'

The third stage of the selection process was rather different and took place at a secret location in the north-east. We arranged things so that the candidates would have absolutely no idea of what awaited them until the day itself.

On 16 December 1994 they were taken by bus to the school run by rally driver Chris Birkbeck at Brotton, near Saltburn on the North Sea coastline. It was an incongruous setting for such a test, given that a supersonic car would be driven in the desert.

Our format was straightforward. The twice British national champion Russell Brookes was strapped into the passenger seat of an F2 Volkswagen Golf rally car, and each of the five candidates would then do four practice laps of the 1.3-mile

The idea of the Brotton test was not so much to see how well the rival candidates could drive a rally car, as to monitor how fast they could adapt to totally unfamiliar circumstances and conditions without losing control. On a bitterly cold day each of them had to complete a number of laps of a muddy course, observed and accompanied by the well-known rally driver Russell Brookes.

track. Russell was there not to instruct but simply to analyse the way the candidates learned to drive the car, although he would answer any questions that they had. These four laps were then immediately followed by three timed laps, again without any help or instruction. If they spun during the practice runs it wasn't a problem, but if they did so during the final three, when the clocks were running, they would automatically be washed out of the overall competition.

Some form of adjustment had been built in to cater for any changes in the course conditions during the programme, but though it did indeed improve as a muddy, initially wet course dried slightly, this did not ultimately have any effect, as the first two drivers set the quickest times by a significant margin.

Russell was a real hero in all this. He did a fabulous job for us, and the report he subsequently prepared was beautifully done.

The big mistake was to assume that the idea of the test was to equate the ability to drive a rally car with the ability to handle a supersonic land-bound racer running in a straight line. There might be marginal similarities between handling a 220-brake-horsepower Golf on the slippery track and making the lightning corrections to a 110,000-brake-horsepower jet car's trajectory on the Black Rock Desert, but the real purpose of the programme was much more practical: it was to throw the candidates into a totally unfamiliar environment, and to see how effectively each of them coped. The medium could have been anything. What was crucial was how they adapted to it.

It fell to Dick Downs to set the ball rolling. He nearly came to grief very early on. The main straight was entered via a tight left-hand bend, and, as Dick braked on the approach, he was carrying too much speed and fishtailed violently before eventually dropping the left front wheel into a ditch. He came to a halt with a dead engine and was obliged to sit waiting while the car was hauled out.

Russell had explained the likely problems the candidates would face: 'These front-wheel-drive cars with two hundred and twenty brake horsepower and limited-slip differentials can be very hard to drive, especially on loose surfaces,

RUSSELL BROOKES

'Andy showed remarkable attributes and learning rate. I highlighted in particular his mechanical sympathy and ability to control slides. After the third lap he never missed a gear-change. He was the only driver to consistently keep the engine working in the correct rev. range. After covering the windscreen with muddy water at the puddle, he was the only driver who anticipated the problem in the following laps by switching the wipers on *before* the puddle. At the end of the session his ability to control a slide without overreacting was exemplary. He anticipated the onset of a slide and responded quickly, balancing the throttle and steering so the car didn't swing about like a pendulum.

'He was the most inquisitive driver. I almost thought the volume of questions was designed to impress me, but equally I had to say they were all relevant. Waving to photographers or making comments during the timed runs struck me as either brash or contrived in order to impress me, but he didn't get into trouble when he took his hand off the steering wheel. In a similar vein was his comment at the end of practice, when he said he knew when to brake because he saw my right foot twitch. At least it showed he had a wide angle of peripheral vision when driving fast.

'There was a little bit of gamesmanship at the start of the timed run. After stopping on the departure line he then proceeded to manoeuvre and reverse the car, each time getting a little further back from the line. I quickly called a halt to that. Although not said, I'm sure he knew that the further back from the departure line you start the higher your speed when you cross the timing line.

'I had no hesitation in recommending Andy, and asked Richard to carefully consider his attributes. He was cautious to start with but progressed through each lap. He undoubtedly had the best mechanical sympathy. He had the best control of the car. He had the self-control to implement instructions. He thought more about the task. He showed no hesitancy when the car was at its maximum speed. In a nutshell, you could say that he was in control of the car at all times, and not the other way round.'

ANDY GREEN

'That was a brilliant day at Brotton, and I'd love to get involved in some sort of motorsport like that. I have never been in a car when a top rally driver drives, so I don't know how fast a professional would have gone round there, but I was most definitely learning all the time. The next step for me was starting to judge the acceleration and braking distances so that I was using all the available traction. What I wasn't doing was slewing the car round the corners, simply because that was a technique I'd never practised before, and it wasn't one I was concentrating on. I didn't develop a technique for getting the back end to come round on a front-wheel-drive car. Just occasionally it happened by accident, and I noticed how much smoother it went round the corner, how much better it was. That was the next thing for me to learn. Whether it would have taken two or three laps or two or three days, I don't know.'

where as one wheel begins to slip and then adjusts to the conditions, the car can pull one way and then the other.' Dick had just discovered this, but to his credit it didn't upset him at all. He had simply wanted to find the limit on his free laps, so that he could pull back from it slightly during the timed runs. Ironically, however, his mistake was to have an unfortunate result for one of the contenders.

The process resumed, after a lengthy delay while Brookes struggled to fire up the flooded engine, and straight away Dick attacked the course as if nothing had happened. It was an admirable bit of driving, and he never again put a wheel wrong as he set the quickest lap times. The hiatus that followed Dick's mistake proved to be Bernie Smith's undoing. None of the drivers was permitted to speak to the others after his stint, so after the long hold-up most, Bernie in particular, assumed that Dick must have been excluded for an off during his three quick laps, and that therefore he effectively now had only three remaining opponents rather than four. He thus elected to adopt the cautious approach and netted a time of 4 minutes 51.132 seconds, which proved to be the slowest. David was placed third on 4 minutes 47.576 seconds and Steve fourth on 4 minutes 48.036 seconds. Downs and Green, however, were head and shoulders above them with respective total lap times of 4 minutes 32.704 seconds and 4 minutes 34.027 seconds.

So we had a result, but not quite as we'd expected. The plan had been to take the three fastest drivers, but the third- and fourth-placed times were so close we decided to take the top four instead.

The most interesting aspect was that, though their times were similar, Dick Downs and Andy Green took totally different approaches. The former attacked again regardless of his initial experience, the latter took the more calculated approach, and ran progressively faster with each smooth lap.

The four remaining candidates – Downs, Green, Ramsden and Warren-Smith – now went through to the final stage of the selection process, teamwork, which was held on 1 January 1995. They thought they were doing an assessment of the project and designing the cockpit. But this was just a ruse to get them to meet the rest of the team. The team didn't know it was a ruse; they, too, thought the guys were evaluating the project and designing the cockpit. It was a double deception, and it worked very well. Again, we didn't want the final decision to be based on a subjective assessment. We didn't want the candidates thinking the team was going to assess them, and we didn't want the team thinking they had to. It was best that neither party knew. On the final night of the evaluation, four sets of the most comprehensive and superbly presented reports with detailed cockpit designs were hand-delivered to Ron's house in Claygate. We felt very bad about consigning them all unread straight into the project filing system. Immediately after, Roger Green circulated his questionnaire, and the team was asked to respond to it by return. A few nights later he telephoned me and said, 'Richard, we've got your man.'

We called a press conference at Brooklands on 2 February, where we told the world that thirty-two-year-old Andy Green would be the driver of *ThrustSSC*, after the most exhaustive and comprehensive driver-selection programme in the history of the land-speed record. Sadly, Roger succumbed to cancer before Andy ever drove the car. Had he been able to see how well Andy performed, he would have been very proud of his namesake.

Andy Green emerged as the outstanding candidate from the six-month selection programme.

My first impression of Andy was that he was very quiet. If you looked at pictures taken during the tests at Brotton he was always at the back, slightly unsure of himself. We recorded interviews with each candidate initially, and he hadn't seemed sure why he was doing it, but he did use the word 'team', which was good.

What was really interesting in retrospect is that he went into this thing absolutely determined to win. His CV showed a remarkable dedication to his chosen profession as a pilot. He had won numerous inter-Services competitions, school colours, single-sculls rowing honours, and was a strong long-distance runner. He was also a highly rated competitor on the Cresta Run. It was manifestly clear that he had a very competitive nature.

ANDY GREEN

'It was very interesting to assess the different approaches of the group at Brotton. Because Richard said we were being marked on car control, I decided there was no point in taking a risk, even in practice. Ultimately they were assessing us from the minute we walked in the door until the end, even if not as formally as during those three laps.

'Overall the thing that was closest to the skills I needed to drive the car was when we had to steer a spot round a computer screen at Farnborough. It was a phenomenally difficult test. Then we did it again after twenty-four hours in the heat chambers, and the surprise was that I did it better the second time round. I recognized much more quickly what control responses I needed. That was exactly like the car; remembering what you did yesterday and where it went right and where it went wrong. As a laboratory test that was very clever. The selection procedure was hard work, but fascinating.

'I found out I had been chosen when Richard called me in Switzerland two days before the official announcement at Brooklands, because I was away doing the Cresta Run at the time. He said, "The competition was very close, but you just got it," so as not to let me get too carried away. About a year later he actually told me the truth. I thought, Are you bullshitting me now, or were you bullshitting me then?'

The land-speed record had been part of my life since I was six years old. For Andy Green, flying always came first. But it was quite clear from the start that he was very keen to get to grips with the *ThrustSSC* programme. He wasn't going to be the sort who just turned up on the day. Nevertheless, at the start there was potential for a gulf to develop between Andy and the rest of the team. He had developed in a completely different culture, one that was alien to everyone else. He was an RAF officer, and was therefore brought up to behave in a very different way. There was never any sense of elitism, but in the environment he was used to there is a distinct difference between the officers and the men in the workshop. He didn't let it affect his integration with the team, which was important because in the *ThrustSSC* project such an attitude would have been completely untenable.

It was also very difficult for him because I'd hoped we would get *ThrustSSC* finished in 1995, and this proved wildly optimistic. Andy effectively had the better part of eighteen months to wait before he could drive the car. In that time he worked very hard. He would try his hand at everything. You'd see him with a soldering iron, trying this, trying that. In the process he earned everyone's respect.

Andy is a brilliant mathematician. If you look at his CV, you will see that he has eleven O levels, four A levels and two S levels. He read Mathematics at Worcester College, Oxford, with sponsorship from the RAF's University Cadet Scheme. He graduated with First Class Honours in 1983, the year we broke the land-speed record. All of that spoke volumes for his character and commitment, and he used his mathematical ability to the full as he worked very closely with the design team throughout the project. In the early days he invested an enormous amount of time in getting to understand the design of *ThrustSSC*. He really integrated well, which was desperately important. We were all working under tremendous pressure, and if anyone on the team had ever got the impression that they were working with a prima donna, then they would very quickly have either walked out or cut him down to size.

Besides integrating quickly, Andy also learned about public speaking, though this was probably not easy for him, given his shy nature. Whenever he made a speech we would generally talk about it afterwards. I stressed the great importance of his choice of words and expressions, and the effect they were going to have. He knew that it was important for him to address people as a member of a team, rather than as an elitist.

I think it's terribly important that people should understand what Andy contributed to the *SSC* project over and above his remarkable driving skills. He did just about every travelling roadshow, and he never charged any expenses. Back in the days when the United States Air Force was chasing the sound barrier with the Bell X-1, it employed a civilian pilot called Chalmers 'Slick' Goodlin. The closer he got to Mach 1, the more money he wanted, until eventually the military brass baulked at the spiralling costs. Goodlin's undoing proved to be an opportunity for a regular pilot called Charles 'Chuck' Yeager, who stepped into the breach and broke the sound barrier for nothing more than his monthly pay.

Andy was the same. We didn't pay him a fortune to drive for us, as if he was a

Michael Schumacher. Hell, we had enough difficulty paying our bills, let alone hiring a star. Andy never received a penny from us. He did it for his monthly Air Force pay, and he put in two years of his holidays to take the time to drive *ThrustSSC*. Working for the Ministry of Defence and living down on site at Farnborough, he would be in the workshop every night and weekend. He put in thousands of man-hours.

The whole project was very much at the mercy of the selected driver. Had he decided to push off for weeks at a time, what could we really have done about it? But Andy was a team player, through and through.

The deal we came to was this: he would be able to claim expenses, if he wished, from this company that was daily on the verge of bankruptcy. He never did. I said to him, 'Andy, at the end of this, if we are successful, you're going to be a global hero. And you are going to be able to make an awful lot of money from advertising, promotions and endorsements. All the attention is going to be on you. We will just be left with the car. I'd like to suggest an arrangement where you get to drive the car, and the contract will state that you can walk away from the project at any time without any recriminations whatsoever. All you have to say is, "I'm sorry, this is it, I've gone as far as I want to go." Please don't feel that you are under any obligation. If you go we will be left with an enormous mess, but we will sort that out.' And we would have been in a terrible mess, too, because Andy was very good and quickly became a key part of the programme. But it would have been wrong to place the driver under a burden of obligation.

Then the question was what would happen afterwards. I said, 'Frankly, you're going to be as famous as Gagarin, and you will be able to pick and choose what you want to do. Whether you want to stay on with the RAF or go commercial and endorse this, that or the other, is up to you. The basis of the contract is that, when it comes to it, the choice is yours. There will be no question of our trying to claw back anything from your post-record-attempt financial benefits or whatever.' And that's what we agreed to.

Andy was free to make enormous amounts of money afterwards, but he has chosen to put all that behind him and to concentrate on his RAF career. A remarkable fellow.

15 A RACE AGAINST TIME

I knew right from the start that raising the money for the *SSC* was going to be even harder than it had been for *Thrust2*. The world had moved into the interactive video-game era, where a project would really have to appeal to a global audience. We had to interact so strongly with the people who were following our programme that they would want to stay with it right through to the very end.

Everything about the project had to be the best. We would never lower our standards, regardless of what we could afford. And there was an immutable principle on which we operated, both on *ThrustSSC* and *Thrust2*: we would never accept money from a tobacco company.

I had always hoped that Castrol would come in with some serious money. That's how I saw us deriving our main income. But it didn't happen. Castrol made it quite clear that we shouldn't expect too much from them. They saw themselves putting in about £50,000 each year, and no more.

I don't say this to disparage Castrol in any way, because we were very grateful for their seed capital for the research programme. But I had always hoped they would take a greater share of the sponsorship than the 10 per cent they did.

As soon as I saw the way things were going, I realized that we needed to bring in revenue from every angle. No longer could we be totally dependent on sponsors and their goodwill, we had to go out and generate income in many other ways. The sooner we got this going, obviously the better it would be, and the more secure the project would become. I was trying to bring in one £50,000 sponsor a month, and, of course, there would be months when I wouldn't get one, so consequently I'd have to bridge that in some way. Invariably I did it with debt, and that was a hellishly uncomfortable feeling. It made me feel as though I was digging a great big hole that I could never be sure of climbing out of in an entire lifetime of penury.

There was no reason why a project as good as *ThrustSSC*, with such potential, should have had to go through that. There had to be a better way of doing it.

The absolutely fundamental thing was this: there were two teams definitely building supersonic cars, ourselves and Craig Breedlove. Only one of us was going supersonic first. The one that did that was likely to knock the other one out

Michael Turner was the first artist to capture the dramatic appearance of ThrustSSC, long before we had started to cut the first metal.

completely. In financial terms, it meant that if you still had substantial debts and were the one that failed, you were going to go bust, because once somebody else had gone supersonic there would be no more money forthcoming for you. It was going to be as simple as that. It was winner takes all, loser gets wiped out.

What made it worse was that we had decided to build a twin-engined car. James Morton and I had originally calculated that *ThrustSSC* would take 35,000 man-hours to build, but eventually it became clear that it was going to take closer to 100,000. Breedlove's car was simple, and I suspected it would be closer to *Thrust2* in build time, which meant about 20,000 man-hours. For every man-hour that Craig put in, we had to fund and put in five. It wasn't difficult to see that, human nature being what it is, sponsors wouldn't be particularly interested in supporting this thing until it was up and running. That's how we saw it. Therefore the funding was going to be a nightmare.

I realized very quickly that we couldn't rely on sponsors, because it simply wasn't going to happen that way.

It was not a situation for the faint-hearted.

So we had a predicament where we were going to incur an enormous liability, because we had to outpace Craig. It was one hell of a thing, because we couldn't control our own pace. This created the most tremendous pressure. At no stage could we say, we're not doing well financially so we'll cut back, we'll lay people off. We couldn't do that, we had to get our heads down and work flat out regardless of the cash position.

We didn't actually start building until late 1994, whereas Craig had been building for a long time, albeit at a very slow pace. Whenever we were failing to keep up with the mounting cash-flow requirement, the overdraft was just growing and growing.

In the old days of *Thrust1* and *Thrust2* I had always preached the doctrine of never using your own money, but we were well beyond that now. We really were well into an all-or-nothing fight to the financial death. The *ThrustSSC* project existed on an overdraft that I had guaranteed, with our house and everything Sally and I owned as collateral.

The problem was that *ThrustSSC* had gone way past the point of no return. A terrific team had been assembled to work on the car. The absolute dilemma was that if we stopped it at all, for whatever reason, everybody would walk away. All of the learning would go with them, and that's the sort of human capital that you can never regain, even if you do manage to spool things up again with different personnel.

Getting there first had become everything, and we simply had to be hard enough to do whatever was needed to achieve that.

One of the best things we did – and it was absolutely the right decision – was to go with G Force for the initial construction. It was a real turnkey operation. James Morton was doing some design work, and G Force worked with Ron and Glynne; all I had to do was run round and find the money. We agreed a rate per man-hour, and the principle that if we did have a bad month they would redeploy the labour on other projects at their own cost. That was a safety net for us, but the reality was that we couldn't afford to have a bad month in production terms. If we did, we would lose the race with Breedlove.

We had identified several potential markets for merchandising. One was our supporters. The second was the sponsors and their employees. And the third would become the Internet.

The key to the supporters' club was a fellow called Robin Richardson. A lifelong and very knowledgeable enthusiast for all things to do with record-breaking, Robin had started the Speed Record Club in the early 1990s as a means of putting similar-minded enthusiasts in touch with one another. Over the years I had got to know Robin and his wife, Sue, and they had come out to Gerlach when we'd held the tenth-anniversary 633 Club get-together on the Black Rock Desert. Robin seemed to me the ideal person to run our new supporters' club. We talked it all out at a meeting in May 1994, when I managed to borrow the

LENGTH	54 feet	16.5 metres
WIDTH	12 feet	3.66 metres
WHEELBASE	28 feet	8.53 metres
TRACK (front)	9.75 feet	2.97 metres
(rear)	1 foot	0.3 metres
WEIGHT (with fuel)	10.5 tons	10.7 tonnes
FUEL WEIGHT	1 ton	
ENGINES	Two Rolls-Royce Spey 202s	
	(the original design assumed Spey 205 engines)	
CHASSIS	Welded T45 steel tube spaceframe	
BODY SHELL	Aluminium, carbon fibre and titanium	
STEERING	Worm drive acting on the rear wheels	
WHEELS	Four forged aluminium, rear pair in staggered formation	
WHEEL DIMENSIONS (front)	34" dia x 10"	0.87 dia x 0.25 metre
WHEEL DIMENSIONS (rear)	34" dia x 6"	0.87 dia x 0.15 metre
BRAKE CHUTE	7ft 6in (2.28) metres ribbon chute plus reverse	
DISC BRAKES	17in dia (0.43 metre) dia. Two on each front wheel,	
	one on each rear wheel, two calipers acting on each disc	
PEAK SPEED ACHIEVED	771 mph	1241 kph
THRUST PER ENGINE	9 tons	
MAX OUTPUT (two engines)	80,000 hp	60 mw
MAX ACCELERATION	1.05g at 600 mph (965 kph)	

DESIGN MAXIMUM FIGURES (assuming Spey 205 engines)		
DESIGN MAX SPEED	850 mph	1370 kph
THRUST PER ENGINE	10 tons	
MAX OUTPUT (two engines)	100,000 hp	75 mw
DESIGN MAX ACCELERATION	1.3g up to 600 mph (965 kph)	

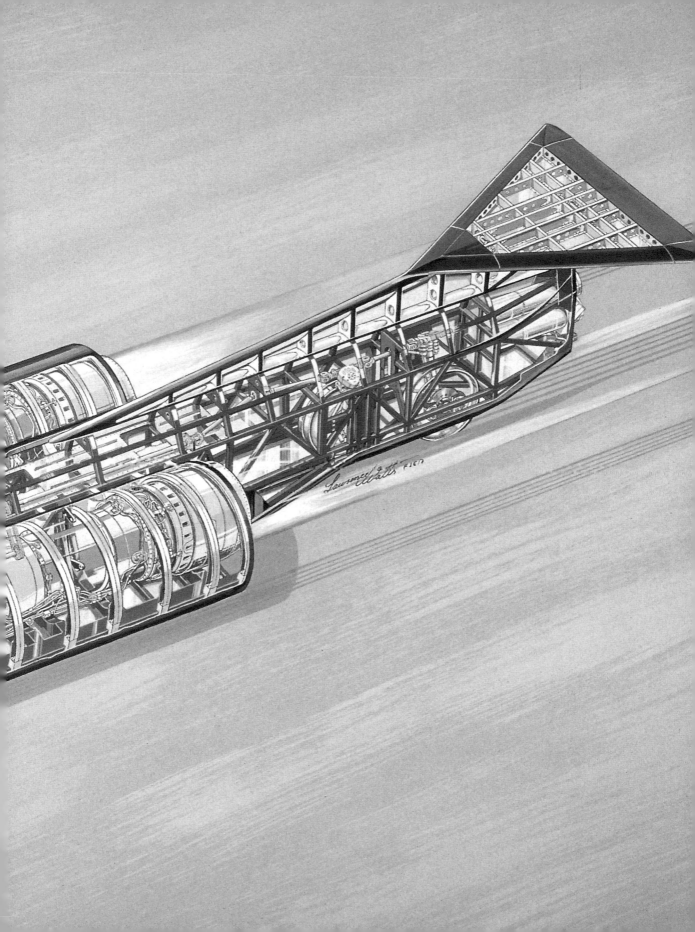

boardroom at the RAC's headquarters in Pall Mall. I was terribly relieved and pleased when Robin said yes. And on top of this he came up with the perfect name for it: the Mach 1 Club. It was a brilliant touch.

It became clear to the people who had worked on the *Thrust2* project that we were manning the *ThrustSSC* project from different sources. This was very important. It was a new project, and if we had started bringing in the old guard it would rapidly start becoming an old project. It had to be new and vibrant, and to have its own identity. It couldn't be a rerun of what had gone before. The workload was absolutely terrible, and people had to be totally committed to doing it. Therefore we left it very much up to the old guard as to whether they wanted to join.

One of the hard lessons we learned from *Atlantic Sprinter* was that it's absolutely essential to involve the public, right from the start. But we felt the same about the old *Thrust2* Supporters' Club as we did about the old guard. Rather than contact its members and ask them to join the new club, we left it up to them to make the move. A lot of them did. But the whole thing had to be different and it had to be new; it couldn't be the same old thing again.

There was another key aspect to the Mach 1 Club. We made a rule that, once they had paid a one-off joining fee, we would never ask the members for donation money. The understanding had to be that this project was not a charity, it was going to earn its money the hard way, and thus earn its independence. There would never be a question of actually saying to them, 'Please put your hand in your pocket and give us twenty quid.'

Instead, we would feel justified in offering them every kind of merchandise, and hoping to God that they would buy some. But that was as far as it went.

The final element was that we would always tell them the truth. We would treat them almost as if we were reporting to shareholders. In fact, the first Mach 1 Club weekend down at Fontwell, on the racecourse close to G Force's premises, was most interesting in that respect. I stood up and gave them fifteen minutes of bad news. And it really did work, because people realized we were telling them the truth, we weren't just saying, 'This is a wonderful project, we are doing really well.' I told them about all the deals that had failed, all the things that had gone wrong. I think it was appreciated, because it built up a tremendous relationship that grew stronger all the way along the line.

Robin and Sue did a fabulous job getting the Mach 1 Club under way, and together with Sally, Andy and our old friends Mike and Ninetta Hearn, we developed our roadshow, which we took all over the country. We would tell people about the project and its aspirations, we would sign up new Mach 1 Club members and we would sell as much merchandise as possible.

We realized quickly that the final sponsorship situation would end up like *Thrust2*'s, with a collection of backers, which gave us more security than a single sponsor that might withdraw when times got hard, but it wasn't until 1996, when *ThrustSSC* was finished, that we really started selling merchandise to sponsors. Ex-RAF man Leigh Remfry had joined us to look after the fuel systems, so when they were complete he transformed into the sponsors' merchandise salesman. He worked really hard at this, but that side of things never caught on in the way we'd hoped it would. I tried to get the sponsors to help us sell merchandise to their workforces, but the message didn't seem to get across. I think some took the view that they didn't want to be dragged further and further into the project.

What was also making life difficult was that, particularly in the early stages of the project, a lot of people were very conscious that the economy was only just coming out of recession. When we were at the 1994 Motor Show at the NEC, for instance, we had to keep the prices of our merchandise pretty low – £3 for a poster, that sort of thing – and people seemed twitchy. But even so we had one hell of a good stand there, and it was a great success. A terrific bloke called Jeff Luff had built us half of a full-scale mock-up of *ThrustSSC*, split longitudinally, like one of those sailing-boat models you mount on the wall. Jeff works in the film props and special effects industry, and he and his colleague Ryan Hodges did a wonderful job. The mock-up gave people their first real inkling of the dramatic shape and scale of *ThrustSSC*, and we signed up more than 1,000 Mach 1 Club members at the Motor Show alone. After that the mock-up became a regular feature of our roadshows, until the car itself was finally completed and we could show them the real thing.

Fortunately a few enlightened souls did believe we were coming out of recession and that maybe it was time to let go a bit again. A very good example of that was John Whelan, managing director of Dunlop Aviation Division. Glynne and I went up to Coventry to see whether they could help with *ThrustSSC*'s wheels and brakes. What he said to us first was pretty depressing: 'We've been through hell with this recession. We've asked outrageous things of our workforce, we've cut them back, and we feel that we've abused our relationship with them simply because of the financial restrictions.' But then he surprised us both by saying, 'Now we want to do something we can all be proud of.'

It was a very brave and far-sighted view that John took. When Glynne and I had gone up to Coventry we hadn't been at all sure of the outcome, but we came away with John's agreement that Dunlop Aviation Division would manufacture the wheels, the brake discs and the calipers – worth over £200,000. That was a great day.

Finally, there was the Internet, which, as far as I was concerned, was a completely unknown quantity. Robin Richardson works for Digital, and he put the idea to Dave Probert, director of their Internet business group, that they should sponsor a website for us. Dave is another very enlightened guy, and he really went for it. Part of the contract with Digital was that we would have the capacity on our website for at least one million hits per day. We had asked him what was the biggest website in the world, and he said it was the White House, with one million hits a day. I told him, 'We're going to beat that!'

At first I just saw the website as a back-up, as a way of enabling more people to become aware of and learn about the project, and to demonstrate its popularity to our sponsors. The more people knew about it accurately and could talk about it with confidence, the wider the story would spread. And, hopefully, the greater would be our chances of pulling in another sponsorship deal. In other words, the Internet website would supplement our sales effort, which was mainly a matter of constantly writing to companies and then making presentations to them when they showed even the slightest interest.

But very soon, once we'd really got into it, we realized that we had actually got something very different. I went to the 1995 British Grand Prix at Silverstone, where we had taken our sales stand and set it up outside the spectator area and the main paddock. What I saw made me realize that the relationship between the public and Formula One was very different. The public was being charged 50 quid a head and they didn't even get a seat in the stands; there was little question of them getting into the pits unless they paid for a special paddock transfer, and there was absolutely no question of any of the great heroes coming into the stands to talk and sign autographs. We were planning to do it the other way round; we were going to encourage participation. Our message was, 'Hey, come and be a part of this. Find out what it's all about. Ask all your questions and we'll tell you what we are trying to do.' It worked really well. I think there were a few who thought *ThrustSSC* was a good idea that would never see the light of day, but gradually our relationship began to build. As Robin handled the Mach 1 Club, steam-train fanatic Jeremy Davey did a fantastic job looking after our growing Internet website, which rapidly became one of the best ever, growing eventually to 800 pages and generating an incredible 56 million hits.

I doubt we could ever have done this if we hadn't previously been successful with *Thrust2*. That had established our bona fides and given us credibility and publicity, and without it I think the step would have been too great. But I do think that people recognized this as a very new, very different sort of project.

Rosco McGlashan knew his time was running out as Craig and I continued production. Ackers had again helped him to modify *Aussie Invader*, and as an indication of the pressure he was under, Rosco said to one of his friends, 'We've got to do it this time. If we don't do it this time I'm gonna drive past the barrels at the twenty-kilo mark and hang myself.'

Again, however, he struggled as the rebuilt *Invader* yawed violently on the Lake Gairdner salt at speeds far below what he needed to achieve. On one run it veered so much that it struck and swallowed a plastic marker cone, damaging the engine's compressor blades. Later, as bad weather stalked him, his crew discovered that off-centre operation of the afterburner ring was changing the line of thrust, and therefore *Aussie Invader II* was skewing to one side. When that was rectified Rosco averaged 597 m.p.h. But his delight lasted only seconds. As he hit ruts from a previous run, *Invader* swerved into a heavy timing light, which went down the jet intake. He was lucky to avoid injury.

From time to time the guys at G Force would raise their eyebrows and ask, 'Where are the wheels? Do we have any suspension yet?' and other awkward questions. One of the biggest challenges was finding manufacturers to help with *ThrustSSC*. Glynne, who lives in Birmingham, was very keen to involve Midlands industries in the project. Thanks to his initiative we reached a point where Coventry University and the City Council started taking an interest. Much of this was as a direct result of *Thrust2*, which is now owned by Coventry's Museum of British Road Transport. Glynne put an evening presentation together, and some fifteen Coventry manufacturers turned up to hear what it was all about. As a result they agreed to make the key suspension components for us. Three months later I drove a hired Transit van back down south to Fontwell laden with what amounted to £100,000's worth of machined suspension parts.

During the build there were two very big and obvious financial hurdles. The first was the suspension, and the Coventry initiative got us over that. The next one was the building of the nose and the double-curvature bodywork that would be manufactured in composites, because of the huge cost of making the patterns, the moulds and the pieces themselves.

We were incredibly lucky here to have Mike Horne on our side, together with his son Chris. Mike's genius with composites was matched by G Force's in manufacture. Later, when Mike was getting the front-end bodywork together in Farnborough, Andy commented, 'I just cannot understand how you guys can measure up in Farnborough, build the parts in Fontwell, and then bring them back up here, and everything fits perfectly.'

But the urgent problem was to make these vast patterns, from which Mike would make the master mould, in which the nose section and the engine nacelles would be laid up in carbon-fibre composite. We were looking at another £100,000 to make these patterns, and we didn't have it. So what to do? We simply couldn't stop the *ThrustSSC* build now.

The hugely successful composite manufacturer Cytec, which had agreed to help us with the *Atlantic Sprinter*'s superstructure, had also decided to support *ThrustSSC* right from the start. That generated a hugely comfortable feeling. But we were still stuck, because the cost of machining these patterns from our computer-aided design data was going to be around £70,000. First we had to get hold of the aerospace foams to make the patterns, and we were quoted £40,000 for this. So just to get these essential patterns was going to end up costing between £110,000 and £120,000, and the irony was that as soon as Mike had made the master moulds from the patterns, the patterns would be thrown away.

At G Force's headquarters, Andy tries the cockpit for size in February 1995.

The Daewoo Technical Centre in Worthing wasn't far from G Force, and they very kindly agreed to machine the nose pattern on their CNC mill. But that left us with the balance of the problem: how to create the huge engine-nacelle and forward-fuselage patterns.

I phoned up Cytec for advice, and somewhere along the line I was put in touch with a specialist boatbuilder in Devon. I said to him, 'Look, I don't know what the hell we're doing here. We have these enormous patterns to make and we can't afford the aerospace foams. Have you got any ideas?' And he replied, 'Oh, it's very simple. You just use MDF board, the stuff you use for kitchen partitions. Cut it into pineapple rings, build your stack and then machine it into shape.'

So I approached the manufacturer that had 60 per cent of the MDF market. They said they might give us 10 per cent off, which wasn't much help. Then I pushed the local distributor to identify a smaller company in the marketplace, because smaller companies are always more interested and aggressive. They came up with a Scottish company, C. S. Forrest Products, that produced an MDF product called Caber Board. I found myself speaking to the marketing director, Joe Martoccia. Joe was interested, and said, 'Yeah, we'll help. We'll send some down. We'll look after you.'

I put Mike Horne in touch with him, and they discussed things. What we didn't realize was that Joe really was intent on making sure we were well looked after, and that we'd get things right first time. Within a week he sent us nine tons of this stuff. It was fantastic! The guys at G Force were over the moon.

The next thing was the question of machining the patterns. I'd talked to a lot of pattern makers and they'd said, 'Well, it needs a large five-axis milling machine.' Somebody put me in touch with a remarkable company called Survirn Engineering in Birmingham. There were two founders of Survirn, Norman Kench and David Houghton, both dedicated motorcycle racers, who had built up this huge and very successful business that supplies patterns to Boeing and British Aerospace. When I explained the situation to Norman and asked if there was anything he could do, there was a long silence. Then he said, 'We'll do it.' He committed to £70,000's worth of work, over the phone. Thank God such courageous people still exist in Britain.

All of this happened over a period of about two days. Now we had Dunlop committing to the wheels and brakes in a programme worth the better part of £200,000; the City of Coventry making the suspension components; Cytec on the carbon fibre; C. S. Forrest providing the MDF; and Survirn doing the machining. It was fantastic, and suddenly we could take fresh heart. *ThrustSSC* was literally coming together.

With all of these projects, however, you've no sooner solved one set of problems than a new set arises. Around the beginning of 1996 we began to run into problems at G Force, partly because we needed a lot more people working on the project, and partly because *ThrustSSC* was taking up the whole of their assembly hall, making it difficult to work on the car. Just to change position or collect your tools you had to walk round it, so it was getting seriously inefficient. About that time John Biddlecombe landed a contract to build cars for the forthcoming Indy Racing League series, borne out of the split between Tony George and the Indianapolis Speedway, and the teams racing in the CART IndyCar series. From now on there were going to be two single-seater racing championships in the USA, and a new horizon was opening up for G Force in the breakaway series.

G Force did a fabulous job, and without them we could never have got going. But *ThrustSSC* was now rather like a boisterous adolescent, and we both knew that it was time for us to leave home.

Andy Green had begun working at the Defence Evaluation Research Agency at Farnborough, and he suggested we should move there. DERA had plenty of hangar space available, and the runways outside. I was sceptical; I couldn't see a Government establishment accommodating a bunch like us. But Andy pushed ahead, and he got us what we wanted. We could move into Q Shed. Somebody up there liked us.

By 1996 we had begun to outgrow G Force's premises. You can see how tight a fit ThrustSSC is as it is manoeuvred out of the door in a partially completed state.

Naturally, the sight of ThrustSSC being craned over the trees attracted media interest, as we began the move to Farnborough.

16 SQUASHING THE PYRAMID

The Farnborough name still means an awful lot. For me, it was reminiscent of flying greats such as John Derry and Neville Duke, and the air shows of the 1950s and 1960s, when so much effort went into aviation research and every year there were new prototypes. It had great appeal for sponsors and Mach 1 Club members coming down to visit, and Q Shed had plenty of room for volunteer help.

Farnborough was less than half an hour's drive from my home in Hampton, and I found I had to guard against spending too much time down there. It was easy for me to get diverted from my main task of finding the money. This wasn't something I could delegate to anyone. Whenever I turned up at Farnborough, people would start saying to me, 'Richard, do you think we should do this? Do you think we should do that?' And I had to say, 'Come on, you guys are the design team, you've got to make that decision. You can't involve me. I will try to help wherever I can, but if I fall down on the money this whole thing falls down. I daren't waste a second.' Generally we averaged fifteen people on the payroll during the build, and my job was to keep the money coming in to pay for them.

The worst months were always August and December; nobody makes any decisions then because of summer and Christmas holidays. In August 1995, while we were still with G Force down at Fontwell, I could sense a financial crisis coming on. I'd had long conversations with the marketing director of Ford, and he was very keen. Towards the end of July he had suggested that a decision would be forthcoming soon. I discussed it with James Morton at G Force. 'There's a better than even chance that it's going to happen,' I told him. 'We've got to take on a couple more guys.' So that's what we did. It was a risk, but I felt confident that Ford would join us.

Then, around 10 August, I phoned the guy at Ford to see what was happening, and was told he'd gone on holiday. I knew that nothing would happen until he came back. We just had to sit it out. Early in September James said to me, 'Richard, we're running up some big bills. What's happening with Ford?'

I was driving down the M4 one morning when the guy from Ford rang. He had the worst possible news. 'I'm very sorry, I've given it my best, but the US board has turned us down. Is that all right?' They all end up by saying, 'Is that all right?'

when you've just fallen into this abyss of despair.

There was a fantastic rider to the story. I turned off the motorway and rang John Denman, our bank manager at NatWest. 'John,' I said, 'we're in serious trouble. You know our financial situation and what we're trying to do. Well, the Ford deal hasn't come off.'

John said, 'You have to pay G Force.'

'Of course I have to, but the reality is that there's no money to pay them.'

Now G Force also banked with NatWest, and John repeated, 'You have to write that cheque.'

'I simply can't. It's illegal. There is no resource to write it on.'

'I am instructing you, Richard, to write that cheque.'

I rang James and told him the Ford deal had fallen through. 'Oh, God,' he groaned, 'and you owe us so much money. We'll have to stop work immediately.'

'No, hang on,' I said. I told him John Denman had instructed me to write the cheque and that it would be with him the next day. I told him to cash it quickly.

It was way above our already enormous overdraft limit. That one guy, John Denman, saved us: he went unsecured on that cheque, and saved the entire project – and probably G Force as well. John's faith was rewarded when we did the Motor Show at Earl's Court that October. The stand took £60,000 revenue from merchandise trading, and more sponsors came in. If John hadn't supported us, we would never have reached that turning point.

Like *ThrustSSC*, the *Spirit of America* build programme was a stop-start business as Craig looked for money, and I knew he found it hard to get skilled personnel. At one stage he had *Thrust2* team members Brian Ball and Phil Goss doing panel work for him, and Ackers was a frequent visitor once he'd left *ThrustSSC*.

The two Rolls-Royce Spey 202 engines were massive units. Composites specialist Mike Horne did a fabulous job on their intakes and the nose section of ThrustSSC.

ThrustSSC under construction in Q Shed, DERA Farnborough.

As Castrol kept up its historic links with us, so Shell eventually did with Craig, but it seemed only when they finally realized that McLaren's *Maverick* project wasn't going ahead. '

People were often surprised that Craig and I kept in touch as we built our cars. We were rivals, of course, and we were both desperately keen to beat the other one to supersonic speed. But in my book that's no reason not to remain friendly, and Craig obviously took a similar view. To me that's one of the best things about land-speed record-breaking; there is none of the emotional intensity that you find in Formula One, where it can be very difficult for people to separate their professional and competitive lives sufficiently to maintain personal relationships.

In our telephone conversations both of us avoided discussing things in detail. Craig might say, 'We've just fitted the fuel tank,' and I would say, 'Where does it go?' And he would say, 'Oh, by the front wheels.' That sort of thing. Eventually I went over to San Francisco and spent some time with him in Rio Vista early in 1995, when we began working out the logistics of what was by then being billed as 'The Greatest Car Race on God's Earth'.

Craig saw himself running *Spirit of America* on Bonneville, so both cars would be running simultaneously, but on different sites. He would talk about the Black Rock Desert, but his heart always seemed set on Bonneville, and whenever he talked about the design of his wheels it was always with Bonneville in mind.

One of the fundamental parts of our design concept was the active suspension. Ron knew from the outset that we'd need a computer-controlled system able to monitor and influence the aerodynamic trim of the vehicle as the speeds reached the upper transonic and supersonic ranges. By the middle of 1995, we'd reached the stage when we needed somebody smart enough to design such a system.

We had begun by working with Cranfield on a system of pitch control, and the systems were being managed by Andrew Day, a keen motor sport enthusiast and a very competent RAF engineer. We were dealing with a very large lift slope, so the pitch had to be controlled with absolute accuracy.

I think this really explains the difference between *Thrust2* and *ThrustSSC*. *Thrust2* was a very clever design, which worked extremely well, but John was keen that it shouldn't become a research vehicle for people to plug their sensors, monitors, accelerometers and God knows what into, simply because he felt that the academics would slow the whole thing down. *ThrustSSC* on the other hand was going to be very heavily instrumented, so we could gather a terrific amount of data to help us with our run-profile decision-making. The entire project would be very dependent on this huge volume of operational data.

Andrew was very upset when the RAF promoted him to work on AWACs and then told him there was no way he could carry on with us. Once again we found ourselves without a systems designer. At about the same time we were in discussion with Pi Research, where Dr John Davies worked. John had experience working with the Lotus and Ligier Formula One teams on their active suspensions, and just after Andrew's promotion he said, 'There's a guy called Jeremy Bliss. He's got an odd manner, but he is brilliant.'

Jerry went to see Ron, and that evening Ron called me. 'He's very good,' he said, 'and he is starting immediately. But I don't see what John meant about his odd manner.' Jerry is a very intense person and gets very wound up about things at times, but he also has an irreverent sense of humour. While he was at Ford it was some time before they clicked to the acronym of the Computer Road Analysis Programme that he had developed. He and Ron understood their boffin's language and hit it off right away.

Jerry lived the project, first of all down at Fontwell and then at Farnborough. If you look at the pictures of Jerry then and now, you can see he's aged about ten years. He gave it the full 100 per cent, and became one of the most important members of the team. The systems he devised for the data collection, active ride, instruments, hydraulic line and parachutes were incredibly complicated, yet we had very few problems with them when the car was operational.

About a year later, Jerry asked me, 'Richard, how long do you think it took me to write that programme for the active ride?' 'I haven't a clue,' I replied. 'A couple of months or so, was it?' He roared with laughter. 'No! I did it on the back of an envelope, and it took me about twelve hours.'

It was literally five lines of code, and that was all. But what a five lines!

JEREMY BLISS, SYSTEMS DESIGNER

'It was John Davies's fault that I got involved. I phoned him up after I'd been at Ford for a year, which was like a major sabbatical. For two days I did absolutely nothing – and nobody noticed. He was working for Pi Research in Cambridge doing the data system for *Thrust*. I was totally bored by what I was doing. Had I heard of Richard Noble? Yes, vaguely. Had I heard of *ThrustSSC*? Er, no. So John told me what was happening and offered me some work. Three weeks later I got a call from Ron Ayers, who asked me to come down for a chat. I went down one Friday at eight and left around twelve-thirty – and I haven't had any spare time since. So it's really Ron's fault.

'The active design, by its very nature, was driven by how the project was. There are things I would have done differently if I'd had a huge budget, but we didn't have. The only thing I wouldn't compromise on was safety. We were using old Lotus controllers, but they were very reliable, they're not known for breaking down, and I didn't think we'd have any problems with them. All our sensors came from well-known reputable manufacturers who had been generous enough to give them to us. At last count we had more than a hundred and twenty of them on the car.

'I thought the *ThrustSSC* team was a collection of egomaniacs, though others disagree. It worked well most of the time. There was always going to be friction, because it was a really loose collection of egos. There was nobody working on the car who didn't think they were wonderful. They wouldn't have done it if they didn't feel that. Toys did come out of their prams. Richard got really upset about it when that happened and thought the team was falling apart. In fact it was forging itself. Arguments that clear the air often form the platform for great relationships. Nobody sat in an ivory tower.'

The rest of the time he was involved in designing the systems, the hydraulics, the electrics. He got into it in great style. What was so reassuring for Ron, Glynne and I was that he also shared our innate concerns about safety. While he was working for Lotus Engineering the racing driver Martin Donnelly had had a very serious accident at Jerez in 1990 in the Formula One car run by Team Lotus. Jerry is very safety conscious, and this merely sharpened his edge. Like all of us, he was terrified of the idea of such a thing happening with *ThrustSSC*. That drove him to even greater lengths to ensure that his fears were not substantiated but, even so, whenever the car ran initially at Farnborough, Jerry would almost never be around. He would be either shopping, or changing a tyre on his car – almost anything rather than watch *ThrustSSC* hurtling down the runway!

The good thing about continuing to work from home was that I could turn out of bed at five o'clock, keep on flogging through to early morning, sleep a few hours and then get going again without interruptions. If I'd been working down at Farnborough I would have had to drive to work, there were always numerous distractions, and then there would be an army of people wanting decisions. And we would probably fail with the most important element of all – the money.

A lot of companies talk about teamwork, but often what they are talking about is not teamwork at all. As soon as you hear anyone say, 'I've got a brilliant team of people working for me,' you know bloody well it isn't teamwork, it's a pyramid, a bureaucracy, with the guy on top making all the decisions.

The key to the *ThrustSSC* project was the way we ran the management. When I taught management for the American Management Association, they would draw a graph showing the levels of management in a normal company, and measure activity against time. They'd have the president at the top and the supervisor at the bottom. The further up the organization you went, the more time was spent actually managing and the less time spent doing something functional. When you got to the top the president spent only 10 per cent of his time doing a real job, which had become a sort of retained hobby. The rest was spent on expensive and unnecessary managing. That's how a bureaucracy works.

That fits in with your typical triangular shape depicting a tall pyramid, where

Late nights were routine during the build programme. As Chris Cowell works on the engine cowlings, Jayne Millington and Jerry Bliss continue to probe the mysteries of ThrustSSC's electronic systems.

the guy at the top spends a tremendous amount of his time fiddling around, making decisions and controlling this tall pyramid. Basically it's desperately inefficient, because everyone on the various levels down the pyramid is waiting for decisions: 'I can't do that because I haven't had a decision yet.' There's an awful lot of politicking because nobody can get to the guy at the top, so decisions aren't made and people lower down find themselves with time on their hands. Often it's a system set up and controlled by one man to carry out his will. Any kind of information that goes up or down in this tall-pyramid organization is incredibly expensive, because it has to travel through all these levels, from the bottom to God at the top and down again.

The other thing with the tall-pyramid system is that the guy at the top never gets anything but good news. The news coming from the front line is filtered to such an extent that when it gets to him it's always good.

But with the flat pyramid we practised in *ThrustSSC* everybody learned that you had to trust each other, and you had to communicate like hell. And it's not only communicating good news, it's communicating bad news. If this system is working, the boss gets nothing but bad news, because everybody trusts each other and tells each other the truth, and that way he knows exactly what is going on. Everyone knows the real truth at all times, and you can all take the necessary steps to avoid further trouble. The system is much more flexible.

Now, if you imagine squashing that tall pyramid down so it's flat, with one guy in the middle and others fanning out on either side of him, you have the flat pyramid operation, and you deliberately set the thing up so that team members are properly empowered and make their own decisions. They only come to you in real extremity, when things are going seriously wrong, otherwise they just get on with it quickly and efficiently. The fascinating thing is that the whole organization moves ahead quickly because they are all making their own decisions, and they soon realize they've got to communicate with each other because they can't make these decisions in isolation. We saw this in the early stages when Glynne would suddenly say, 'Richard, Jerry is driving me up the wall. He's trying to put all his systems boxes where I've already put parts of the chassis frame.' So Jerry and Glynne had to communicate closely. As did everyone else.

The key to the success of the whole system was the decision not to have a chief engineer. The chief engineer's role could be defined as that of managing the specialist engineers and taking an overview of their work. But why shouldn't the specialist engineers manage themselves? That way you avoided the danger that the chief engineer might be tempted to put his stamp on the project, though he might be less experienced in some of the specialist disciplines.

I really tried very hard to get everybody to work as a team, and that often gave rise to problems. There were current or ex-RAF guys, like engine specialist John Rowles and his successor Al Harkness, or the Remfry brothers, Leigh and Paul. They were used to working in a tall pyramid, where somebody outlined their exact responsibilities and told them precisely what to do. They were very happy in that kind of environment. But put them into a flat pyramid and at first they were lost. For them, it was like working in a jelly. They had to make their own ground rules and their own discipline, and it was very difficult for them at first, but they adapted, and in the end it worked damned well.

The problem initially was that whenever I turned up at Q Shed the thing went bang! Back up into a tall pyramid, like a jack-in-the-box. So force of circumstance made it sensible for me to stay home as much as I could, to keep the money coming in. I would go to Farnborough once or twice a week, so the guys were forced to get used to flat-pyramid working. It wasn't as if I could have helped much with the design side of things anyway; it was way beyond me by that stage and I had so little time to learn the technology.

It takes people eight or nine months to get used to working in this way, because everybody has his own ingrained working habits. The secret of it is to be very confident in terms of your ability, and the important thing is to communicate like mad. If you are going to do something, tell everybody you're going to do it, so if there are any objections they're raised before it becomes too late.

Our flat-pyramid structure was crucial to the way we ran the project, but the social side of the organization remained very fragmented. Everybody was going flat out, but the whole team hadn't bonded at that point. We had this monster taking shape, but there was no success yet, and success is the crucial bonding agent. We just didn't know each other particularly well.

That may sound funny, since there we were, all working on this great big monster of a car. But the build was a nightmare, a seven-day-a-week battle against the clock. There was very little time for socializing.

What we didn't fully appreciate as we neared the end of the build stage, and the first trial runs, was that the team's failure to bond properly was going to lead to a lot of difficulties on our first trip to Jordan, difficulties exacerbated by technical problems and poor weather. We still had a lot of growing up to do as a team, and most of it would be stressful. But I'm convinced that if we hadn't run the *ThrustSSC* project as a flat pyramid we would still be building the car, and we would be £10 million down the road with nothing to show for it.

17 OPERATIONAL AT LAST!

Andy had begun working at DERA Farnborough on *Joust*, an air-combat simulator programme. Besides trialling real concepts, such as the front-line RAF Tornado against the export version of the MiG 29, which the Russians had just put on the market, he was working not just on the development of the next generation of fighter aircraft, but, at times, on the generation beyond that. The work was a satisfying blend of simulator design work and trial-flying of the concepts, each part requiring a very high standard of ability. This was all a great way of ensuring that he stayed razor sharp, since it was basically a complete electronic model of an aircraft and its weapons system and capabilities. It flew precisely like its full-size counterpart, with all of the systems linked together to simulate a formation, if required. There was one very important extra factor that was perfect for us: though the simulator was computer-driven, there was a manual requirement. A man had to control the overall system, and he would be as fallible as if he were in a real combat situation.

'It's called Man in the Loop,' Andy explained one day. 'This is arguably the best combat simulator in Europe, perhaps the best in the world for this kind of work. You start off with a new concept, a new aircraft, or a new missile, and rather than just programming something into the system and seeing how it will work, we can actually fly it with people such as myself, with a real air crew and with the scientists who have had quite extensive experience working with the air crew. So we can develop the next generation of tactics for the next generation of weapons. The pilot will use the strengths and weaknesses of his aeroplane and equipment as effectively as possible.'

Farnborough's Systems Integration facility also produced a *ThrustSSC* simulator. Andy began driving this highly sophisticated piece of equipment towards the latter part of 1995, but he was always careful not to become over-familiar with it. 'The problem with over-training on a simulator is that you end up training yourself for the simulator rather than training yourself for the real thing,' he explained. The simulator enabled us to finalize the design of *SSC*'s cockpit and instrument layout. Andy was not just adapting to the car, the car was adapting to him.

OTHER VOICES

ANDY GREEN

'I spent a long time working with Jeremy on the instrument panel, working out what the critical failures would be and what was trivia. That determined what warning lights and instruments I needed. I worked it out on a computer spread, printed it all out on a sheet of paper and cut them out and shuffled them round. I'm not a great believer in computer-aided design, but it worked well in this case, as we could take the disk and a slab of aluminium and get the whole thing cut out in one go. It worked superbly.

'Craig's cockpit in *Spirit of America* was so cramped I couldn't fit in when subsequently he offered me the chance when I visited his camp on the desert. Even he had to lever himself in. *ThrustSSC*'s cockpit felt quite a tight fit, but it was designed to be comfortable. The biggest single limitation was the width, and I actually strapped myself in cross-handed. But, in any case, I drove it with my elbows tucked into my sides. I'm sure Richard could have squeezed in, but he never gave any indication of wanting to.

'I was absolutely overawed by the speed when I drove *ThrustSSC* for the first time on the simulator. I couldn't believe how quickly it accelerated, even without using the afterburner. The great benefit of this was that, having done it five or six times, I started to see that I had got to watch this, this and this while it was accelerating, and I put the afterburner in here, so look at this, look at that. Very quickly I started to see the pace at which things happened, and the pace at which I needed to respond.

'That first time I was way, way behind it. It's just the same with flying an aircraft simulator the first time you get in. Despite the fact that you've been trained on all the systems, you get in and you're way behind because it's all happening so quickly. Once you've practised it a few times you rapidly begin to catch up.

'The tremendous benefit of having a simulator available for training was that there was so much to assimilate and it helped you to do that. We could also use it for research. Ron Ayers was running all the data sheets on the performance of the car, and we could actually cross-check those with the simulator because it was using all the same data but a completely different set of calculations. Encouragingly enough, we were coming out with exactly the same set of figures.'

Meanwhile doubts were accumulating about the McLaren *Maverick*. When we had invited the media to see a static test of one of our Rolls-Royce Spey engines at the Proof and Experimental Establishment at Shoeburyness in the middle of 1994, I announced that we were looking for around £5 million for the whole *ThrustSSC* project. I knew at the time that Ron Dennis, McLaren's managing director, was seeking £25 million, and I've often wondered precisely what he thought when he read the papers. I'm told that £5 million was just about enough to buy you the rear wings on a midfield Formula One team's cars. Some said that our low costs dealt the *Maverick* project a mortal blow.

Others suggested that the death of Ayrton Senna at Imola on 1 May 1994 had robbed the project of some of its finance. According to rumours, although Senna had left McLaren at the end of 1993 to drive for Williams in Formula One, he had helped to finance Ron Dennis's research programme for *Maverick* and was considering driving the car. Dennis had yet to nominate a driver, but he had said at the initial launch that the driver would be British, because it was an all-British project. He also said that his leaning was more towards a pilot, with experience of military aircraft, rather than a racing driver. But there was plenty of speculation that the *Maverick* project would have fascinated Senna, and this was fuelled by Dennis's insistence that 'Ayrton will one day drive again for McLaren'. Was Ron just putting a brave face on losing Senna to Williams, his greatest rival, or did he know something he wasn't going to let on about?

Ron Dennis and I came face-to-face for the first time at the 1995 Goodwood Festival of Speed. We had a sales stand there with Jeff Luff's full-scale mock-up, and we had an astonishingly successful weekend, selling about £9,000's worth of merchandise. There was a dinner on the Saturday evening, attended by 400 very successful people, and Lord March very generously said that we could take the money raised by a prize draw. We got the team together, with all the G Force guys too. 'We've really got to do this properly,' I said. 'We've got to make the point to these people that we need serious money.'

So everybody had a plastic bucket, and off they went round the tables, chatting up the diners. People were writing their names on £10 and £20 notes, and putting in £100 or £150 a throw. When Gareth, one of our designers, asked Ron Dennis to put money in, Ron looked up at me and said, 'Richard, I will give you a thousand pounds now, at two to one, that you don't get this car running on a desert by next summer. If you fail, you've got to give me two thousand pounds back.'

I said, 'Right, Ron, you're on.' And we shook hands on it.

I wrote him a letter the following day just to thank him and to remind him of the terms of the agreement, and that was that.

Ron wrote to me in September 1996 to say, 'Richard, yesterday it was the official end of summertime and I hear you are about to go to Al Jafr. But you haven't run the car and therefore you owe me two thousand pounds.' I'm sure he'd actually taken advice on the precise definition of summer.

I sat down and straight away wrote him out a cheque for £2,000, though it was seriously painful given our precarious financial state at that time. I sent Ron the cheque – and he never cashed it. I thought that was brilliant. It was really nice of him, because he must have known how tough things were for us. He's a wealthy man, but £2,000 is £2,000. To us then it was money from the overdraft.

I thought a lot of him for that gesture.

In July 1995 the big day came when *ThrustSSC* was taken to Boscombe Down for its first static engine tests. Here Andy would climb aboard the tethered car and fire up the Speys for the first time.

We were all very edgy as the great moment drew near, but it turned out to be something of an anticlimax. The engines weren't breathing properly and kept surging. Eventually we reasoned that, because the car and engines were static, the Speys weren't getting the ram effect they needed. The solution was quite simple: both Rolls-Royce at Bristol and DERA at Pyestock advised us to make up a special bellmouth that fitted into the jet intake to promote improved flow under test conditions. Mike Horne got cracking with it, and we were ready to try again a couple of weeks later. We made our way back to Boscombe Down, only to be told when we arrived that an RAF Hawk needed to use the facility we had booked. The problem had arisen after we'd left Farnborough, so they hadn't been able to tell us in time to delay our journey. Since we were begging these resources, we had to drop down the queue. Then, while the Hawk was being tested, a Hunter also needed treatment. So it wasn't until three o'clock in the afternoon that we could move in. By then it was pissing with rain. As Ron Ayers said, it didn't seem quite the day it had started out as.

By about six thirty we'd got *ThrustSSC* in position. Mike's bellmouth was fitted to each intake in turn, so that Al Harkness and Chris Cowell could tune and balance each engine to produce maximum power in harmony with its twin. There was no more surging. The sight of the car sitting there in the pan, with each of its engines blasting out 21,000 pounds of thrust in reheat, was just awesome.

As we showed the finished *ThrustSSC* to the public for the first time at the

An early static test at Shoeburyness demonstrated the sheer power of ThrustSSC's Spey engines. The noise was deafening, and the ground shook.

Goodwood Festival of Speed on 22–23 June, Craig Breedlove was making plans to shake down *Spirit of America* on the five-mile Space Shuttle runway at Edwards Air Force Base in the Mojave Desert. There had been some last-minute hitches, but he wasn't far off running. Somehow we had all but caught up in the great supersonic race. There was a bit of a panic in the *ThrustSSC* camp around the middle of the year, when somebody reported seeing the completed Maverick, but it turned out just to be the full-scale mock-up which the press had been shown three years earlier. People I know said that from their conversations with Ron Dennis during the ensuing months it did indeed seem as though the project was firmly on hold. 'We will wait and see what happens to *Thrust* before we decide what we are going to do,' he said publicly, though his private comments suggested that he foresaw disaster for us.

In many ways I felt the same way about *Maverick* as I did in the *Thrust2* days about an American drag-race veteran, Sammy Miller. He drove very quick rocket dragsters and was always talking of a land-speed record attempt. I lived in dread that he might suddenly appear with a car and put the record out of our reach. He never did. Likewise, I worried that McLaren had been working in secret on *Maverick*, and would use their direct access to substantial funding to spring the big surprise and suddenly unveil the finished product long before we were ready.

With the successful static tests completed, our first run was scheduled to take place on runway 25, right outside our Q-Shed headquarters, on Bank Holiday Monday, 28 August. Scores of Mach 1 Club members and numerous dignitaries were in attendance, and the sense of anticipation was tangible, for this would be a day of reckoning, the day when so many of the long-posed questions would be answered. Did the rear-wheel steering work? Would the car run straight? Would one engine exert priority over the other?

Inevitably there were delays, and it was getting towards four thirty in the afternoon when the car was finally lined up on the runway, ready to roll. Momentarily it fired up, but then Al Harkness quickly shut it down. The minutes crept by one by one, until there were none left on Farnborough's six o'clock curfew. We had a leak on one of the engine's fuel couplings, and the big day ended in anticlimax, without *ThrustSSC* turning a wheel under its own power.

A month later we were ready to try again.

A week of high-pressure testing began with a small degree of embarrassment. Andy started with a low-speed run at a gentle 40 m.p.h. We were using Dunlop Aviation wheels and rubber tyres for the runway, and, as Andy braked heavily on completing the run, the front tyres burst. Of course, that was what made the news that evening: 'Supersonic car stymied by punctures at forty m.p.h.'

ThrustSSC was being run with very stiff suspension settings, in which the springing medium at that speed was effectively the sidewalls of the tyres. Glynne had asked Andy to use the brakes hard, because the carbon discs needed to be really worked in order to reach optimum operating temperature. But the brakes were more effective than we had anticipated, and when the brakes locked the

ANDY GREEN

Andy ponders a pair of punctured front tyres, after the carbon disc brakes proved far more efficient than we had expected.

'The brakes were two to three times more effective than we thought, because of the application. There were a whole bunch of synergies: they all worked so well together that they gave me very quick brake response, much quicker than either I or Glynne had been expecting. Unfortunately, because of this we burst the tyres on the first run. We changed the tyres, went back and did it the second time, and found out exactly where the limit on tyre braking was. After that, we changed the tyres a second time once we'd finished the braking test, and at the end of the Farnborough test programme they still looked brand new. No wear on them at all.

'With carbon disc brakes, when they were totally cold and I was running up the engines at the end of the runway, they needed a huge amount of pressure because the friction was very low. As they heated up, the friction went up. It was predicting the rate which gave us problems. After a day doing nothing but brake tests, I adapted to applying brake pressure based on the deceleration rate of the car (typically around point three five g) and then holding the brake pressure this required (again typically around six hundred and fifty psi). The car would stop with plenty of room to spare and no tyre wear. The runway runs were always a little nerve-racking, though. When I drove out onto the end of the runway I could see the far end very clearly – it looked a lot closer than seven thousand feet, and I was going to have to reach two hundred m.p.h. between here and there.

'When I told Richard that slowing from one hundred and sixty m.p.h. with only three thousand feet of runway left on one of the runs was "a little sporty", he laughed and told me of his regular two-hundred-and-forty-m.p.h. runs in *Thrust2*, stopping a few feet from the end each time. I once worked out the figures – because of its ten ton weight, *ThrustSSC* was harder to stop from one hundred and sixty m.p.h. than *Thrust2* would have been from the three hundred m.p.h. he briefly touched during the Greenham Common crash! Needless to say, I never mentioned that to Richard – he would only have worried.'

In September 1996 we were finally able to run ThrustSSC under its own power at Farnborough.

front wheels, the tyres shredded and burst. On later higher-speed runs we used the parachute and then the wheel brakes, placing a lighter load on the tyres themselves, and the problem did not recur.

Glynne wasn't worried. 'We've learned that the brakes are more powerful than we thought,' he said. 'That's a good fault. We can do something about that. It's when they're not powerful enough that you have to worry. We just restricted the amount of hydraulic pressure that we used on the braking, and carried on without any problem. Typical development-engineering learning.'

Ron also made another telling point about the brakes' efficiency: 'A two-hundred-mile-an-hour stop on a runway is counted in the Air Force as a severe emergency procedure. We're doing it daily as a planned procedure.'

These initial runs were to acclimatize Andy to the controls and to establish that all of the car's complicated systems worked properly. But by the end of the week he had completed a further seven runs, at speeds of up to 160 m.p.h., progressing in carefully planned stages, while Ron, Glynne and Jerry monitored the car's performance carefully, like trainers with a million-dollar racehorse. Run number seven had been achieved with the 'max mil' power rating, an abbreviation of the RAF term 'maximum military', meaning the maximum without reheat.

Andy used the afterburner only on the last two development runs, eleven and twelve. On the latter he took *ThrustSSC* from 160 m.p.h. to 190 m.p.h. in less than a second, momentarily touching 200 m.p.h. Now for the first time he could appreciate the power of the car he would drive towards the sound barrier.

His enthusiasm was also in reheat, now that the long wait to try the car was finally over. 'It's a marvellous machine.' He kept laughing. 'Fantastic.'

It was great to see him so animated, and the team had worked well together, preparing the car so that we got the main part of the Farnborough test programme done in just two days. The only things that held us up were aircraft movements and weather. Once operational, the car didn't hold us up at all. With Jayne in the tower controlling all of our airfield operations, both we and Air Traffic were

As with Thrust2, we slowed ThrustSSC initially via a parachute. From 200 m.p.h. downwards Andy used the wheel brakes.

surprised by the efficiency of the team. Curiously enough, the majority of people in Air Traffic were very sceptical about our chances of success, despite the team's excellent performance during the runway tests.

The noise level of that one-second reheat run was simply fantastic. As it echoed off the famous Farnborough black sheds, I just thought, Wow! That's something!

This was fabulous news for the project. We now knew that we had a car that worked, with rear-wheel steering that worked, and a driver who could rise to the challenge. For a challenge it had been, especially on that final run.

The reheat run was also intended as a final test of the rear body of the car, with its partial titanium panelling, to ensure that it could withstand the heat of the exhaust gases and the acoustic buffeting that around 42,000 pounds of thrust produced. Glynne explained the situation to Mach 1 Club members. 'With the engines running flat out you get around a hundred and seventy-five to a hundred and eighty-five decibels of noise, and the effect on that panelling is quite profound. If you watch a video that we have you can see test panels of quite thick titanium literally flapping like tissue paper. It's staggering the effect that the power and noise can have. That's why titanium is the only metal we believe can cope. The panels were also perfectly OK during full-power tie-down engine tests. So far here it's all hanging together nicely.'

For Glynne, perhaps more than any of us, the Farnborough tests were a source of relief, for after all the months of doubt they proved that his controversial and innovative system of rear-wheel steering worked extremely well with rubber tyres on tarmac. During the final run Andy engaged maximum power at 80 m.p.h. before going to full reheat. The nozzle on the left-hand engine opened a fraction before that of its right-hand partner. Both stabilized almost immediately, but he had to make a rapid steering input to cope with the momentary yaw.

OTHER VOICES

ANDY GREEN

'The steering proved no problem at all, after the first couple of times of getting used to it. That was another thing that Glynne and I were both delighted about, and I was enormously impressed by how smoothly the whole of his system actually worked.

'I could feel that the front end was staying put while the back end tended to swing out behind it. I could feel that, but there wasn't much perception of the rotation being about the front wheels because I was close enough to them so that the rotation point felt somewhere between me and them. It was difficult to say just where, but I could most definitely feel the back end moving. But after the first couple of times of doing it, and obviously you've got to take the mass and momentum into account as well, it was no problem at all to put in the right rate of steering input to get the response I needed.

'It was about run eight when we started getting it up towards max mil, and the performance became absolutely scintillating at ninety-five per cent max mil power. Once it got to accelerating at max mil it was accelerating at one g, putting on twenty m.p.h. per second. For a ten-ton vehicle that really was amazing, and you really could feel the power. The whole vehicle just leapt forward.

'When we are at military power, it's comparable, I suppose, with a lightweight Phantom in full afterburner. But, of course, as soon as you stick the afterburners in, it enters a world of its own.

'The final run was great. At one hundred and ninety I started throttling

This was Andy's office at speeds of up to 771 m.p.h. He played a key role in designing the layout of the instruments and controls.

back, because it takes a finite length of time to pull the power back, and the car hit its two hundred in that time. The approximate timing is that zero to one hundred took something in the order of six and half, seven seconds, and the hundred to two hundred took about three to three and a half. The rate of acceleration was still increasing as the afterburner was lighting. We never actually got full power on the car; we were about a second away from fully stabilized afterburner. I looked at the g meter later and it was actually just about to peak in power as I throttled back.

'We all knew on paper that the car had this tremendous potential, but to actually go out and drive it, or to watch a ten-ton vehicle put on a hundred m.p.h. in just over three seconds, you think, Yeah, that really has land-speed-record potential.'

It was vital to know how the car would react to a yawing force. And thanks to that split second when one nozzle opened before the other, we now knew just how the car behaved. Andy coped with it very simply, by giving just a little twitch on the wheel to cope with the yaw.

The steering had been designed to have no feedback. It wasn't the same as a car or an aeroplane. David Crolla had vetoed any castor return – which is what makes a road car's steering self-centre as you come out of a corner – as confusing to the driver. It meant that the car went where the steering wheel was pointed, and Andy had to unwind manually whatever lock he applied. Despite all that, he got to grips with it remarkably quickly. He approached the whole thing in a very steady Andy sort of way, which was taking small steps and perfecting each. He didn't seem to get the fatigue that I used to experience. When I was at the wheel there was always an emotional element. I had virtually no disciplined background; Andy had 1,000 hours of flying fighters. From his point of view it was all about discipline. It was not about tally ho; none of that at all. It was about not making the next move until you know that the previous one is absolutely right. Andy showed similar restraint on the road – he once told me that he was very controlled then to make sure that he never got stopped for speeding. I envied him that.

We now faced a big push to modify the car in the light of the test runs, and to complete the other necessary work prior to running out on a desert surface at really serious speeds. The team was working seven days a week, and the hangar was always full of busy people.

Every action in Q Shed generated more paperwork at Hampton. Our house filled up with invoices, delivery notes, statements and accounts – plus, of course, Mach 1 Club mail, which more often than not ran to over a hundred letters each delivery. Sally presided over all this, unflappable as ever, somehow keeping on top of the administration while managing to produce meals for our family of three children. Our own communication had become reduced to a series of panicky conversations, often at three o'clock in the morning: 'Darling, did you remember to invoice Castrol?' 'Omigod, no!' That sort of thing.

Breedlove didn't go to Edwards after all, which gave us some further leeway, but he arrived at Bonneville in August and he had reached a reported 360 m.p.h. before retiring with a number of technical and personal problems. A fanatical animal lover, he was devastated when his beloved dog was run over and killed, and he couldn't get out of the place fast enough. We soon learned that he was, after all, going west, to Black Rock. It was what I'd suspected he would end up doing all along. As for us, we were headed into the unknown, to the Al Jafr desert in Jordan.

Going to Jordan was a way of getting round the problem of the season being so short in America; the conditions were suitable for running only during September and October each year. If you missed that slot for whatever reason you were in serious trouble, as we'd discovered after the 1982 accident at Greenham Common had delayed our departure for Bonneville. We guessed that Craig wouldn't travel abroad, so if we could run more than once a year, we could develop our car and our team faster than he did and close the gap further.

Back in the *Thrust2* days we simply didn't have the funding to investigate sites around the globe. Now my brother Andrew had spent a year looking at deserts: twenty-three in total. He'd gone to places such as Verneuk Pan in South Africa, where Malcolm Campbell had run *Bluebird* back in 1929; he'd also been to Algeria, Tunis, Morocco and two sites in North America. We wanted a course at least ten miles long, with a hard, flat alkali surface and plenty of run-off area at either end. There had been some promising sites in Pakistan, but they were in an unstable tribal area. It boiled down to only two suitable sites: Black Rock, where we intended to make the major runs; and the Al Jafr Desert in the Hashemite Kingdom of Jordan.

We'd first heard about Al Jafr from a chap called Ken Waughman, who'd been there doing a topographical survey with the Royal Engineers just after the war. He had never forgotten driving across the Al Jafr mud flats. 'It was like being in an aircraft taking off,' Ken told us. 'You felt you were literally floating. You'd just set the hand throttle, put your feet up and away you'd go. The surface was as smooth and flat as a billiard table.'

Once he'd gone out to Al Jafr to see for himself, Andrew liked what he saw. It hadn't rained there for five years. We took that as a good omen.

Al Jafr offered serious advantages. We could operate out of the King Feisal Air Base, so we had good accommodation, a hangar in which to work on the car and a flat desert that was likely to remain dry until well after Christmas. The surface was similar to Black Rock, so we wouldn't have to drag it as we'd done at Bonneville, but like the desert in Nevada it would need to be cleaned of any of the stones and debris colloquially known as 'fod', which would be a painstaking job. There were also some depressions caused by Bedouin groups crossing our intended multi-lane track system; Andrew led an advance party to have these filled in and packed down.

The name of the game was that we had to push on hard with what remained of our money. We wanted to get *ThrustSSC* up to 600 m.p.h., then we could come back and prepare for an attempt to go supersonic at Black Rock. But first of all we had to get out to Al Jafr. We knew from the *Thrust2* days that, if you decided to go by ship, you could lose all your equipment for up to a month on the high seas. There was then the prospect of things getting lost, and of at least a week to collect everything on site. In the race with Breedlove this would all take up time that we hadn't got. So we had to go by air.

The key was thus not just to find an interim site, but how to move all our equipment out to Jordan and then to America with minimal delay. The total package involved *ThrustSSC* and its special trailer and tractor, the pit station control centre which was essential to the running of such a technologically advanced car, and the two Supacat towing and refuelling vehicles. Then there was the Jaguar XJ-R Firechase rapid-intervention vehicle, the Merlo 4x4 all-terrain forklift, and the Land Rover Discoveries for general support. All this plus the two HGV tractor units and food for thirty days, the spare Spey 205 engines, and the huge quantities of tools and spares totalled 93 tons. All this would have to be flown, and there was only one aircraft capable of flying it – the Russian Antonov 124. It was the world's largest commercial freighter.

The only company I'd ever heard of that operated these giant freighters was HeavyLift, so I called them and spoke to Graham Pearce, the commercial director and a real entrepreneur, who had built up the company from virtually nothing. It's great to deal with such people, because they have courage and they understand what you're going through. I was hoping he might give us a 50 per cent discount. I'd no idea how on earth we would finance any of it. I didn't even know what the costs were. But somehow we just had to have the use of an Antonov.

Graham asked me to come and see him, and at the end of our discussion he said, 'Here's the offer: we will provide the aeroplane and the crew, you provide the landing fees, the navigation fees and the fuel. The rest of it is on us.' It was a stunning deal, and to make it even better Royal Jordanian Airlines came to our help by providing the 250,000 litres of fuel to get us to Jordan and back.

Before that, however, we'd had the pleasure of a visit from His Majesty King Hussein to Q Shed. It was during the week-long Farnborough Air Show in September. We'd been approached by the organizers about doing a demo run at the show, but sadly the car was in pieces during the final preparations for going out to Al Jafr. The show had brought chaos to our production schedules. All the roads in and out of the place were gridlocked from the early morning on, and our

Plane swallows car. HeavyLift's Antonov 126 consumed not just ThrustSSC with its truck and trailer, but all of our back-up equipment, too.

suppliers were unable to get through. Once on site at Q Shed it became impossible to leave until late in the evening.

During the show I was invited to the Royal Jordanian Chalet, where I spent twenty minutes talking to the King. His Majesty is a jet pilot with his own collection of fighters, and he was very interested in what we were doing. Before he had to go, I invited him to visit us at Q Shed.

Back in the shed, the noise level was intolerable. The flying displays had just started, and work was only possible wearing ear defenders. In a lull between flights, the telephone rang. At the other end was an agitated air-show director, telling us the King was on his way over. We dashed outside to see a twenty-four-car convoy arriving. His Majesty spent half an hour with us, and met the entire team, though conversation was almost impossible because of the noise outside. As he left, he turned to me and said, 'Thank you, Richard. I'll see you in Jordan.'

Just before we left we had a bolt of good fortune when Tivoli, the software and control-systems manufacturer, came in with a cash boost. I'd been tipped off by a marketing specialist that a deal might be in the offing, and that it could be a big one. But the more I was told, 'Trust me, Richard,' the more I worried. Those are the last words anyone wants to hear in these situations, because they are usually a prelude to disaster. This time, however, the deal really was going ahead. Frank Moss and his partners, Scott Harman and Bill Watson, put in a shade over £200,000, and by God it was welcome. They understood what we were trying to do, too, which made a terrific difference. Right before we went to Jordan, Frank flew his team into Farnborough by helicopter and brought us the rest of the money. It was the shot in the arm we so desperately needed.

We were heading off to Jordan determined to steal a march on Craig, and speculating that we might even break our own world land-speed record.

The spirit was very high. Little did we know what lay in store.

18 THE CULTURE CLUB AND THE SILVER SPOONS

Camel trains were a frequent hazard on Jordan's Al Jafr desert.

We arrived at Al Jafr's Air Base on 26 October 1996, to learn that Craig had just survived a terrifying accident. During one high-speed run on the Black Rock Desert, *Spirit of America* had turned onto its left side and then described a 180-degree arc before coming to rest. By some miracle nobody was injured, though apparently he ran over the spot where a camper had been parked. By sheer chance its owner had moved on just before the run commenced.

I sent Craig a message of commiseration. An accident was the last thing that any of us wanted. Anything that cast a question over the safety aspect of these attempts could be the kiss of death for potential sponsors.

Craig had estimated his speed at 675 m.p.h. at the time of his accident, so his car was clearly capable of such speeds. The question was whether *Spirit of America* had the aerodynamic stability to do the job. Craig claimed that a gust of side wind had lifted one of his car's rear wheels, tipping it onto its side, but we thought he'd simply accelerated too soon and reached the limits of his car's stability. As far as I was concerned it was worrying to see a fellow competitor in trouble, but it also endorsed my firm belief that our twin-engined concept was now the only valid one for cars seeking supersonic speed.

Safety was always our priority. The original design specification for *ThrustSSC*, written early in the life of the project, stated clearly that we intended to set a supersonic record *safely*. The project would have stopped if any of the team had lost faith in our safety precautions. The crucial question was: what would happen to the driver if something went wrong at maximum speed? Could he eject at 850 m.p.h. at ground level? The answer, quite simply, was no.

So could we protect him if there was an accident? Every precaution was taken. Andy was held in a moulded seat with a five-point safety-harness attachment, and was surrounded by an extremely strong welded steel box, complete with a two-inch-thick fire wall. He would wear fireproof clothing, and the cockpit was equipped with a Halon extinguisher, a water-spray extinguisher and a thirty-minute supply of compressed air.

But would all this make any difference in a crash at 850 m.p.h.? We had to assume it would not. So, if Andy could not eject, and we could not confidently protect him, the emphasis had to be placed firmly on primary safety, i.e., accident prevention. A detailed analysis of every possible failure mode resulted in some very extreme precautions.

On the all-important priority of keeping the wheels firmly on the ground, we relied on Jerry Bliss's active suspension. He had incorporated no fewer than five layers of fail-safe logic-circuitry to ensure that no component or system failure could result in the car becoming airborne. A sophisticated abort system would ensure that a sudden increase of aerodynamic download could be achieved if all else failed.

If either engine suffered flame-out, the resulting asymmetric thrust would be catastrophic. This danger was overcome by developing special strain-gauged thrust-bearing trunnions in conjunction with NPL. The output from the trunnions was read by the onboard computer and if there was a substantial difference between the two engines, Jerry had programmed a computer to shut them both down immediately. Wheel-bearing failure could not be contemplated, so the temperature and vibration spectrum was monitored for each bearing. In the event, the SKF angular-contact ball-bearings selected by Glynne proved to be admirable. Even at maximum speed the bearing temperature rose by only about 20 degrees centigrade. Although the structure was extremely strong and rigid, some thirty load cells and strain gauges were positioned to check the loading on key parts of the structure.

More than 120 sensors were used for safety or diagnostic purposes. Their output was datalogged on two onboard computers, which also monitored one another. The computers monitored the live data, identified any incipient problems, decided on the correct course of action and implemented that action within milliseconds. Jerry was responsible for this whole complex system. He called it the nervous system, or reflex system, of the car.

We didn't stop there. Operations manager, Martyn Davidson, ensured that the team was able to handle this very complicated vehicle, and training was provided where necessary. The Firechase crew – Mike Hearn, one of my long-standing friends who had been part of the *Thrust2* team, and Brian Palmer, the transport manager – were trained by the Gatwick Airport Fire Brigade. Jayne Millington ensured that our communications procedures were strictly observed.

Tired engineers make mistakes. On this first visit to Jordan we would soon find our 'fatigue limit', when mistakes occurred. We could not afford errors as the speeds rose. Long hours were going to be necessary, but simple rules were implemented. If the team was working late at night, there would be no runs early next morning, even if that meant losing a weather window.

Finally, we had to ensure there were no errors due to misunderstandings or carelessness. When planning a run, the engineering team would study the design team's proposed run profile. The decision to proceed had to be unanimous. When runs were imminent or in progress, any member of the team could stop them by calling 'abort' over the radio. Even when a record and a one-hour turnaround were being attempted, the data from the onboard computers was downloaded and safety-critical quantities – wheel loads, bearing temperatures, etc. – were checked before the return run was authorized.

As a result of this rigorous attitude, *ThrustSSC* would safely complete all of its sixty-six runs.

On the face of it Craig's enforced withdrawal with a damaged car offered us the chance of a breather, but I knew that we couldn't afford to relax. Instead, we now had an opportunity to pull ahead for the first time since we had entered the race.

Quite early on it became clear that the plan to take *ThrustSSC* back from the desert to the King Feisal Air Base each night was impractical. It was taking too long to load the car on and off its trailer. But within a remarkable forty-eight hours, Richard Bailey of the Huddersfield-based company Aireshelta had arranged to freight out a giant yellow inflatable hangar, which allowed us to set up a workshop on the desert. This was so successful that the arrangement continued for the remainder of the project.

Two team members were delegated to overnight guard duty, accompanied by two air base sentries whose powers of English were in inverse proportion to the hospitality they showed guests in their small tent. The welcome extended by the Jordanians to our strange car and its attendants was universal and touching. They couldn't do enough for us. His Royal Highness Prince Feisal Al Hussein went to great lengths to assist us and make us welcome. At one stage General Mamoun, the commander of the Al Jafr base, came out with twenty-five volunteers to help with the defodding of the desert, even picking up stones himself. Major Nawrez, who had been deputed to co-ordinate our attempt, was another who excelled himself; it turned out that he was a Jordanian Geordie, having lived for two years in Sunderland! But day-to-day responsibility lay with the indefatigable and completely unflappable Major Saleh. Also in this category was Martyn Davidson. We'd first met when he was range safety officer at Pendine during our rocket trials. Martyn somehow migrated to Farnborough in time to supervise the move from G Force to Q Shed, against a seemingly impossible timescale. He did such a good job that I quickly invited him to become our ops manager, and he would be the main reason why we were able to get operational so quickly both in Jordan and, later, in America. He is one of those very calm, organized people, and we soon learned that the only visible sign of stress he showed was the studied ignition of a large cigar.

Once an initial problem in the fuel system had been corrected, Andy was able to reach 230 m.p.h. on his first run on 12 November, but the rear end of *ThrustSSC* sustained an impact loading of more than twenty tons after crossing the Bedouin truck tracks that cut across our course at right angles. We later discovered that this route was the main illegal highway to Saudi Arabia. Softening the gas dampers in the suspension improved the ride sufficiently for Andy to reach 325 m.p.h. four days later.

All the pounding that *ThrustSSC* was receiving revealed shortcomings in the durability of the rear-wheel steering, and a further run on 21 November had to be aborted after Andy was unable to hold the car on course and veered across the white lines we used to mark the lanes we had prepared. The rear wheels were toeing out, causing the car to veer off course several times. As soon as it became apparent that he wasn't going to be able to bring it back, Andy aborted the run. It turned out that the friction bushes in the steering linkage had slipped. As a temporary 'fix', the bushes were reset and pinned to the drive shaft to prevent further movement. But underbody video cameras were indicating a disturbing degree of 'shimmy' on the rear wheels.

Andy was pushing on in his steady way, and if he was frustrated by the recurring problems which prevented him from driving the car, he didn't show it. Nor did he ever sit back; he put in hours and hours of fodding.

He didn't complain when we discovered a classic cock-up in the workshop, which had come about as the team tired in very hot temperatures. After completing a run, Andy had reported that the steering felt heavy. It was only on close inspection that we realized what had happened. A bar which had been welded across the rear brake calipers to stiffen them on the desert had inadvertently been welded to the steering, locking the system and preventing any wheel movement.

As this was being rectified, Mike Hearn, by now known as 'der Fodmeister', led a fodding party. Everyone took his turn clearing stones away from the course. The way to do this was to walk every inch of the course in line abreast; when you saw a stone you got down on your knees and gouged it out with a screwdriver. We cleared 170 miles of track by this painstaking method; Ron likened it to clearing the A303 between London and Exeter. When he offered the seemingly redundant observation that ninety-four tributaries led on to the desert, everyone looked up at the sun blazing amid wispy clouds in the stunningly blue sky and laughed.

It rained that night, but the desert remained dusty and the *ThrustSSC* was ready to fire its Speys just as the orange-pink sun prepared to nod good-night in its swift drop from the skyline. We should have run sooner, but there was a delay because a Bedouin refused to move his camel off the track until Ron gave him a cigarette. He had spotted some packets in Ron's car. These belonged to somebody else, and the Bedouin took a while to realize that he was dealing with a dedicated

Sunset on Al Jafr, Jordan One, 1996.

non-smoker who had no idea what he wanted.

Andy aborted the run when the steering again gave trouble and he veered across several lines. The steering-gear quadrants' drive pegs had yielded under the battering the car was receiving from the desert, allowing the wheel to flop and shimmy yet again. Glynne

ThrustSSC ready to run with air start umbilical.

consulted Ken Norris, who was out visiting us, and they decided to fit new and stronger pins. The cameras again confirmed the wheel shimmy. Glynne discussed the problem with Professor David Crolla back at Leeds University, and David agreed to the addition of steering dampers, and adding five degrees of castor to the rear-wheel suspension.

Al Jafr's surface was giving us a lot of problems. Andrew and his advance party had prepared a track, but in the period before our arrival, Bedouins crossing the desert in their trucks had recreated transverse ruts. When Andy crossed these tracks, even at relatively low speeds, the car would be off the ground for seventy feet or more. Each time it came back down, or to be more precise when the uneven ground came back up to meet it, the car was getting a terrific battering. Switching from torsion-bar front suspension to gas struts had allowed us to protect the car as best we could, but this was still a very severe handicap.

As well as these ruts there were a lot of stones on Al Jafr, and they became denser at each end. We had to be terribly careful that the *ThrustSSC*'s engines

This is what we had to contend with at Al Jafr. Where Bedouin tracks crossed Andy's course, ThrustSSC would take off, crashing back onto the desert after flying for seventy feet or more.

didn't hoover them into the intakes when Andy was starting a run, which is why the car never did dragster-type starts. Ron became gradually more concerned that we lacked sufficient run-off area at each end, should anything go wrong. There was plenty of space, but beyond our ten miles of prepared track the desert got very stony, and then rocky. If Andy had overrun the course, we risked inflicting serious damage on the car. We decided that we weren't going to be able to beat my old record within our safety parameters, and after that we concentrated purely on getting *ThrustSSC* up to high peak speeds.

All we could do was simply push on and fix any problems as they arose. It was this damn race thing again. There was no way that I was going to squander this chance when the pendulum had finally begun to swing in our direction. I wanted us to capitalize on our position as much as possible.

It was clear to me very early on that we had other serious problems besides our technical difficulties. The most obvious was that the team itself hadn't properly bonded, and the problems that had been just beneath the surface in Farnborough now came out into the open.

Initially I suspected that people felt it was all a holiday, after months of almost non-stop work in the push to complete the build programme. I knew from past experience with *Thrust2* that what lay ahead was even harder work. Then I felt that a boozing culture had built up, though others disagreed totally with me. I felt it may have been some kind of reaction to our lack of progress. Part of the problem was similar to the situation at Bonneville in 1981 with *Thrust2*. Everyone was so fired up by the project, and so convinced by it, that some really believed we would be in Jordan for around ten days or so, and would then go back home with a good result. We had a fighter pilot, all the *Thrust2* knowledge behind us, weren't we a terrific organization?

But unfortunately record-breaking isn't like that. Great expectations can be an awful thing, especially as, in this case, there was an almost complete lack of fulfilment.

We also suffered a spate of injuries. Robert Atkinson lost the end of a finger, and was very lucky not to suffer worse, when a pneumatic radio mast fell on him; Rob Hemper fell off the transporter and broke his wrist; Ninetta Hearn burned herself; Dee Campbell-Coombe fell and broke a leg at Petra, but defied all our efforts to get her sent back home. Glynne had a spell of feeling unwell, so he, too, was packed off to hospital in Ma'an. There was a standing joke that they had dedicated a special *Thrust* ward.

None of this helped, but the underlying problem was a cultural one, really, because we were a very mixed lot. There were the technicians; Sally and me, together with Mike and Ninetta Hearn, the civilian element of the team; the RAF guys; and the contractors: all trying to get on with one another in the extreme heat, when the project was often making uninspiring progress. Some found it difficult to trust one another, or thought that somebody better should be in this job or that. I'd just have to say to them, 'Look, there isn't anybody better, for Christ's sake. That's it. Fred is the man for that job, he's built that bit of the car, and he's here whether you like it or not.'

We had employed four contractors on the build at Fontwell, and later at Farnborough. Out in Jordan they made up the hard-working core of the workshop team. Contractors are like mercenaries, selling their skills to whoever will pay for them. Aircraft contractors are used to being given work and then being fired when the contract ends. The point is that if you are a contractor you're used to being abused. You are used to being given the lousy jobs, and you know that when you work for somebody it's not going to last for very long. Therefore you never bond with anybody. There's no point, because your job is only short term.

What we were trying to do was to bond these groups into a team, and the contractors objected like hell. Of the four contractors that we hired, only Nick Dove made it through to Black Rock; he made an enormous success of running the workshop and then being crew chief out on the desert. The other three did a huge amount of work and made one hell of a contribution to the project, but they never bonded with the rest of us. We started to have serious problems. I felt there was a drinking problem, and a huge macho-driven culture was building up, which was exhausting the team and undermining the project. Soon it would become a safety issue.

The contractors apparently referred to themselves as the Culture Club, and one of them called Sally and me the Silver Spoons. It was relatively good-natured. As a joke Andy called Jerry Boffin, while he in turn was referred to as Dog or Driver-bloke, and Jayne was Desert Witch. That was a good sign that the bonding was starting, but the saga of 'handbagging' delayed things from gelling fully. With *Thrust2* we'd had the Silly Boy Award: a big wooden badge given to anyone who made a glaring mistake. That had been done in a spirit of good fun. In Jordan people who screwed up or were perceived not to be pulling their weight were known by the contractors as Handbaggers. That too should have been humorous, but it all got a little bit unpleasant when one recipient took it badly and understandably refused to see any humour in having to carry a handbag around with him for a day. That further split an already divided team.

The underlying problem was that we were making poor progress with the project in an uncomfortable environment that lacked alternative entertainment. And perhaps there was the embarrassment of being associated with a project that looked as though it would have to be wound up on our return to the UK.

The main thing was that we simply didn't know each other well enough. It was just like *Thrust2* at Bonneville all over again, but with macho undertones. Whether the contractors thought that I didn't do anything, and that they were the only ones doing anything, whether they were naïve enough to think that, I just don't know. But what happened was that because we weren't delivering and meeting expectations as a team, the drinking culture seemed to me to take hold.

I was very worried about all this. I didn't want to intrude in people's private lives, and they needed to have private lives since we were all living on top of each other. What they did when they weren't working was not my concern. I believed strongly that as soon as we started making more obvious progress again, the team would finally bond. Nevertheless, I could see that it was having one hell of a debilitating effect.

Things came to a head when one of our Land Rover Discoveries was crashed in ·circumstances that I was very unhappy about. Some team members took it as just another setback, and a joke about roller-discos in the desert began circulating, but it wasn't a laughing matter. I called in two of our contractors and told them I was sending them home.

Everything settled down amazingly quickly afterwards. It was astonishing, actually, because literally overnight the whole project changed. The drinking culture collapsed, and people were out playing volleyball whenever we hit any downtime. But as if the disappointments weren't enough, BBC Radio broadcast a ridiculous and wholly inaccurate report that Andy had left the project because of the difficulties. It was precisely the sort of nonsense we didn't need.

As a backdrop to all of this I had to come to terms with the fact that I was no longer the driver. I had become neutered – I suppose I had actually neutered myself, which was even more painful. Without the thrill of driving the car, I was stuck with enormous problems, mostly financial or operational, having to race round in small circles, trying to edge the thing forward and keep it pointed in the right direction. There seemed to be no end to the problems in the hot desert, and the prospect of a lifetime paying off debt. There was seldom a clear way forward and no personal satisfaction whatsoever.

ANDY GREEN

'The trip to Jordan certainly never seemed like a holiday from the shop floor. We were looking forward to a change of scenery and our first chance to test the car on the desert, but those of us working on *ThrustSSC* were all too aware just how much work still needed to be done. Richard had probably not realized that when we flew to Jordan we knew that we still had at least ten to fourteen days' work left to do before its first run.

'The so-called drinking culture never existed. Richard was obviously very concerned about the difficulties within the team, although the rest of us were not as worried. The problems that we had to deal with, preparing the very rough and stony desert tracks and the technical problems with the car, were far more troubling than any minor differences between us. What Richard never appeared to appreciate was the strength he had built into the team by recruiting a very professional group of people. We didn't need to get on well together or even to like each other. We were there to do a job and as professionals we were going to do it regardless of our personal relationships.

'The drinking that Richard was worried about was nothing more than a group

Two generations of Thrust drivers.

of the team spending the evenings in one of the houses, having a few beers and chatting - there was nothing else to do and nowhere else to go out in the desert. The injuries were also troubling him, although there was no single cause for them. Two of the serious ones came from people tripping over at Petra whilst sight-seeing on a rare day off. Perhaps we were just tired after weeks of very long hours. The team wasn't coming apart at the seams, it was just getting on with the job in its own way, and had yet to bond fully.'

All along the idea had been to go out to Jordan and damn well stay out there, come hell or high water, until we got the right result. We would cater for ourselves, and we took a lot of food with us because our aim was simply to sit it out and make it work. But if what we experienced was not quite hell, the high water wasn't long in coming. On the night of 25 November it began to rain, and as water came cascading down Ron's tributaries, much of our course disappeared under it. Two days later the situation was clearly hopeless, and after a hasty evacuation we were forced to head ignominiously for home.

As we boarded the Antonov, Rosco McGlashan was preparing to grab another chance to attack our record with his *Aussie Invader II*. Rosco had said that his third attempt would have to be the last. As you would expect, his sponsors were getting restless. But he isn't the kind to stop pushing while there's still hope. He was grabbing the chance of getting ahead of us, while planning to push on in 1997 with a heavily revised and quickly built version of *Aussie Invader II – Invader III*. It was shorter and sleeker, and powered by a SNECMA 9K-50 afterburning turbojet, capable of producing 19,000 pounds of thrust. With more power than *Thrust2*, he had a serious chance of beating our 633-m.p.h. record. Having failed ourselves at Al Jafr, we wanted to see him succeed, setting a new target for us to aim at, of 650 m.p.h. or so.

We flew back from Jordan a very quiet team. This was Bonneville 1981 all over again, but in many ways it was far worse. This time there was no 'British car and driver' record with which to offset disappointment. If Hugh Wickes had been around it wouldn't have been a case of, 'Richard, you promised us gold and you brought back bronze.' It would have been, 'Richard, you promised us gold and you failed to even qualify.'

We were in very serious trouble.

All the time people were comparing *ThrustSSC* with *Thrust2*. The *ThrustSSC* team was terribly proud of what had been achieved, and always wanted to show that it was streets ahead of anything *Thrust2* had done. That had to be healthy. But the problem was that we'd only reached 340 m.p.h., while at the equivalent stage *Thrust2* had peaked at around 500 m.p.h. And this was just the external manifestation of our problems. We were really in a hell of a mess. We'd spent all of our money. We still had considerable creditors, though the Tivoli money had allowed us to get the balance sheet looking almost right before we went to Jordan.

Now we entered an extraordinary phase. Everybody was very disappointed. We hadn't even come back with 500 m.p.h., let alone the 600 m.p.h. we were looking

Our best speed on our first visit to Jordan was a disappointing 340 m.p.h.

for, and the problems with the steering did nothing to allay the suspicions of the rear-wheel-steer sceptics that we might have a basic design fault. It must have been a terrible time for Glynne in particular. His work was an obvious target.

We had to survive. The logical thing to do, what any rational businessman would have done, was to say, 'Right, let's cut the team right back to just those who are absolutely essential, and let's exist while we try to turn the thing round.'

I thought this was absolutely the wrong thing to do, because gradually we were starting to come right as a team, and if we had bust the thing apart then, sooner or later we would simply have to go through the whole bonding process all over again. Because we were in a race, we simply couldn't afford to let that happen. We had to stick together as a team, and somehow keep the thing going. The sponsors didn't want to know us, we weren't good news, it was all very downbeat.

What helped us through this black period was the Mach 1 Club.

Weekend after weekend we held open days down at Farnborough, where we had moved to P8 Shed. And every weekend the Mach 1 Club members came down in their droves to see us. We had around 4,000 members at this time, so there were all these people coming through the doors and buying truckloads of merchandise. It was wonderful.

We auctioned off life-expired bits of the car, and they just kept buying. At that stage it was the Mach 1 Club and its purchases that kept us afloat. By selling them merchandise we gave them something they wanted, and in return they gave us the income we so desperately needed. I'm terribly proud that throughout the entire *ThrustSSC* programme we never missed paying the payroll once. I'm also proud that the Mach 1 Club contributed 20 per cent of our overall budget, and in effect became the project's major sponsor.

I went to see Graham Pearce at HeavyLift again, and explained that we needed to go back to Jordan. 'That's OK, I understand,' he said. Then, as an aside, he asked, 'What do you think it cost us the first time, Richard?'

I had no idea, so he told me: 'One hundred and seventy-one thousand pounds.' Yet here he was, prepared to do it all over again. HeavyLift is a joint venture with the Russians, and they were getting a bit shirty about a second trip, so Graham explained that he would take us to Jordan and back on the same basis as before, and that he would do the same to America, but we would have to make a contribution of £65,000 as well as the fuel. I didn't know where that money was coming from, but it was a remarkable deal that was worth more than half a million pounds to us.

That, I think, typifies the real spirit of British enterprise and corporate enlightenment. The project just couldn't have been done without HeavyLift. It was a bloody good public relations story. There was this tiny little organization, which had no money, somehow flying out in the world's largest freighter. I believe it paid off for HeavyLift, too. They got enormous media coverage, and I'm sure it was good for company morale. The first time I wandered around one of Graham's Antonovs they were preparing to load a Pepsi bottling plant. That was hard for the media to get excited about, but transporting *ThrustSSC* was something else.

We were slowly making it through our toughest period, and early in 1997 we got another of the breaks I'd been after for two years. I'd been trying very hard to bring in BTR, the parent company of both Dunlop and Hawker Batteries, two of our key technical partners. I had been to see them, but I'd been told, 'All we're interested in is ensuring that the share price stays high. We will happily spend whatever PR money is necessary to ensure that, but we're not interested in corporate PR.'

That was how it stood until Norman Finn, the development director of Hawker Batteries, came along to see us one day. In the course of conversation, when the BTR topic came up, he said, 'Well, how much do you really want for a space on the side of the car?' So I replied, 'A hundred and fifty thousand pounds.'

Norman saw Ian Strachan, the chairman of BTR, two days later, and Strachan said yes. It was absolutely extraordinary. What Ian wanted to do was to show the City that BTR had changed. In the past BTR had made its living from buying companies, tidying them up, then selling them, like a warehousing operation. But as a result of the recession it was very difficult to find those sort of fat, badly managed companies with good growth potential, so they were forced to move into a proper trading situation. BTR's whole culture had changed, and this was one way Ian was going to prove that to the City.

What we couldn't know, and what might have been terminally disheartening if we'd known it then, was that BTR was to be our last major sponsorship.

With the BTR money we could get a lot of the bills paid off, and restore the balance sheet from a position of dire collapse to just plain unhealthy. We pushed on with the development of *ThrustSSC* in the light of what we referred to as Jordan One. It was most important to correct the rear steering. One of the major changes Glynne made was to have two more Dunlop rear wheels machined with twin keels on the tread. This was similar to the Second World War way of curing shimmy on an aircraft tail wheel – it's strange how these technologies re-emerge. By May 1997 we were ready to go to Jordan again, and this time we were determined to come back with something worthwhile. Once we'd settled our debts there wasn't much of BTR's £150,000 left, and we were so desperate that we even took the money we owed in VAT with us. If you're going to fail, then you might as well fail spectacularly!

Our backs were right up against the wall, and there was no coming back without a good result. If we didn't do well for the second trip running, the car would have to be sold for scrap when we got back.

We established ourselves once more at Al Jafr late in May 1997. This time, in direct contrast to Jordan One, the teamwork side of it suddenly clicked, just as if a switch had been thrown. After Jordan One we'd all started getting closer to each other, and perhaps people appreciated that we had kept the team together despite all the financial problems.

Brian Palmer, who was responsible for all transport, once again ran a superbly efficient operation. Within two days of touchdown the camp was operational; during Jordan One it had taken a week. The whole team had come together in a way I hadn't experienced before.

On 25 May Andy made his first run, with a gentle peak of 136 m.p.h. before building up to 300 m.p.h. By 4 June, after further runs, Andy had pushed up to 479 m.p.h., our fastest speed yet. Thus far we had experienced only minor glitches with the electrics, and we were elated. But I spoke too soon when I said, 'That was a very predictable run. Nothing broke!'

Later that day he hit 540 m.p.h. Though we didn't realize that something serious was wrong until the team went to jack up the rear end of the car after the run to mount it on the tow dolly, Andy had realized we had a problem when a

ANDY GREEN

'We'd sought a lot of advice from people within the industry about driving a car with rear-wheel steering. Professor David Crolla at Leeds University looked at it from the academic's point of view and said, "These will be the dynamics of the vehicle and this is what the wheels need to do; there might be some confusing inputs to the driver," and just left it at that.

'Former Grand Prix driver John Miles at Lotus Engineering took completely the opposite approach: let's see what the driver is actually going to have to cope with in terms of the car being a drivable vehicle. He did all sorts of things that never occurred to us, such as driving our converted Mini in reverse just to see what effect it had. He found it was completely stable with the rear wheels going first.

'Now, on *ThrustSSC* the centre of rotation was about the front wheels. To turn it, you had to put in negative acceleration. That meant that to turn it right, you actually had to accelerate the vehicle to the left about the front wheels and as the back end started to go left, so the front would go right. This is oversimplifying it, but once the back end had been accelerated to the left you had to slow it down so it didn't swing too much. As the front started to move right, the back end would go left a little more, slow down, and then eventually go right, too.

'I had to be careful, because if I then reversed the steering to make the car go to the right, if perhaps I'd put in too much original movement, the car was already beginning to go right even faster because I'd put in a new initial input over the first. If I then thought, Oops, that's way too much, and decided I needed to reverse the steering again to the left to counter that, I'd lose control. If I wasn't very smooth and careful, I had about three inputs before the car went out of control. A second and a half, two seconds, it didn't take very long. On the couple of occasions when I got slightly out of time with the car, I could feel the back end starting to react completely out of phase with me. Then I'd got two choices, either admit I'd lost it and shut down, or stop those inputs straight away. According to figures from Lotus, if I made inputs greater than one hertz — the standard unit of frequency equal to one cyle per second — the vehicle would go completely out of phase with me and become uncontrollable. It was the classic thing that whatever you wanted it to do, it would do exactly the opposite, because you couldn't catch up with its reactions.

'The fastest inputs you can make are around three to three and a half hertz. There was no positive advice in the early stage, but given that by the two hertz band you'd be out of phase with the car, what advice we did get suggested that sticking to one hertz was the answer. I thought, Yep, that explains why it handled oddly even at fifty to one hundred m.p.h. on the runway at Farnborough.

'John Miles's findings arrived at the end of the week I first drove *ThrustSSC*, so I spent a lot of time studying them and trying to get the feel for the car on the runway. I would make an input, stop, wait to see what the response was and then correct it. But there was compliance in the system, and any compliance is destabilizing. It was the old shopping-trolley effect. If you just push one down a supermarket aisle, it almost always veers and hits something on the way down.

'At low speeds, *ThrustSSC* would weave gently around its back end. Hard though I tried, I could never get it to track an exactly straight line at one hundred and fifty to two hundred m.p.h. It was like trying to balance a pencil upright on the end of your finger; you can keep it upright if you keep moving your hand, but you can never get it to stand upright keeping your hand perfectly still.

'To begin with, on Al Jafr, the faster I went the bigger *SSC*'s zigzags would get until I was out of control. If I got just a little bit off line, I'd be fifty feet off straight away. I couldn't wait a second to control that. The problem with

the rear-wheel steering affected the fine control stability, but the coarse control stability came from having the engines and the weight up the front and the huge long tail and its fin. That's what Ron imbued the car with originally, his big-fin stability which meant that it was never likely to yaw suddenly into a ground loop. So *SSC* was stable aerodynamically, but unstable in fine control mode. It had the stability of an arrow in flight, but it was a slightly wobbly arrow. Fast jets exhibit exactly the same tendencies, but they all have extra computer-controls for stability. Switch them off, and the jets will pitch and bob around the sky.

'I soon became aware that one second pause – input – one-second pause – input – wasn't working as the speed got up to around three hundred to three hundred and fifty m.p.h. During Jordan One that wasn't a problem, because the steering itself wasn't working well enough and we were getting the wheel shimmy.

'As I worked up to more than three hundred and fifty m.p.h. during Jordan Two, I recognized that the car's divergences from a straight line were getting bigger, and there was nothing I could do about it. The following day we were due to use the afterburner for the first time at Al Jafr, and to aim beyond four hundred m.p.h. The faster I accelerated, the faster was the rate of onset of the fishtailing. That night I came to the conclusion that the driving technique I had been using, making inputs at a rate of no greater than one hertz, simply wasn't going to work. Therefore, it was going to be a major problem. My big concern then was how I would keep *SSC* on line. As well as the steering, I had been controlling directional stability on the throttle, backing off when necessary to slow down the rate of build-up of problems before accelerating again when I was back in phase with the car. But now I didn't know what I was going to do. There was nobody else on the team to talk to about it, because it was a problem unique to me. At the time I knew there was a problem, but it was only much later that I could begin to explain it properly. I just knew that my current technique wasn't going to hack it, and all I had was a graph that said the dragons lived above one hertz. I thought about it, then went to bed, but it was a really hot night and nobody slept well. I got up at two in the morning, and went for a walk outside to try to cool down. But the conclusion I came to was that I couldn't see any way of controlling the car. Above one hertz lived dragons; below one hertz I wasn't going to be able to correct the car's divergence fast enough. What were my options? I could have had a chat with the team and told them what I was going to do. But that would only worry them, and there was nothing they could suggest anyway. Only John Miles might have understood what I was struggling with, but in any case, an electrical storm had put all the phones down.

'Eventually I decided that if it came to a straight challenge between me and the car, I had to try to win. I needed to spot a divergence as the initial yaw movement started, but before the car actually began to yaw. That meant using inputs around three and half hertz. I had to twitch the car to stop it yawing. I had to think one step ahead of it, make the adjustment before I waited to see what the car was going to do. That would either work, or I'd lose control. I was due out at four o'clock, so I either had to make a decision there and then, or stay up all night worrying about it. I decided that out-thinking the car was going to be my best shot. I was going to find out whether I could react as quickly as the car could diverge.

'At this stage I was beginning to wonder whether the car was at all drivable. While everybody else seemed perfectly happy because we were ramping up the speeds, I knew it was getting harder and harder. The definition of undrivable is when the demands on the driver are greater than the driver's ability. By most technical definitions *ThrustSSC* was undrivable. Test pilots have a scale in which one is fabulous and ten is uncontrollable, like trying to hold wet spaghetti vertical. *SSC* was up in the seven or eight territory. My question was: could I actually drive to eight and a half?

'By lunchtime later that day I had driven two runs, one with minimum afterburner, the other with maximum, and the good news was that my technique of very high-frequency inputs – above two and a half hertz – had worked to keep the car relatively straight by twitching the wheel whenever I felt a yaw divergence building up. Of course I still had to put in the basic steering inputs at one hertz and below, so I found myself driving the car by using two totally different frequencies of input: below one hertz for steering to follow the line and above two and a half hertz to stabilize the car. And if they ever started to overlap, I would lose control within two or three seconds.

'When I was up at two that morning wandering around, I wondered whether I was going to have to say to Richard, "I don't think we have a project any more, I can't drive the car." And with the best will in the world he would have had to say, "Maybe we've chosen the wrong driver." When the day's runs were over I didn't get ecstatic. I'd found a new driving technique that worked, but I knew now that it was going to be tough. That's why I never really enjoyed driving the car. It was much too much like hard work to actually enjoy it.'

number of captions lit up in the cockpit and steering the car became much more difficult. He was able to drive it normally, but his calm, 'Oh dear,' at the end of his voice transmission told its own story.

What had happened was that first one, then the other rear-suspension mounting bracket had broken at over 500 m.p.h. as a result of the continuous hammering the car was receiving from the Al Jafr desert. As these failures occurred one of the suspension struts penetrated the car's framework above the broken bracket, punching through the skin of the box-section structure and jamming there, taking the full weight of the back end of the car.

We knew we had a car capable of achieving our goal. Further development pushed our speeds into the 500 m.p.h. region when we returned to Jordan briefly in the middle of 1997.

That saved Andy's life.

If the suspension had totally collapsed at that point, the back end of the car would have fallen to the ground and, at well over 500 m.p.h., the front would have lifted off and the project would have come to a disastrous end.

As we towed *ThrustSSC* back to the Aireshelta, behind one of the Supacats, we could actually see the rear wheels flopping around. We used the little tractors to tow and turn *ThrustSSC* round because, had the car been turned round via its own steering, the lock was so limited that it would have described a very wide arc. We would hitch up the back end of the car to one of the Supacats, lifting the steerable rear wheels off the deck, and could thus manoeuvre it much more easily and save time between runs.

It was a serious shock to discover that, despite all our efforts to develop a safe land-speed-record car, we'd nearly had a disaster so early on. We learned from the event and made the necessary engineering changes.

The problem would take some days to fix, and we

were already running into problems with the high ambient temperature. The electronics didn't fare too well in the heat, which obliged us to run very early in the morning, before the ambient temperature exceeded 25 degrees centigrade. The prospect of 600 m.p.h., our target speed, was looking remote. The design team had a long meeting, at the end of which it was decided that the best course was to pack up and head back home, make lasting repairs, and prepare for Black Rock. I would have preferred to make repairs and stay out, but it was getting more and more hopeless trying to run the car at very high speeds on Al Jafr. Andy was flying all over the place, and the rear end of the car was getting horrible treatment on the rough, hard desert surface. Moreover, the temperatures were rising as midsummer approached. Reluctantly I agreed we should head back to Farnborough

I wasn't really surprised that Andy was so calm about it all – you only had to look at his background flying fighters, which are often temperamental. If you had a problem in one of those and got the thing down safely and walked away, so what? It was an incident that was behind you. Andy did what he'd always done, which was to give his very best in the circumstances. He was very aware that if the rear suspension had dropped it would have increased the positive incidence of the car, and at 500 m.p.h. that would have made it fly. But all he said on the cockpit tape was, 'Oh dear.'

Despite the suspension breakage the team was very excited. We had now begun to reach credible speeds, but more than that we'd really started to get to grips with *ThrustSSC*. Once again Andy had done a fabulous job, and we could take real pride in what we had achieved. We had now closed the gap on Breedlove, who hadn't run since his drama at Black Rock the previous October. Everybody seemed to be on a high, with the feeling that we really had a good chance now.

I hated to do it in those circumstances, but I had to call them all together just before we left to fly back to Farnborough. I was seriously worried about the future, because of that old record-breaking bogey: lack of cash.

'Look,' I said, 'I think I have to tell you just where we are. I had hoped we would get over six hundred m.p.h., but we didn't. Five hundred and forty isn't going to get people excited back home. It couldn't happen because the desert was too rough, so don't take it personally. But I want you to understand where we are.'

Up until then I'd never really talked about money, because the problem with money is that people tend to get worried about it. 'Christ, we've only got that much left,' that sort of thing. But now I wanted to share my worries about the situation with the whole team.

'The reality of it is that to get us to America, to keep the organization going while we're out there, and in the two months before we go, is going to cost six hundred thousand quid, or nine hundred thousand dollars. Now somehow we've got to make that money, and we haven't even reached six hundred m.p.h.

'We've also got only July and August to raise this money, the worst months for seeking sponsorship. And if we don't go this year, that's the end of the project. It's all finished. We cannot keep going for another year without a result.'

At that point I thought we were out of our depth. I really didn't know how we were going to make that money in two of the worst months for sponsorship decisions. I just hoped that some big company would come in and take the gamble as BTR had, and say, 'Right, we'll put up four hundred thousand.' When we got home, I rang Tivoli, who told me they were very pleased. 'We couldn't have got that level of publicity for that kind of money any place else. We've done the job, we've got ourselves known in Europe.' But very shortly after that they were bought by IBM.

Now we were in this terrible situation. Although we had a tremendous amount of work to do to repair the car and prepare it to run in Nevada within two months, the real problem was that somehow we had to make £600,000 in forty-three working days. It was seriously daunting.

The opportunity was there for a company to step in, with the really hard work and the development all behind us, and to grab some glory late in the day when the risk was much less. But sponsors were getting more and more difficult to find. We had only three major ones: Castrol, Tivoli and BTR. So now we faced a huge level of graft to raise the vital cash.

We went straight into an intensive programme of Mach 1 Club days at Farnborough, weekend after weekend, and they were buying £5,000 or £6,000's worth of merchandise each time. All of that helped.

I asked Peter Ross, our support manager, to post the current percentage of funding achieved on our noticeboard. Everyone knew that we needed £600,000, so they could all see where we stood. It climbed to 14 per cent, then 15 per cent. By the first week of August it was 16.5 per cent. Then it crept up to 27 per cent, and there it just stuck.

Chris Cowell, our highly experienced engine man and always one of the most level-headed and dependable members of the team, said quietly to me one day, 'Richard, at twenty-seven per cent, we're not going to go, are we?' What could I say?

What was so desperately dispiriting was that we'd created a brilliant culture, an organization that could do things; that could do just about anything. It could work its way round almost any kind of problem, it could duck and weave, but it did need a modicum of money to keep going, and if it didn't keep getting that lifeblood it just wouldn't survive. I felt very strongly that if we could get the fuel for the Antonov, then we could somehow do it, even if we had to sleep in tents! We were talking about 250,000 gallons of Jet A fuel. Around £140,000 at pump prices.

I went round every single oil company. They were all very nice, very friendly. And they all said no. Or they didn't come back, which, as we had learned, is a cold corporate way of saying no. The fuel we needed was dirt cheap Jet A-1 paraffin. God knows what it cost to make. A penny a gallon? Ten pence a gallon? Nothing. So why was it that every oil company refused to help? They didn't even offer discounts. Why? It was only 100,000 quid. Was it part of that old problem we had with ARV? Does the country consist of a collection of cosy monopolies? And had these monopolies decided they weren't going to help us? It reached an all-time low when the BP board sent us a rejection letter enclosing a little brochure about how 'BP cares'.

The oil companies were all very defensive, and several of them explained the good work they did in the community. But it was clear that, for us, it just wasn't going to happen. It was a terrible time. We were pushing on with all the final arrangements, making commitments and booking things. My brother, Andrew, had his team out on the desert surveying and establishing the track, and he was sending back faxes saying, 'Can we afford to pay for this? Can we afford that? Should we do this?' I kept telling him, 'Yes, Andrew, I've put the money on one side. Go for it!' Even though we only had 27 per cent of the money we needed.

Breedlove saw all this happening on the Internet, and I suspect he began to tell people we weren't coming. The rumour going round in Nevada was that the British weren't going to show.

We'd got so close, but now it looked as if it was all going to grind to a halt. The ignominy of not going would be ten times worse than going out there and failing. It was all so frustrating. What do you do?

If you go and protest loudly – say, go on breakfast television and moan about it – nobody gives a cuss. Everybody says, 'There's got to be a very good reason why Shell and BP aren't going to back that lot,' or, 'That bloke Green is going to kill himself, and we don't want to be a part of that.' Banging the table is totally counter-productive, so you've got to be smarter than that.

I sent out a distress call to all the 231 companies that had supported us, mostly

with product sponsorship or equipment loan. 'Look,' I said, 'it's only two thousand pounds a head, and we can go.' The response was very poor.

We thought a great deal about this, and it seemed to be the moment to go for the Internet. We already had 800 pages on our website. In the month since we'd come back from Jordan Two, our webmaster, Jeremy Davey, had set up a remarkable Internet trading system. In conjunction with Microsoft, our bankers NatWest and the Irish software company Trintech, we now had the ability to trade electronically on the Internet, without the need for a credit-card swipe. We were the first in the UK to do so. Jeremy now suggested that we should put out an appeal through the Internet. We put out a piece on the web that night. 'Look, we are in very deep trouble,' it read. 'We've got to get out to America, nobody will help us with the fuel, but if we get that we can probably busk the rest. We're offering you *ThrustSSC* fuel certificates, signed by Andy Green, in twenty-five-dollar lots. Will you help us?'

The amazing thing was that people started buying these certificates in huge volumes, which peaked at around 30,000 gallons a day. Suddenly, from being becalmed, we were sailing ahead again at high speed. With electronic trading the thing just went like a flash; all the money trickled straight into the NatWest account. Flash trading – that's the Internet for you!

The *Daily Telegraph* got to hear of all this, and put out a series of pieces which basically said, 'We find it very odd that nobody has supported this British project.' Their readers started sending in money, which peaked at 15,000 quid a day.

All of a sudden, from staring defeat in the face, we made the better part of £400,000 in twenty days. Then Castrol came in with a loan of around £70,000, and they took a £20,000 logo space on the nose.

Like Cinderella we were going to make the ball after all, but I was damned if we would be coming back before midnight.

In this record-breaking game nothing ever runs smoothly. Against the odds we had found the funding to get to the Black Rock Desert. But even before we set off we learned that the Gerlach motel rooms we'd booked with Bruno Selmi had been let out to other people. Craig Breedlove was also in town as he prepared to go head-to-head with us, and he had attracted publicity so the media were there already in full.

We had been late paying the deposit on our rooms. Andrew had been in an invidious financial situation and had been unable to pay the deposits for the hotel rooms as he simply hadn't got the money; all the work he was doing out in

Nevada was being done on a shoestring budget, and he was having to promise everyone that we would pay soon. Suddenly, we had left it too late. I never got the feeling this time round that Bruno really wanted us, even though he'd doubled the size of his motel accommodation in Gerlach between 1982 and 1983, when *Thrust2* was operational. I suppose from his point of view we were a pretty dodgy bet this time. I think he really wanted the media, because they offered extra opportunities, such as installing phones in their rooms. When the moment came, Andrew was told flatly that the rooms weren't available. We had a car, we had the money to get out to Black Rock, but now, suddenly, we had nowhere to stay.

Andrew raced round and got hold of a lot of beds and bedding and managed to rent a number of apartments. When the main team arrived everybody was pretty upset about this, because many were actually sleeping on floors. I had to say to them, 'Look, this is the reality. You tell me what else we can do. I'm not going to spend money renting motorhomes, the money has to go into the project. We'll just have to do the best we can with what we have.'

It was heartening that so many warm-hearted American friends welcomed us back so enthusiastically and rallied round to help. Dink Cryer of Carson City Dodge, for example, heard that we were short of transport. The Rover Group, which had generously lent us Discoveries in Jordan, had withdrawn as soon as I asked them for financial help. 'So, tell me what you want, Richard?' Dink asked. He provided us with a series of Dodge pickups, and bought a crew bus for us. From time to time we reduced the weekly car-hire bill by borrowing a number of Dink's Chrysler Neons.

Tom Revilgio's company, Western Nevada Supplies, provided a vast amount of equipment, supported our accommodation costs in Reno and helped us in all sorts of other ways. Tom is one of those people who's impossible to thank. 'Think nothing of it, Richard,' he told me. 'I know you guys will pull it off if anyone can – I just want to be a part of it.'

19 A PEG IN THE GROUND

We had a car that we knew was going to shatter the land-speed record. Now we set out to prove it to the rest of the world.

Our initial runs on the Black Rock Desert were low-speed affairs to make assessments of *ThrustSSC*'s systems and the state of the surface. They reminded us just how much smoother it was than Al Jafr. It was, of course, the surface for which the car had been designed. We began running on 8 September, with a leisurely 148 m.p.h. pass, working up to 517 m.p.h. in five runs. On 11 September Andy peaked at 550 m.p.h. and then went over 600 m.p.h. for the first time, equalling *Thrust2*'s average from its first record run, with a peak of 624 m.p.h. At that speed Andy said he was just loafing along. A wheel came off one of our Palouste turbine starter units, which were used to start the Speys, so we didn't try too hard to do a turnaround within the hour.

Andy took that first run nice and gently, accelerating up to 500 m.p.h., then throttling back to minimum afterburner, before cutting the afterburner altogether and slowly coasting down to check the handling. On the second run he was taking *ThrustSSC* in and out of burner, between 580 and 610 m.p.h., to control the speed. This constant-speed driving, which proved very difficult at these relatively low speeds (too slow for burner, too fast to maintain without), could be very destabilizing for the car. The most it deviated was ten feet off the line, and it came straight back on again, so it looked as if the car would run absolutely dead straight, although at higher speeds this would prove not to be the case.

We were keeping all four wheels on the deck. In Jordan, when we did get up to reasonable speeds, you could sometimes find all of them off the ground due to the unevenness of the surface. You couldn't control the car in those conditions. And every time the car landed back on the Al Jafr desert there was an impact, the hard surface sending shock loads through the car. Black Rock didn't have the undulations of Al Jafr, and there was that slight 'give' in the surface. When Andy did his first run there he said it felt like running over a carpet. The surface seemed much more powdery than it had been back in 1983, but a lot drier despite recent heavy rain. At 630 m.p.h. *Thrust2* had been peaking and struggling, whereas *ThrustSSC* still had plenty in reserve.

Pit station was home to the design team and operations. It became the ThrustSSC desert nerve centre.

The right stuff.

Andy would start each run slowly to avoid hoovering up great quantities of desert into the engine intakes. He would get up to 70 m.p.h., then accelerate to max mil, maximum military power without afterburner. The car would pick up speed pretty quickly, until, at 120 m.p.h., he would select minimum afterburner. By the time he reached 200 m.p.h. he had selected maximum afterburner and *ThrustSSC* was really beginning to move. It took him a fraction over 11 seconds to go from 300 m.p.h. to 550 m.p.h. My daily duties encompassed taking the media to the press pen, which was situated to one side of the measured mile in the middle of the course, and there we could watch the car appear over the horizon, a little over two miles away, already doing well over 600 m.p.h.

Thrust2 was at its most stable under savage acceleration, so I had driven it on all of our Black Rock runs with my right foot flat on the floor. We had determined entry speed to the measured mile by the simple expedient of varying the start point, like stretching the elastic on a catapult. The further back I started, the faster I would be going into the measured mile.

We adopted a completely different procedure with *SSC*, using a full thirteen-mile track for every run, with Andy determining its speed at all times with the throttle. Sometimes the point at which he would go to the afterburners would be different, or he would only hold maximum afterburner for a specific time before throttling back, depending on the run profile the design team had chosen. This was a new approach which had not been tried before, and our 'accelerate–cruise–decelerate' profile amazed Craig Breedlove and his team. They were much more familiar with the 'flat-out-to-the-middle-of-the-mile' technique.

RON AYERS

'All of our aerodynamic research using computational fluid dynamics and the rocket sled gave us sufficient data to design the car. It also gave us an approximate idea of how the car would actually behave when running at high speed. However, we knew that such experiments could never give precise information, and even small errors concerning the potentially enormous aerodynamic forces could be catastrophic. We were also aware that the transonic region, the "Bermuda Triangle of aerodynamics", was unexplored at ground level, so there could still be some totally unforeseeable problems that might lead us to disaster. It was thus necessary to supplement our early research with a carefully constructed and tightly controlled test programme for the car, both in Jordan and on the Black Rock Desert.

'Before *ThrustSSC* became a record-breaking vehicle, it had to be a research vehicle. First, I constructed a skeleton programme which specified the peak speed, or peak Mach number, for each run. In the transonic region I was very cautious and assumed that the Mach number increment between runs might need to be as small as point zero one. Such caution was necessary, as flow patterns and aerodynamic forces could conceivably change very rapidly in this complex region. Only if results gave us reason to be very confident would we take Mach number increases as large as point zero two. At lower speeds, larger increments could safely be used.

'This enabled me to estimate the number of runs we would need to set a supersonic world land-speed record on the Black Rock Desert. These were my predictions, made in July 1997.

	Optimistic	Pessimistic
Up to M = 0.9	11	11
From 0.9 to supersonic record	8	16
Subtotal	19	27
+ 20 per cent repeat runs	4	5
Total runs	23	32

'The "optimistic" total assumed we could use Mach number increments of point zero two in the transonic region. The "pessimistic" figures assumed we needed point zero one increments. It was also assumed that the fastest run of a supersonic record would peak at M = 1.06. The twenty per cent repeat runs were to allow for the development problems that would inevitably bedevil a prototype vehicle.

'In practice, *ThrustSSC* ran twenty-eight times on the Black Rock Desert. Two of these were low-speed taxi runs to return the car to the pit station when it had finished at the wrong end of the track, so the number of operational runs was twenty-six, which was very close to my most optimistic prediction. This is an indication that my worst fears (of transonic buffeting, or unforeseen transonic problems) were not realized.

'For each run a "run profile" was designed. This was a detailed specification of the speed against time and distance for the duration of the run. This gave Andy a detailed set of instructions to follow for the run. On page 258 there is an example of the profile for a supersonic run. Note that there is a "high-speed cruise" phase, which gave Andy the maximum chance to explore the handling characteristics of the car at high speed, and this provided the design team with the maximum experimental data from our myriad onboard sensors to help plan subsequent runs. These profiles were agreed with Andy, discussed by the whole design team and only adopted when everyone was happy. Apart from aborted runs, Andy followed these profiles with uncanny accuracy.

'This tightly controlled research programme was a totally new departure for speed-record attempts. Indeed, it was more like the programme for testing a prototype aircraft or guided missile. That had been my job over thirty years earlier!'

*Andy Green with
Ron Ayers.*

I felt very confident that we had the technology, but I was concerned about the car's reliability. *ThrustSSC* had active ride, a very complex hydraulic system and 120 channels of data collection, all of which were dependent on the two computers. If those two computers went down, we were stuffed. There was the one that had come from Lotus and the other which had been used by DERA in a Scorpion tank, so they were pretty ancient. Were we expecting too much from them? Computer One dealt with all of the safety systems and thus would shut the car down if it sensed anything it didn't like; Computer Two handled data acquisition. Twice Computer One automatically shut down the car at exactly the same point in a run.

You can imagine the situation. Ironically *ThrustSSC* was being held back by its technology, and what little money we had was being frittered away as we struggled to sort things out. Whether we ran or not, it was costing us at least $5,000 a day to be at Black Rock. Fortunately, Jeremy Bliss and Robert Atkinson sourced the problem and effected a lasting cure.

If we had our problems, we were not alone. Craig had run *Spirit of America* a couple of times, but had to withdraw temporarily when he blew up his engine. While his crew went back to Rio Vista for a spare, Craig learned that one of his sponsors had pulled out. He had my full sympathy. I knew how he must be feeling. He kept fighting back, however, and I knew we hadn't heard the last of him.

Though the surface of the desert was perfect, it was a terrible environment for delicate machinery. You only had to leave a window open a fraction and everything would be coated with a layer of dust like talcum powder. *ThrustSSC* was charging through clouds of this stuff, creating a dust trail 500 feet high. Worse still, it was an alkali dust, and that starts to corrode any kind of bright metal. If you looked inside the car, the whole damn thing was covered in a film of yellow alkaline dust.

Despite my concerns, and the occasional heart-stoppers with the computers, the car proved surprisingly reliable, considering its complexity. A lot of that was due to Jerry and the unsung heroes in the background. Robert Atkinson, who was in charge of the computer hardware, put in an enormous amount of work. During the build programme he had been doing a day job in Bournemouth, then jumping in his car and coming up to Farnborough to work nights on the car. He worked out that he had driven 70,000 miles in the process. Rod Barker and his colleague Steve O'Donnell, from Met Research Flight, also put in an enormous amount of time. Jerry was very impressed with Rod and spoke highly of the design he came up with for the or-gates, small microswitches in the active-control computer. 'It was', he observed, 'a very sweet piece of design.' Jerry doesn't impress easily. Rod and Steve knew that we couldn't afford to bring them out to the desert, so they just decided they were coming anyway, and by God did we need them! Bits of the electronic intestines were constantly having to be resoldered. Jerry and his systems team shunned the publicity, but it was very seldom that runs were held up through electronic problems.

ThrustSSC was also reliable mechanically. The engines gave us no problems at all, and that was a great testament to the expertise of Chris Cowell and Steve Wiltshire, our crew ever since Goodwood in 1996, and the work they did setting up the Speys; and to Chris and Robbie Kraike and the hours they put in fettling the throttle linkages. At Farnborough these had been in pieces continually until we were certain they were perfect. We couldn't risk another situation where we had only partial reheat.

I had several other concerns. Things happened thick and fast, some bad, some good. There was the day I reversed over my Digital lap-top, which definitely fell into the former category. For an hour or two it was to be a killer crisis.

I had been working so hard that there had been simply no time to back up whatever was on the computer: the correspondence, the contracts, the financial plans, the accounts; the whole damn thing.

The way I operated was to carry around my pilot's case, with the key things I needed in it: the lap-top, all our money and my notepad. On this particular day an ITN cameraman had been filming the roll-out from the Aireshelta and needed a lift down to the press pen. I was headed that way, so I said, 'Quick, get in the car.' We threw all this into the back of my blue Chrysler Neon, and I put it into

Our camp on the Black Rock Desert, dominated by our Aireshelta – the world's largest inflatable hangar.

From the air, pit station is visible to the left of the Aireshelta.

reverse. I'd forgotten that I'd left my case right behind the rear wheels until there was a sickening crunch. Then the implications began to sink in. Accounts: gone! Contracts: gone! Financial plans: gone! Budgets: gone!

I just thought, Christ Almighty, what am I going to do? Later, after that day's run, I dragged my mangled Digital lap-top out of the boot and handed it to Jerry Bliss. 'You've got to help me out,' I pleaded with him. Jerry roared with laughter. 'You've bloody done it this time.' We took the battered remains into the pit station, where he very carefully levered out the hard disk and put it into Glynne's computer. Thank God, it was all right. Somebody was truly on our side that day.

Since the handbagging thing in Jordan our 'cock-up' award had changed. Robbie Kraike, an ex-Navy submariner, had been determined to join our crew and brought with him invaluable training as a firefighter. He and his wife, Suzie, became intrinsic members of the team. Just before leaving for Nevada, Robbie had spotted some furry dice in a shop near his home in Alton, and they now became the symbol of stigma for anyone who blundered spectacularly. I got to wear them for a day after the lap-top incident.

Week by week we followed a regular routine. We'd rise early, breakfast in Gerlach, then head out to a team briefing on the desert, which would outline the day's schedule once again. We would work on the car or else run it; then, following a debriefing after any runs, the design team would meet in the afternoon to discuss the following day's plan of action. On days when Craig was ready to run, Martyn Davidson, our operations manager, would toss a coin with Breedlove's cousin Bill to decide which team would run in the morning and which would run in the afternoon. Martyn described himself as the British champion tosser. Because of Craig's technical problems, it turned out that we didn't need to share the desert very often.

Safety was always the priority. Transport manager, Brian Palmer, together with Mike Hearn, was fully trained and equipped to deal with fire during every run.

One day a fellow called Colin Hill faxed me from the Isle of Man to say, 'I'd like to help and bring some friends out. Is that OK?' I replied that of course it was, he'd be most welcome. Then he said, 'I've been reading about your financial problems in the *Daily Telegraph*. I'll bring you out ten thousand dollars.' Well, in that case he was even more welcome.

Colin is a successful businessman, specializing in carbon fibre, which was first created at Farnborough. He'd apparently consulted his dogs to see whether he should do this; they gave him the right answer, and out he came. He had sensibly talked to the man from the *Telegraph* and got himself an enormous amount of publicity, and very good luck to him. It was a great story, and I think it encapsulated what *ThrustSSC* had come to mean to enlightened people back home. Sponsors didn't want to know about us, but real people did. And these real people were prepared to put their money down.

When we got back home, Colin invited us to take *ThrustSSC* to the Isle of Man. Ten per cent of the island's population turned out to greet us.

Besides money, one of the most taxing concerns was the media. Paul 'Black Adder' Remfry did a wonderful job looking after security and access to the desert throughout the attempts, and very quickly he had to put a wall around the pits. With the help of Mach 1 Club volunteers we got a superb 'security machine' going. Press people were welcome, but we expected a certain standard of behaviour.

Immediately after the morning briefing and the roll-out of the car, my job was to go out and meet the journalists at the second entry to the desert, then escort them out to the press pen. I would address them with the same story each day, explaining the ground rules, asking them to follow me out there at no more than 30 m.p.h. in order to keep the dust down to a minimum. When we arrived, we would collect their car keys, because once *ThrustSSC* was preparing for a run we'd agreed with the Bureau of Land Management that there could be no uncontrolled vehicular movements on the desert. The entire desert had to be closed off, and patrolled by our two Pegasus microlights. I ended by offering to sell the journalists back their car keys, once the runs were over. I would then escort them to the pit station, where they could conduct interviews with Andy and other members of the team.

People who know me well will tell you that I have a precarious relationship with the media. These projects are difficult enough without the pressure of having to do them in public. But the sponsorship element means that you are obliged to

Further back-up came in the form of our Pegasus mircolight spotter aircraft.

give the media considerable access. This I find sincerely uncomfortable. It's very difficult to do a project anyway, and you never have the time or the resources to look after journalists, to actually brief them or to educate them properly. Often the quality of the people we have to deal with is not good. Many don't understand what the hell they're talking about, and even when you try to explain to them they still don't. They go for the instant-reaction type of story, ignoring the real one underneath.

One day CNN marched into the pits, their guys just expecting to film. I said, 'Hang on, what gives you the right to do this?' From their reaction I deduced that their attitude was effectively, Well, you're sponsored, aren't you? Look at all the logos. Therefore we can film. You need us.

It's almost a form of prostitution for the media. You are sponsored, therefore you are there to be exploited. You've got a bloody great Castrol logo, so you'll want all the coverage we can give you. And you'll oblige by doing whatever we ask.

I had my hands full running the project, without all this hassle. We eventually reached a provisional agreement with CNN, but their representative said, 'Right, I want five hours' filming.' I said, 'I'm terribly sorry, you can't have more than twenty minutes.'

He duly came into the pit station, and suddenly I saw him filming our contract with Breedlove, which happened to be pinned on the wall. I hit the camera! You couldn't have that sort of thing. It was totally intrusive. That document was confidential to the team. I wouldn't expect people to come into my office and start reading and copying my faxes.

This guy was very upset. 'How dare you hit a CNN camera!' he roared at me. 'How dare you film confidential contracts!' I roared back. 'You're out.'

Later he came back and apologized. 'Fine, no problem,' I said. 'Let's just forget the whole thing.' But the reality of it was that these guys were making serious money out of us, while we were struggling to keep the project going.

We'd already had an unsavoury incident in Jordan, when a film crew had bluffed its way into a high-security area on the King Feisal Air Base at Al Jafr and proceeded to start filming, after telling everyone that I'd approved it. I had done no such thing. They were eventually apprehended; General Mamoun informed me afterwards that he could actually have had them shot. They were let off after making grovelling apologies, but I just couldn't believe their arrogance. I felt that their behaviour was disgraceful.

The worst thing was when I discovered there was one journalist/photographer out on the Black Rock Desert with a specific contract to cover any disaster. That made me feel very uncomfortable. The only way to deal with this guy was to allow him on site with everybody else, and make sure he never got what he wanted.

Some of the journalists are extremely professional, like those on the *Reno Gazette*. They really understand what it's about, and they don't intrude. When the moment comes to ask questions, they ask bloody good ones that really set you thinking. They know what they're talking about, and it's a great privilege working with them. They are the classic example of how I think you should behave. You don't make a nuisance of yourself, you don't intrude, and you study your subject.

The problem is that such specialists are a rare breed. In general the media are undisciplined, undependable, arrogant and tend to think we're doing it for them, which we're not. I have no problem at all dealing with knowledgeable and professional pressmen. But once you are dealing *en masse* with guys who have no conscience, who are going to take up precious resources and be excessively demanding, that's when I start to see red.

We had one very unpleasant incident with a guy from a national newspaper who could have placed everything in jeopardy. The Bureau of Land Management had been very anxious after Breedlove's incident the previous year, and had insisted that nobody was to move on the desert while one of the cars was running or preparing to run. This guy absolutely knew that; he knew the rules, because he had been on site for weeks as I spelled them out daily. What made him think he could drive across the desert and head for town as a run was about to begin, putting the whole project in jeopardy? What gave him the right to do that?

The BLM had every right to pull the project's licence because of that. It was very clearly written that no vehicles should move. If they had pulled the licence at that point, I would now be bankrupt. Because of that guy's egotism, I would be bust. And we would not have broken the sound barrier. What would have happened to him? Nothing.

Years of effort could have been jeopardized by that. Incredibly when, later, I was asked about the story by the guy's editor, he said to me, 'A very likely story!'

In early September I was confident enough to call for the timekeepers. I had agreed to share the cost of the Sports Car Club of America crew with Craig

Breedlove, but I was beginning to have real doubts about their ability to handle this complex arrangement. They were friendly enough, but they kept raising fundamental issues, which undermined my confidence. I stayed in the arrangement as long as I could to support Craig, but in the end I felt that it was critical to have a timing system that nobody would subsequently question. So I bit the bullet and called up our old friends Dave Petrali and Mac McGregor from the United States Auto Club, who'd done such an impeccable job for us with *Thrust2*. Though it cost a substantial amount, which we hadn't budgeted for, to employ USAC, the expense would be nothing if the outcome was in doubt.

Dave was clearing out his garage when I called him. He was on the road to

Before and after every run I would give a briefing on our progress to the media in the press pen.

Black Rock the following night. Later he told me that he had been following the project on the Internet. The only reason he hadn't joined the Mach 1 Club was the fear that it might compromise his impartiality if the call came.

We had a scare on the thirteenth when the tracks revealed only three wheels in contact with the desert, but it turned out to be another software glitch in the active suspension, not the onset of more steering trouble.

The focus of attention moved round the car. It was on Glynne in Jordan, on me when the money wasn't coming, on Jerry with the computers and the active and on Robbie Kraike with the parachutes. Everyone seemed to have their spell under scrutiny. We were developing the car to a greater and greater standard, and from time to time something was found wanting and the focus moved there. It was inevitable.

You couldn't compare our progress with the progress in the *Thrust2* days: we had a different team and a completely different project. The sort of things that would cause serious hiccups in the *Thrust2* organization were just dealt with routinely by the *ThrustSSC* team. It was a bigger project with greater momentum, and perhaps the attitude and professionalism of the team were different. The project was so much more complex that things that were relatively big in the *Thrust2* scale of things just assumed a smaller proportion in the *ThrustSSC* scale.

The problem on the thirteenth put us a run behind schedule, but it gave us an opportunity to take the car out of service for extensive inspection. Ron told the media, 'Downtime is not a bad thing at this point. We've had a cracking week and the team needs a break.'

The first time we ran with official timekeeping, a week later, Andy averaged 553 m.p.h. through the mile. Two days later he peaked at 650 m.p.h. and averaged 618 m.p.h. We knew we could break the record on the

Readying ThrustSSC for a run.

return run, but Computer One played up again and we overran our hour. It was one of those things, made more agonizing when Andy averaged a fantastic 687 m.p.h. on the return, faster even than the 675 m.p.h. Craig had claimed as his peak the previous year. Andy took the disappointment in his stride. 'The car's running so well that I now comment if it goes a foot off the white line I follow on the desert,' he told the press. 'It's accelerating so fast that I'm having to back off the reheat to avoid exceeding the speed we'd planned for the day. Black Rock is a fabulous place to run. On this surface you really feel as if the car has no limit.'

The turnarounds were crucial, given that the rules only allowed us those sixty minutes. Here the Supacats came into their own. Besides being used to turn the car round, ready for its restart, they acted as fuel bowsers, so we could re-fuel the car very quickly as other team members made a detailed inspection

of *ThrustSSC*'s structure and systems, looking for potential trouble. At the same time, Andy would debrief with Ron, Jerry and Glynne.

The following day Andy actually went faster than my old record again, but for the second time we couldn't make the return within the allotted hour. On his first run he took *ThrustSSC* down the course at 693 m.p.h. Coming back he shattered the 700 m.p.h. barrier for the first time ever, at 719 m.p.h. But the parachute had torn off at the end of the first run, forcing him to overshoot. By the time the team got him dragged back to the intended start position, twenty minutes later, we'd run out of time.

Andy started and stopped at the same place for each run, but sometimes, if the parachutes failed, the car could end up as much as a mile and a half past its intended stopping point. This meant that we sometimes

Our Supacat 6x6 all-terrain vehicles became an indispensable means of manoeuvring ThrustSSC on the desert and refuelling it before each run.

Leigh Remfry and Steve Wiltshire refuelling ThrustSSC prior to a run.

had to tow *ThrustSSC* from its stopping point down to the start of the return run. More often than not, however, Andy was able to control the deceleration so perfectly that the car would come to a halt right over the point Ron had selected for the restart.

Our chute failure this time was maddening, but we put it down to experience. Nobody had been in this territory before. 'It was no big deal,' Andy said. 'Actually, it was rather boring, because I knew I'd have a long walk home.'

We kept *ThrustSSC* in the Aireshelta the next day, modifying the chutes so they ran quite straight behind the car. In Jordan they'd been pulling the back of the car sideways, and Andy was having to correct all the time. Then, on Thursday, 25 September, we were ready again for the big push.

Up until now we'd been fantastically lucky with the weather, which in the past had been so cruel to us. We encountered terrible white-out dust storms every so often, but otherwise the gods were being surprisingly benign. Now a light rain had been falling since dawn, but it didn't seem to have affected our thirteen-mile course at all.

On his first run Andy averaged 700.661 m.p.h., a slower ground speed than his best the previous Tuesday, but a higher Mach number due to the colder air temperature. At this stage all runs were being done on Mach number as we were so close to the speed of sound. We waited for the return, all nerves keyed to breaking point. Then along came *ThrustSSC*, charging down the desert, chased by its own dust cloud, and at the end came the words we were all anxious to hear when Jayne Millington said, '*SSC* is safe, safe, safe.'

There were other words, too, this time from Dave Petrali. 'Speed through the mile, seven-twenty eight point zero, zero eight…' I schooled my face as all around me exploded into screams of delight, then Sally and I embraced. We'd made it.

Andy had shattered our old record, with an average for both runs of 714.144 m.p.h. And he'd also shattered Gary Gabelich's 630.388 m.p.h. kilometre record, which we'd just missed with *Thrust2*.

'This is a peg in the ground saying this is the best car in the world, serviced by the best people in the world,' Andy told the reporters crowded around the pit station. 'Now that I've driven it at transonic speed several times, I can actually feel

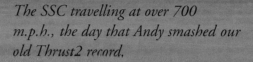

*The SSC travelling at over 700
m.p.h., the day that Andy smashed our
old Thrust2 record.*

*ThrustSSC, cementing our
first record with a very strong
return run at 728 m.p.h.*

the shock waves forming over the car, and I know now that taking it to supersonic speed will be safer than crossing the road. I have the best technology in the world looking after me. It's a question of identifying the risks and minimizing them. Fear doesn't come into it. I am more convinced than ever that *ThrustSSC* will break through the sound barrier, with ease.'

It was a simply fabulous performance.

OTHER VOICES

ANDY GREEN

'I guess the hardest aspect of our work up to that point was keeping up with it. We were all working long hours, and it was the judgement, as much as anything else, of how hard you had to work preparing the car without tiring out the whole team.

'I drew my own line, and decided where I stepped back. If it got to the stage where I was there at ten o'clock at night the boys would say, "Go home, you've got to drive the car tomorrow." If there was work still being done at ten o'clock at night, maybe we shouldn't have been driving the car tomorrow. It was the judgement call. But if it got to the stage where I was feeling too tired to be fit to drive the next day, I'd just say, "Sorry, I'm going home." I'm dead lazy; I enjoy eight hours' sleep.

'It felt terrific when we achieved the seven-fourteen record. Absolutely terrific. It was a marvellous boost to the team to go out to Black Rock, take out what we'd promised was the world's most powerful, safest, best-developed land-speed-record car and actually get the two runs within one hour. We knew it was capable of doing it and we were quite happy stepping the speeds up in ten- or twenty-mile-an-hour increments, but, of course, to make the world sit up and take notice you've got to do it twice within one hour and have it officially sanctioned.

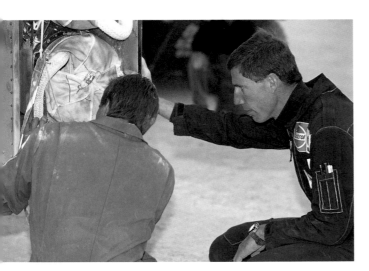

The braking parachutes became a cause for concern as ThrustSSC speeds exceeded 700 m.p.h.

'To begin with I didn't know it was such a big increase because I'd been driving to air speed not ground speed. The car was very well behaved. I was just delighted that I hadn't screwed up driving it.

'We had, however, made a major error.

'Outwardly, we were still talking about setting the record and exceeding the speed of sound in a safe car, but in reality we had made a major mistake in the last few days. We had been running the car ten to fifteen m.p.h. faster on each run, with the tail fully down and cycling the active suspension fully tail up and then back down at predetermined points during the run, to gather aerodynamic data. This relied on careful data analysis after each run — eventually we would reach the point where the front would start to get light, and raising the tail with the active suspension would be essential to keep *ThrustSSC* on the ground. Unfortunately, the day this happened, we were having some minor computer problems and were trying to get two runs within the hour for the first time. We forgot to check one critical piece of data — the front-wheel loads — and this was the run where the shock waves had started to cause the load to fall rapidly. I went only ten m.p.h. faster on the next run, but that was enough

'Later I went out to inspect the tracks, as I often did after a set of runs. There was a section during the high-speed cruise where one of the front wheels was barely touching the ground and the other was leaving no mark at all. Unlike Jordan, this was on a completely flat surface; *ThrustSSC* was flying at the front. I went to see Jeremy. He had seen the same results on the data. The static weight of six and a half tons at the front of *SSC* had been reduced to just a couple of hundred kilogrammes on that run. Fortunately, Ron's natural caution in increasing the speeds very slowly, and my determination to follow the run profiles as accurately as possible, had paid off. It had saved my life. But we should never have got that close, and I felt responsible for allowing our operations to get to that state. We had a very subdued design-team meeting that afternoon, after our second major scare, and after that our data checks took priority over everything else. If we didn't get two runs within an hour, we didn't really mind too much so long as we were sure it was safe to run again. We'd had our final warning and we'd heeded it.'

The sign outside the Black Rock Saloon.

Left to right: Glynne Bowsher, Mike Horne, Ron Ayers, Jerry Bliss, Nick Dove, Chris Cowell, Andy Green and Martyn Davidson, in one of the design-team meetings that analysed the latest runs and determined the profile of those to come. These run profiles were prepared the day before and based upon Ron's performance-prediction programme. Mphg refers to ground speed, mphi to indicated air speed, A/B to afterburner and ESD to engine shutdown.

715 MPHI PROFILE AT 12°C MACH 1.015, 769 MPH GROUND SPEED

OBJECTIVES – *Explore further into the transonic region.*

CONDITION OF CAR
Normal running condition with active locked at 4" up 650 mphg, then active linearly increased to full extension at 800 mphg.
Tailplane at +3/4 degrees.
No special instrumentation.
Five video recorders: tailplane looking fwd, tailplane looking rear, cockpit display, leading rear wheel (looking from ahead), front wheel. Rear brake hydraulics disconnected.

715 MPHI PROFILE AT 12C
Normal accel programme to Max A/B. Reduce A/B to cruise at:

715 mphi	to end of measured mile. Despool to idle
530 mphi	Deploy chute
150 mphi	Apply brakes – 0.1g assumed
100 mphi	ESD

PREDICTED FIGURES	DISTANCE (MILES)	TIMES (SECS)
Acceleration to 715 mphi	4.69	69
High-speed cruise	2.29	11
Deceleration	6.04	77
Total	13.02	157
Chute failure case	15.31	
Fuel consumed 642 litres		
Max accel	1.08g	Max decel -1.22g

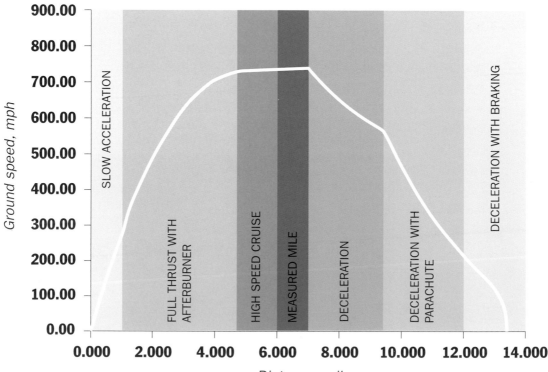

I was asked countless times in the build-up to this tremendous success how I would feel when Andy broke my record. I won't lie; giving up the driving, watching somebody else drive the car, was not an easy thing to adjust to. Not at all. I suppose the thing about the *Thrust2* record was what somebody once said to me: it was symbolic of Britain coming back. It had all gone wrong for Britain in the 1960s and 1970s, but back in 1983 we had hit back and turned the corner. So there was an enormous buzz from that. But *ThrustSSC* was very different. When Andy became the fastest man on earth I was just so thrilled, so delighted. It was the greatest land-speed record ever. The biggest ever increase over an existing record. A jump of over 80 m.p.h!

By the time the moment came I was willing to trade my record in return for being part of something like this. Losing my crown was precisely what I'd been working night and day for six years to achieve, after all. I'd expended so much energy to get rid of it.

I found myself wondering briefly how Craig and Rosco must be feeling. Craig had had nothing but trouble. The problems with his engine ingesting debris and then his sponsor pulling out had been compounded by a malfunctioning afterburner, which kept his speeds way down. Some said it was crew trouble, others that it was project trouble. I really felt for him, because I know how difficult these things can be. While we were making dramatic progress, everything seemed to be going wrong for him.

Rosco, meanwhile, was encamped at Lake Gairdner, awaiting dry weather. Then our success simply blew away his dream and everything he had worked towards for the last six years. He must have been bitterly disappointed, yet he still sent us a sincere message of congratulation.

There were two funny things I remember in the immediate aftermath of Andy's success. We were all elated as we gathered at pit station; I grabbed hold of Jerry Bliss and said, 'Jerry, you're a bloody genius!' He shook my hand and laughed, and then said, 'I'm not talking to you, you're a has-been.'

I'd asked Sally a couple of times, 'Will you still love me when I'm not the fastest man on earth?' She looked at me and smiled. 'Darling, I loved you before you were the fastest. So yes, I think I probably will.'

It was a great day, but we didn't realize then that the magnitude of our success would so nearly contribute to disaster.

The moments during a run, and when we were waiting for Andy's speeds to come through from the timekeepers, were always the most nerve-racking.

20 SUSPENDED ANIMATION

I think that quite a lot of people expected us to quit after we'd smashed the old *Thrust2* record, as if we were going to be content with the biggest speed increase in history. Sometimes when you succeed at something there is an immediate temptation to relax, even momentarily, but we had no intention of succumbing to that. We had come for the world's first supersonic record. That was always the goal. The new record was merely a stage towards it, however impressive. The maximum speed for which the car had been designed was 850 m.p.h. The speed of sound is typically 750 m.p.h., and we expected to end up with a new record somewhere between those two figures.

The record-breaking roller-coaster continued to sweep us from one high to the next low, and the latter wasn't long in coming. We kept the car in the Aireshelta for a number of engineering days immediately after the new record, and suddenly one hell of a row blew up over the trim in which we should run it.

The active suspension was deemed to be a key part of *ThrustSSC*. Its purpose was to act as a computer-controlled means of defining the angle at which the car ran to the ground and compensating for any potentially destabilizing changes in the car's aerodynamic loading. The 'active' was a compromise between ploughing and flying. If the nose of the car dug too deeply into the desert, the rolling drag would be astronomical. If the nose began to lift, the car could take off. We needed a controlled angle of attack.

Within its Aireshelta lair, ThrustSSC was well protected from the occasional sandstorm.

If there was any tendency for the nose to lift, the active suspension would raise the tail of the car, thus forcing the nose back down and maintaining aerodynamic stability. Likewise, it would not allow the nose to plough. The design was not what is called a closed system, however, so there was never going to be a situation where it would read the loads on the front suspension and vary the incidence automatically. The design did start off as a closed system, but we quickly realized there was a real danger that such a system might run away with itself and cause the sort of horrendous accident that we were all so concerned to avoid.

What we ended up with was a system that measured the vehicle speed, and then varied the suspension setting according to the speed reading.

ThrustSSC had always been designed with its active suspension as an intrinsic part. Now, led by Andy and Ron, there was a move afoot to abandon the system.

The outward manifestation came on 3 October, when we were running without official timing. The USAC guys had gone down to Reno to pick up a specially calibrated thermometer which would allow them to make absolutely certain that any supersonic record we set would stand without the slightest question. Petrali would use it in conjunction with his timing equipment to record the exact ambient temperature at the very moment the car passed through the measured distance, thus permitting a precise calculation of Mach number.

Andy was scheduled to make two runs, aiming for Mach 0.95 and Mach 0.96. *ThrustSSC*'s active suspension had been disconnected. He peaked at 560 m.p.h. on the first, but the car felt skittish and was drifting 20–30 feet off the line, so he decided to slow down. It felt safe on half afterburner, but only marginally stable at full afterburner. If he couldn't control it on full power then he wanted to stop and find out why.

He likened it to a racing driver tuning the aerodynamic balance of his car, and kept things light with a joke: 'Basically it's a lazy thing with drivers,' he said. 'If I can just put my foot down and drive in a straight line then it's good for me. If I can't, then I make the engineers work!'

The car was becoming divergent in yaw although the power output was perfectly symmetrical. It was skittish because the change in trim was generating a much higher download on the front than on previous runs, which was further destabilizing an already slightly unstable car.

The design team had changed the attitude of the car and the tailplane incidence. Ron confessed that we had paid the price for changing more than one thing at a time. The team decided to restore the tailplane's original position, and to run with just the increased download on the front. Ron described it as a balancing act. 'We expect to learn as we go. There's no textbook that we can get the data from; we are writing that as we go along.'

What had been suggested was that *ThrustSSC* should be run with the tail in the fully up position, effectively removing the active-suspension element that controlled its pitch angle. As Andy accelerated through Mach 0.85, the load on the front wheels would peak and then rapidly reduce. The active system left the tail fully down until Mach 0.85 and then gradually raised it as *ThrustSSC* approached Mach 1, to prevent this lightening of the front-wheel load. With the active system switched off and the tail locked fully up, the load was building up to well over ten tons on the front end, making the car dramatically unstable. Unlike *Thrust2*, which started to fidget around coming out of the measured mile with all the drag at the front, this build-up of load on *ThrustSSC* was causing it to be yaw divergent and making it completely uncontrollable. Andy had done exactly the right thing aborting the two runs. 'This is test driving, it's supposed to be like this,' he said.

He had tried for Mach 0.95 again on his second run, but had aborted that at a peak of 628 m.p.h. (around Mach 0.85), well before the measured mile. *ThrustSSC* was unstable, with 12 or 13 tons of load pushing down on the front wheels. A camera underneath told us what was happening: the car appeared to be ploughing ruts in the desert surface and getting very low to its belly. Perhaps as a

Ready to roll.

result, it was starting to veer to the left. All it proved was that there was too much download in that configuration.

Behind the scenes there had been an awful row in the design team about the decision to run without the active. Jerry Bliss had walked out. It was an unfortunate situation, but one reason why the project had advanced so far and so fast was that the design team had total responsibility for everything related to the car and its operational profiles. I'd said to them, 'Look, I'm out of my depth here, it's your show. I don't have time to learn the technology. Please don't involve me, because I probably won't understand. If there's a crisis and you don't know what to do, tell me. Otherwise, it's your baby.'

Andy had been concerned because he felt there was a weakness in the active system. He believed that under certain circumstances the active-suspension arrangement might actually drop the rear end of the car before it jacked it up. That would have been enough to make it fly.

Jerry had disagreed strongly and was desperately upset. I think he felt that Andy had used his position as the driver to influence the design-team decision. From Andy's point of view it was understandable because he believed there was a risk that *ThrustSSC* might fly: it was a very human thing to do, because he was the one taking the ultimate risk.

OTHER VOICES

ANDY GREEN

'The decision to run without the active system was a design-team decision. We looked at the consequences of running without the active suspension simply because I always felt it was another potential thing that could go wrong. But we knew we might well find that we would want to switch it back on. We needed to look at the data.

'It was a suggestion to run without active, because we were concerned that, with the changes we had already had to make to the car, a complete hydraulic failure could prove fatal. If there was a complete active collapse — a complete hydraulic collapse — then we had to have another safety system. We'd already raised the back end of the car a little, and that meant there wasn't room to have the active fully extended and then, in the event of a hydraulic failure, to further extend the rear suspension with the back-up safety system; we would have to balance the two, which was an incredibly difficult thing to do. There were two completely independent systems operating simultaneously, one going down as the other went up. I couldn't see how we were going to do that. Jeremy reckoned he might be able to do it, but he wasn't certain. So I said, "Well do we actually need it?" Ron had a very similar idea at a very similar time and said, "I was thinking the same thing, I'm not sure we need it either. Let's talk about it."

'So we tried it to see what happened, and it was just too much for the car. We got to the peak load and the car started squirming. If we'd had a little less load on the front we might have been able to manage, although it seems very unlikely. But it wasn't worth pushing the car, and me trying to drive through that every time, so we put the active back in but reduced its authority. Instead of running two and a half inches of ride height, we mechanically locked it halfway up at four inches minimum, and then the active did the extra two to two and a half inches. This was a compromise. The load was still going up at Mach point zero eight five, but not to the uncontrollable twelve to fourteen tons previously. The load would then start to fall again, with the active cutting in to stop it falling too far. The difference was that now, if the hydraulics did collapse, the higher minimum ride height would prevent the front wheels leaving the ground and *ThrustSSC* flipping.

'In Jeremy's position, I would have felt exactly the same as he did at the time. His perception was that it was already decided, and that wasn't correct. Ron and I had not agreed that it was what we were going to do. We had met to present it as an option, but unfortunately it came across as a decision that had already been taken, because we explained ourselves very poorly. I apologized to Jerry for that on several occasions. I was a great believer in the design-team concept, and was very concerned when Jeremy no longer wished to be a part of it. He was, at that time, incredibly busy, and he felt that there were other things he could more usefully do on the car, but I desperately missed his advice and input. The last thing I was going to do was overrule anyone in the design team; these were the people whose expertise was keeping me alive and our discussions were a way of watching out for each other's mistakes. I depended on them absolutely.

'Jeremy and I developed a very close relationship during the build of the *ThrustSSC* as there were a lot of discussions about the systems, the cockpit displays and controls, and the overall way this very complex machine would function. I know that Ron and Glynne felt isolated by this relationship, although they realized that it was inevitable.

'Once we got to Black Rock, with systems and structure largely complete, the problem became one of performance and development, and Ron and I started working very closely together, so that then Jeremy felt left out of the decision-making. Again, this was inevitable: Ron was our performance guru and I had to work with him to produce run profiles that I could actually drive, and drive accurately. In any case, the design team had to approve the profiles and everyone had their chance to make changes. Perhaps Ron and I presented it as a *fait accompli*, but it was hard to see how we could have done it differently.

'In fact, it was the wrong thing to try, but at least we found out that we could get away with a limited active system. That worked and we had a car that was safe at all speeds, even if we had a hydraulic failure. It made me feel happy and it made Jeremy feel happy, because his active suspension had been demonstrated as being necessary. The disadvantage was that it made the car slightly more unstable at the six hundred and thirty, six hundred and fifty m.p.h. point, but I was reasonably happy I could cope with that. It made the last few runs very hard work, but it was worth it.

'Once we'd sorted this out we were into the stage where routine test runs were seven hundred m.p.h. and above. The *Reno Gazette* quoted us as running low speed on the Friday because we did only six twenty-eight! The guys had done a fantastic job producing a car that was safe and reliable enough to do slow-speed testing at six hundred and twenty-eight m.p.h.!'

JEREMY BLISS

'Andy turned up and said, "I can't think of any safe way to do it other than this," which was locking it up fully. The lift was jumping up very rapidly as soon as you started moving into the transonic region, from five-fifty onwards. That was fine, but I just wish he'd talked to me about it first. He turned up at the meeting and said, "This is what we are going to do." So I said, "Do what the fuck you like."

'If I thought it would have been dangerous I would have fought it. But it was clear that I was up against Green, Bowsher and Ayers. They'd all decided already, so whatever I said was just going to heat the air.

'Apart from a couple of odd occasions I'd had no problems with Ron or Andy, though Glynne and I had our difficulties. Now I told them all I was quitting the design team because it had made a decision I simply couldn't believe in. What was the point of me being there if they weren't going to listen? I was disappointed with Ron going that way, but I kind of expected it with Andy. I think the project was taking a lot out of Ron, and I doubt that his opinion would have been the same had the situation arisen earlier in the trip. I thought that drivers should stick to driving and engineers to engineering. I didn't want to drive the fucking thing and I don't think he should have interfered so profoundly with the engineering side. Despite what he said, I don't think Andy liked the idea that there were civilians involved. He believed that the Air Force way was the best way. That's my personal feeling. However, in everyone's defence, I would say we were all fired up and we seemed to be taking it in turns to make dumb decisions. Sadly, on that day, three people decided to take a dumb decision at the same time.

'I thought, just like everyone else, that it would be all right with the active locked fully up. I was as surprised as them when *ThrustSSC* swerved so violently. Everyone wanted to keep it quiet, but it was all part of the story. It was Nick Dove who came up with the idea of using the shorter strut. I wouldn't let them rearm the active with the longer strut because there was too much potential for the active to destroy the back end of the car if it suddenly had to go to full extension. Even if it overextended with the shorter struts it would have done so only by an inch and a half, which would bend things but not break them.

'The design team met the following day. Ron, Glynne, Andy, me, Nick Dove, Chris Cowell and Mike Horne. Contrary to what the outside world might have believed, that was the design team. It wasn't just two men. Nick suggested the shorter strut, which was much better than the only other suggestion, which would have taken a week to implement. Now, if the system collapsed, the car would still generate enough downforce on the front wheels to keep the car on the ground. But it would be even more difficult to drive. A rear-steer car is inherently unstable and the *SSC* was an absolute bastard to drive. It was extremely difficult. I still think a rack-and-pinion steering would have lent itself to tight tolerances better than the worm-and-sector design we used.'

Andy and Jerry had established a very close relationship. Andy saw Jerry as the one guy who really understood the whole car; Ron and Glynne were compartmentalized to a certain extent on either aerodynamics or structures. Jerry was Andy's age, too, whereas Ron and Glynne were older. So I think that Jerry felt betrayed by the active decision, almost as if Andy had effectively said, 'Stuff you, Jerry Bliss, this is what we're going to do.'

After a long session with Jerry, I managed to get them all back together in a late-night meeting and smoothed things over, and gradually the teamwork came back again. I could appreciate just how Jerry felt, but walking out didn't help anyone.

The project's safety depended almost totally on the design and engineering team acting as a team, thoroughly discussing everything and agreeing the car modifications, run policies and profiles. If they ceased to work as a team and just took instructions, then the project would have lost that essential safety balance that protected the entire team. Under those circumstances it would be difficult to continue the project.

Nick Dove came up with a compromise solution. He realized that if he took out the longer shaft at the top of the rear suspension's hydraulic cylinder and replaced it with a shorter one, then under similar circumstances the shorter shaft wouldn't allow the suspension to make that initial drop that had so worried Andy. Now Andy could safely run with an increasing download; as that began to fall again over Mach 0.85 the active actually jacked the back of the car up to maintain a safe load on the front wheels. It was a clever bit of analysis, and everyone was relieved, not only because we'd solved a technical problem, but also because it had averted an emotional crisis. Had there been rather less emotion around, Nick's idea might have emerged earlier and we would have saved time. But by this stage we were all extremely tired and fraught.

The length of the parachute strops proved to be critical. If the strops were too long, ThrustSSC could be yanked violently from side to side during deceleration.

This incident really focused us, and we tried even harder to be very careful to avoid any temptation to make up time by taking two steps where our normal practice would have been to take one. We continued to edge the Mach number up point by point. All we'd done to date had been based on our *Thrust2* experience. But now we were into uncharted territory, 100 m.p.h. faster than *Thrust2* had ever gone, and we were beginning to encounter all sorts of new problems. The exhaust flames, for example, were beginning to curl round and meet at the back of the car, burning the parachutes.

The important thing was to keep all the emotion out of it. We were determined to avoid any temptation to say, 'Hell, let's just push ahead.' That was probably the biggest difference between ourselves and *Spirit of America*. The danger was in saying suddenly, 'Hey, it looks good. Let's give it another two points on the Mach meter and then we can all go home.' That's when we could hit real trouble.

What fascinated me was that we weren't getting the aerodynamic buffeting everybody had predicted. The question was, were we not going to get it at all? Or would it suddenly kick in at Mach 0.99? It might even be that the car would go supersonic really easily, against all expectations – but whatever happened we had to proceed step by step.

We began to discover all sorts of extraordinary effects the closer we got to Mach 1. Nobody has yet been able to explain them satisfactorily, because we made very few runs at that speed. One of the things we discovered is that the wheels were rotating more slowly than the car's forward speed. I'm sure that Ron will continue to investigate the data we acquired, because his is the inquisitive engineer's mind that doesn't like questions without answers.

The key thing is that, because of the active ride, the load on the front suspension was always predictable and controllable, whereas on *Thrust2*, as we subsequently discovered, the load was decreasing the faster we went. But what was happening was that the airflow and the shock waves under the car, and possibly ahead of the front wheels, were absolutely pulverizing and destroying the hard desert surface. So both the front and rear wheels were running along in some sort of crumbly ruts, some of them as deep as four inches below the desert surface, yet they were still carrying the load.

As the design team began pulling together again, we knew we had learned a valuable lesson, and not a moment too soon. After the 714-m.p.h. record, everything we had tried had worked, and if we hadn't actually become complacent, we had become just a mite too confident. Jackie Stewart once said that whenever an inexperienced team – and we were still inexperienced at the speeds we were achieving – is successful, they suddenly think they are invincible and they relax. Without us realizing it at the time, that was what we had started to do. The design team had been starting to break up, and it actually broke over the active issue. The scare with the active system showed us that we were fundamentally tired and jerked us back to reality as if we were on a leash, just as sending home the two contractors in Jordan One had shaken everyone up. Success had threatened our vigilance.

One of the most important decisions we made in the entire project was not to have a chief engineer. I know Andy disagreed, but that put an absolute obligation on all the guys in the design team to talk to each other and work together.

Back in the design and construction stage there had been a time when Glynne complained that nobody was communicating with him, and I had intervened to tell everyone to phone him the following week. It worked. Now I called everyone on the design team together and demanded to know their problems. Our system depended upon a completely different kind of management where everyone was held responsible for their own sections. They managed themselves, but every now and then they needed leadership. I was facing personal bankruptcy, and there was no way I was going to let anyone wreck the machinery we had all built up together. Once I realized the machine had been broken, getting everyone talking to each other again and hammering out the differences was the only way to fix it. Jerry Bliss got it right when he said, 'I honestly believe that after breaking the *Thrust2* record we let egos confuse the situation and we lost our way. We regained it when Andy swerved across two tracks. We didn't expect that. We thought it would be safe, and it wasn't. And at that time the whole team thought, Shit! And then we all got back together again and we started acting like a team, and not like a bunch of egomaniacs.'

ThrustSSC was back in action again on 6 October, when we watched Craig Breedlove run at 531 m.p.h. before it was our turn again. Andy averaged 714 m.p.h. and 727 m.p.h. respectively. The first gave us our required increment to Mach 0.95 at last, the second was a hair below Mach 0.97. A stripped bolt in one of the rear-wheel access panels prevented him returning within the hour, but for once it didn't really matter. In its further-revised trim, the car was running properly again, and both Andy and Ron were happy with it once more. Andy felt that the new set-up was slightly better than the one used on the record run, and that we now had a trim that would allow us to run at supersonic speeds. Jerry seemed happy, too. We were back on track again.

Richard Meredith-Hardy, one of the intrepid microlight pilots who did such a fine job for us patrolling the desert to ensure that no uncleared vehicles, or 'bandits' as Jayne Millington called them, had sneaked onto the desert, was aloft in *Pegasus Black* with Bev Slaughter of Castrol during both runs, and they reported that they could see a shock wave emanating from both sides of the car for about 150 feet, and trailing slightly. It was the first sign of the supersonic shock wave. Andy said he could hear it going over the cockpit, though he couldn't actually feel it. It was an eerie sound, he told us: like a banshee wail.

'It's very rare to see shock waves except in very humid conditions,' Ron said, 'but it sounds like one under the car. It may be sucking dust off the ground which gives a flow visualization. I won't know until I see pictures.'

Andy was asked how stable the track was, and he replied, 'The track was completely stable. It hasn't moved all day.'

We had regained our sense of humour, and we had learned our lesson. We had avoided disaster by the skin of our teeth. Our design team was like a group of mountaineers roped together: as they had slipped they had nearly fallen as one, but each individual was just strong enough to hang on until rescued, and now they were climbing again. We had the summit in sight.

21 BOOM OR BUST

We actually went supersonic for the first time on Tuesday, 7 October. I personally am convinced of that, and so are one or two other team members, but we have no official evidence to back up our conviction because it was an untimed run. We had done it quietly, if you can say that about the sonic booms that some claimed to have heard. We simply closed off the Black Rock Desert, made apologies to the media, and made a run at short notice, so few people knew we were out. That was the day it became absolutely clear that we really did have the potential to drive through the sound barrier.

Once the design team had proved that we had to use the active ride, and that any further progress was totally dependent on it, that was our last big lesson. It would be very wrong to suggest that it was an anticlimax when *ThrustSSC* finally lived up to its name and went supersonic. But we just seemed to achieve that last stage very easily.

On Monday, 13 October we set out to do it officially, timed by USAC, in two directions and within the allotted hour. We achieved two of those goals, but there was to be an agonizing twist. On his first run Andy achieved a fantastic speed of 749.876 m.p.h., the fastest *ThrustSSC* had ever gone, mere fractions below Mach 1. But there was a delay. A transformer had worked loose, and as the sixty minutes ticked away we lost the run. There was enough time remaining for two more if we were quick, however. As Andy started the first of these, I held my breath. As usual, Jayne Millington was the runs controller. A squadron leader herself, she was ideally suited to the role, while also able to help out on the car in numerous technical areas. Her voice came over the radio, '*SSC*, you are cleared supersonic. Your discretion.'

Andy roared through the mile. When they came, the figures were fantastic: 764.168 m.p.h.! The fastest yet.

It seemed an age before Dave Petrali in the USAC timing stand finally and calmly gave us our Mach number. When he did, it was precisely what we wanted to hear: Mach 1.007. We were officially through the sound barrier! *ThrustSSC* had gone supersonic!

The problem was that we had to stifle our elation; we couldn't celebrate yet. We had to make a third run within the hour to act as a new return in order to make it official, and we now learned that Andy had overrun by just under a mile and a half, after yet another parachute had failed as a result of heat damage from the engines' afterburner flames. The Supacat was dispatched to drag him back to the start position for the new run, but this took agonizing minutes.

At the press pen, Sally and I had to endure an awful drawn-out wait in front of the assembled media. What made it worse was that we were eating into time allocated for the *Spirit of America* team – but in a fabulous, sporting gesture Craig simply said, 'Give them the playa!'

ThrustSSC was no dragster. To prevent the engines hoovering up the desert, Andy always had to accelerate very gently to 70 m.p.h.

The minutes crept by. Then Andy came roaring back past us a third time. On the cockpit tapes, just before he took off, he'd said, 'We've got a minute and a half to get this car rolling. As soon as I see Nick I'm going for it,' but nobody knew whether he was within the time limit. Then there was Dave Petrali with the speed: 760.135 m.p.h. We already knew that we'd beaten Mach 1, because we'd heard the sonic boom. But had Andy started too late? Or had we just scraped through? It was mental torture. If he'd scraped through then we were home and dry, it was all over.

Jayne radioed the timing stand for confirmation. A few moments later we heard Petrali's reply: 'I'm sorry, I cannot confirm. You missed it by about a minute.'

We'd failed. By precisely 49.6 miserable seconds. Less than a minute denied us our place in the history books. It was a crushing letdown.

The team was terribly disappointed, but we knew that, if we could do it once, we could damn well do it again. We just had to pick ourselves back up and make sure it worked properly the next time.

During these supersonic runs *ThrustSSC* was taking a terrible beating. The acoustic battering on the rear panels was springing rivets on every run, and there was a real risk of damage to the internal bracing. There was so much repair work to be done, plus modifications to the parachutes, that we couldn't possibly run on the Tuesday and would have to work hard to be ready for Wednesday. Up to 1,200 rivets were replaced on those rear panels and cracks in the titanium tail were stop-drilled to prevent them spreading. Some internal stiffeners on the underbody panels had to be replaced. Robbie Kraike spent all day and half the night working on the parachutes to protect them from further heat damage.

Wednesday, 15 October, dawned bright and sharp. I'm sure some people will find it hard to believe, but that morning I had no feeling that we were on the threshold of a historic moment. I didn't have any thoughts of Sir Edmund Hillary or Chuck Yeager in my head, nothing like that at all, as Andy Green prepared to take *ThrustSSC* back into territory that only he had ever charted.

The truth is, I suppose, that these things are only romantic on paper, or after the event. Believe me, there was nothing remotely romantic about it at the time. I had been at it for so long, and there was this 'mustn't cock up' sort of mentality to it, just as there had been fourteen years earlier with *Thrust2*. That always intrudes into it. The rest of the world might have seen what we were doing as a romantic joust with the unknown, but when you're actually out there on the desert you're so close to reality and you're just concentrating so much on doing it properly and not cocking anything up. There just isn't the luxury of time to relax or think any such fancy thoughts. You are simply stuck out there, focusing on the job, while the media keeps hammering you with questions.

I'd been up since before five o'clock that morning. The pressure was simply enormous, and had been for many weeks. Like the rest of the team, Sally and I had never stopped working. It wasn't just looking after the media side while we were running *ThrustSSC* during the day. There was the financial

Early morning, and final preparations are made before a run.

side as well, and we were doing that late into the night and often into the next morning. This didn't leave time for sleep. As soon as I got back from the day's activities on the desert, at six or seven o'clock in the evening, there'd be work to do. Then, at about nine o'clock, I'd usually go out to the desert again, to the pit station, in order to send and collect any e-mails. There was a constant flow of these. It didn't help that at the very time I'd want to be winding down in America, in England things would be winding up at the start of the day because of the eight-hour time difference.

That morning I just grabbed a bowl of cereal for breakfast and then headed out for the desert by about seven o'clock, in time for Adam Northcote-Wright, who'd taken over from Martyn Davidson as head of operations when Martyn's leave expired, to give the day's briefing. I didn't say much, if anything. As far as I was concerned the ground had been covered adequately, and I'd been in on the previous evening's design meeting, so I knew what we were looking at. The machinery was operating smoothly, like clockwork, and everyone knew what they had to do. Today's target was very straightforward: two runs averaging at least Mach 1.01. As usual, there was a bit of banter, but everyone was very focused. After Monday's near miss, we were all very aware of what the day might represent.

Immediately after the briefing and the roll-out of the car my job was to meet the media at Access Two, the second entry point onto the desert, and take them out to the press pen. For me this was always a difficult time, and that day was the worst because I was getting very anxious. We were all getting seriously tired, to the point where I began to wonder whether somebody might make a stupid mistake. I was worried sick that it might be me. We also had to contend with the fact that several of our key people were living on extensions of extensions of their time. Within the next few days I knew that a lot of them were going to have to go home.

Nick Dove wanted the car in the workshop for a full inspection within the next three or four runs. That would have taken up at least four days as the team worked on its complex systems, and four days meant another $20,000. We were already well beyond the edge financially, which was something that never ceased nagging in the background. It didn't intrude at all that morning, though. We just had to do it, and that was that. It was once in a lifetime. I wouldn't even contemplate a situation where we'd have to call it off because of the money. You'd regret that for the rest of your life – that was your one chance and you blew it because you were worried about the debts. We were half a million dollars in the hole, but there was no way we could stop now.

One of the things I will always remember from that day in particular was Jayne Millington's voice. It took tremendous courage day after day to go through the nervous tension of leaving Andy to get into the car and drive it.

I could appreciate just how Jayne must have felt. Watching something like that from the press pen was a really unnerving experience for me, too. Prior to the *ThrustSSC* programme, of course, I'd always been the one doing the driving. I suppose it's that old thing where you can do something as a child without the faintest idea what effect it has on your watching parents; then, when you're a parent yourself, you go through it all from a different angle with your own children and begin to appreciate what emotions your actions must have evoked.

I was quite seriously worried and frightened by it all, which may seem strange given what we had achieved with *Thrust2*.

Most of the people around me in the press pen were just terribly excited, pure and simple. As you'd expect them to be. After all, how many times do you get to watch the only supersonic car on earth blasting across a desert in the middle of nowhere? Of course it's superficially exhilarating. But then I was much closer to it all. And I'd seen what had happened to the scale model of *ThrustSSC* at Pendine's rocket test track: that had been a horrifyingly graphic illustration of what those gigantic aerodynamic forces could do. The success of subsequent tests had been crucial to our decision to go ahead and build *ThrustSSC*. But the trouble with these things is that people can develop a very blasé view of them. 'Yeah, it's all right. It'll do another run. It'll be OK. Don't worry.'

The reality is that we were a responsible, safety-conscious organization, and that basically we were all aware of what could happen if it went wrong. Watching from the midpoint of the desert you could see that car accelerate with maximum afterburner from around 200 m.p.h., and by God it *went*! Several days earlier I'd been flying a light aircraft down that course, and I was absolutely appalled to see that none of Andy's tracks was straight. The deviations were very obvious. That was when I truly appreciated what a hell of a job he'd been doing, because the reality is that under those circumstances many drivers would simply have given up. The car was clearly not directionally stable at high speeds, and he had to fight it right through Mach 1.

Nick Dove would say at the end of a run that Andy was absolutely vibrating, he'd been so stressed up. So it was a fantastic personal achievement.

We just don't know what caused the problem, but every time Andy hit 590 m.p.h. the car would leap sideways 30–50 feet out of line. Every time, always

JAYNE MILLINGTON

'Coming from a position of complete ignorance, and knowing nothing about land-speed record-breaking, I was initially a little bit concerned, because obviously the magnitude of the project was such that it was clearly no amateurish venture. As I knew so little about the project, I think such concern was natural, but nevertheless it was what Andy wanted to do, and I certainly

Throughout every run, Jayne kept the team informed of progress as she and Martyn Davidson controlled all movements on the desert.

wasn't going to stand in his way because I knew he would never put himself in a position where there was any great risk of danger. As we became more involved with the project, I went to great lengths to find out every detail; no design aspects of the car were hidden from me, and it helped that, after a fashion, I understood most of it, even though *ThrustSSC* is not a simple beast. I went to great lengths to understand it, because I thought that only through understanding it could I actually come to terms with the fact that they were designing a car with safety in mind. I was very impressed from the start, as soon as I met Jeremy and Ron and realized the extent of their ability and their research. I knew it was going to be as safe a project as was humanly possible. I also knew that Andy was not the sort of person to take unnecessary risks. My initial concern quickly gave way to a calm acceptance of what was coming.

'It helped to be involved. I think the worst thing in the world would have been to be on the sidelines. I knew I had something to give, so I was quite happy to be involved. That worked on the practical side with the wiring and the systems work, helping out Jeremy and his team – particularly when Robert Atkinson lost his finger in Jordan One.

'It was also a great thing to be able to give what my RAF experience had given to me, which was for me to operate the radios and become a more pivotal team member, helping Martyn Davidson out with his excellent operational management.

'In terms of being worried while Andy was driving, I wasn't, because I was so completely immersed in what I had to do. I would have let him down if I'd been worried. It would have impaired my ability to work, and, of course, the RAF has taught me that the job comes first, and that's what I do every day as a fighter controller. So, like Andy, it was an extension of my day job.

'I think some people were a bit worried when Jeremy suggested I be runs controller. I think they wanted to shield me from the emotional pressure, which was touching. And in retrospect it was understandable, because they didn't understand what my day job involved. But it was great to be a part of the team, and I think that without the military people, such as Martyn and Adam, a lot of the logistical problems wouldn't have been overcome. The last thing anybody wanted was people being regimented, but I think we rose to the various challenges in a disciplined manner. I'm particularly thinking of the dreadful day when we had to evacuate at the end of Jordan One!

'Andy and I always talked things through, and on many occasions he invited me out to see his tracks. Though I wasn't part of the design team I was usually in pit station when they were debriefing with the video material. So I knew what was going on, and Andy made sure I knew because I would have found out anyway, one way or another. The tracks were a bit of a dead give-away whenever I was out fodding. He dealt with things exceptionally well, and he had a plan. He knew what he had to do to control the car. I wasn't in Jordan Two when his

Andy and his girlfriend, Jayne Millington, who had her own fan club amongst the American scanner-equipped watchers on the Nevada hillside.

problems with the car's steering seemed to be at their greatest, so there might have been more heart-to-heart then, or else I might have had to give him a little more space. But by the time we got to Nevada he knew exactly what to do.

'Both of us wanted to project a professional approach, but I think that came naturally because we knew that it was a serious business. There was room for a little bit of humour, but when we got down to it, we were first and foremost professionals. Five per cent of my brain was thinking, Hmm, that's my partner out there doing that. But the rest of it was just devoted to listening and ensuring that I would be equal to it when he called, if he called.'

*Looking along the run with
ThrustSSC in the foreground.*

to the left. It reached a point where, at 590 m.p.h., he would turn the wheel right in order to oppose *ThrustSSC* going left; it was just so predictable. Whether it was a question of shock waves establishing underneath, or some other aerodynamic effect we'll probably never know.

Then there was the constant battle damage that *ThrustSSC* was suffering on every run. We really were hammering it, and there was vibration from the ground, from the engines and from the transonic buffeting, plus the thermal effects from the jet exhausts. It was a tremendous battle for the people involved with the engineering and electronics and computers, which often needed frequent attention, sometimes during the one-hour turnaround. Thankfully, we were a highly motivated and professional team.

ANDY GREEN

'At seven hundred m.p.h. the loads between each front wheel differed by more than a ton, which they didn't do subsonically. There were a lot of shock waves around the front of the car, which may be why it behaved so oddly.

'The transonic Percival Jet Provost trainer aircraft was limited to around Mach point seven three; it had thick wings over which the airflow would start to go supersonic near this limit. As a training demonstration we used to dive the aircraft to exceed Mach point seven in order to produce shock waves. If there was a mile or two an hour difference in air speed over the wings it could cause a shock wave to form over one wing and not the other. The difference could be the result of the thickness of a coat of paint or a rivet that wasn't completely flush. That would give you a shock one side and not the other, and a shock stall where one wing would drop. It can happen to jumbo jets if they fly too high.

'The same thing may have happened with the car. The loads on the front wheels would be almost perfectly matched until around six hundred and thirty m.p.h., Mach point eight five, when the shock waves started to appear and the front-wheel loads would start to diverge. There were other factors, too, but when the car started to diverge it was accelerating very quickly through the transonic region and the net result was that it would diverge left around five hundred and ninety indicated m.p.h. Give or take five m.p.h., the wail would start over the canopy as the shock waves formed, and at that stage the car would be at its most unstable and start to go left. Sometimes it was dramatically bad, and it was always worse going from south to north, perhaps because that part of the desert surface was softer. Sometimes I hardly felt it. Each time I would try to stop the yaw rate building up by making a quick input to counter the divergence.

'From six hundred and fifty m.p.h. plus, once it was over the hump, the car became almost completely stable again. If you looked at the tracks within the measured mile, they looked as if they'd been drawn with a ruler. On the test pilot scale of undrivability, if it was seven or eight in that tricky period, it was probably at three or four in the measured mile. Much easier to cope with.'

During the downtime on the Tuesday we'd taken the opportunity, while panels were off the car for some remedial work, to have a look at the structure in the parts where the main bending moments were, just behind the cockpit. We were enormously relieved to find that they were as sound as the day they were built, despite the terrible pounding the car had received in Jordan. It was a tremendous tribute to Glynne's chassis.

The faster we went, however, the more strain we were putting the car under, so we could never be complacent. We never knew what might suddenly fail. It took sixty runs before a transducer in the active system failed. It had never happened before, but suddenly the pounding had become too much. We just never knew what lay over the next horizon, where the next weak spot might be.

Glynne Bowsher bore the brunt of the criticism of his controversial rear-wheel steering, but coped admirably with the stress and uncertainty before we were able to prove his radical concept.

So while I was standing there in the middle of the course, waiting for those momentous runs, all this was going through my mind – as everybody else seemed to be preparing for a couple of minutes' superficial entertainment.

Every time I saw *ThrustSSC* accelerating like a bullet for the mile I'd think, God Almighty! Christ, that thing really is shifting! Then Andy would come past. On film it all looks so effortless and so easy. Standing there, watching it coming up, knowing that at 590 m.p.h. it jumped 50 feet off line, knowing that every single one of our previous tracks was as wavy as hell, was very different. We'd been conditioned really by seeing it do the same thing so many times, looking absolutely steady as a rock as it seared by like a huge black American locomotive. So dependable and so reliable that it almost became commonplace. But it had once seemed commonplace for Donald Campbell's team, too, until it all so suddenly went wrong. I've never felt so helpless as when I watched *ThrustSSC* hurtle past. Despite all the care, all the effort and all the struggle that had gone into the project, it was now out of our hands. Once the car was at speed, there was absolutely nothing any of us except Andy could do.

With *Thrust2* I'd been right at the centre of the action, now I was a spectator. With *ThrustSSC* I was quite relaxed when it was running up to 650 m.p.h. The car gave the impression of actually going very, very straight, and being nailed to the deck. In point of fact it wasn't like that at all, but somehow it created that kind of illusion.

When we started going into the 700s, however, I started to feel this fear. What worried me more than anything was the idea that we might have created an organization that would press on until there was an appalling accident. If we had created such an organization, it was my job to jump in and stop it quick and say, 'That's it, we're going home.'

We had taken every safety precaution we could think of. Primary safety is all about making the design as perfect as possible in the first place to minimize the chances of an accident. By the layout of *ThrustSSC*, we knew we'd come up with a fundamental concept that should have been stable aerodynamically. We knew there was a good, solid 1g loading on the front wheels, so we knew the car wouldn't fly.

Then there were the secondary safety aspects, which were concerned with what happened in the event of an accident. We had protected Andy by cocooning him in a fireproof cockpit between the two engines. We also had the Jaguar Firechase to act as a high-speed accident-intervention vehicle, and the Merlo could lift up to ten tons. In the event of the car overturning it could be on hand very quickly to lift the car to facilitate Andy's rescue.

We had survived two mishaps that could have been fatal, and the design team was finding its feet again after it had reached breaking point. Here we had a car that was right on the edge, doing something that had never been done before. We truly didn't know what was happening underneath *ThrustSSC*. We knew that it was digging this huge broad hole in the desert, where it was smashing up the surface across its own 12-foot width and beyond that, as it created this bloody great shock wave 150 feet wide on either side. We knew the front wheels were going round

Fast intervention was essential if anything went wrong. Just as they had in the Thrust2 days, Jaguar came up trumps with the famous XJ-R Firechase, fully equipped by Kidde.

Andy streaks towards the measured mile, on the first leg of the supersonic record run, 15 October 1997.

slower than they should be, even if we didn't quite know why. There was also an awful lot we didn't know. How could we? Nobody had been here before.

At the back of all this, I knew, too, that we had only this one chance to break the sound barrier. We just didn't have enough money to carry on. I'd been very shaken by the lack of response from British industry. We had one hell of a project, but they just hadn't responded. They didn't seem to be interested. We were reaching 100 million television viewers every night in most countries around the world, and generating, at its peak, more than three million hits a day on the Internet. Accesses had peaked at 11 million a week, and overall we would total 56 million. And the sponsors weren't interested.

I was very proud of our Internet figures; we had delivered the 1 million hits per day that I'd promised Digital, and more. That was a fabulous achievement in itself and testament to Jeremy Davey's absolute dedication to the task.

I was amazed that the sponsors' response, even at this stage, was so poor. We were looking for a five-figure sum to help us through, we were knocking on the door of the world's first supersonic land-speed record – and British industry didn't

Perspective is lent to Andy's progress by the USAC timekeepers' motorhome, just by the entry to the mile.

want to know. There was the tailfin, the prime sponsors' spot on the car, ready to be photographed all round the world, and nobody wanted it. They seemed to prefer to spend their money on Formula One, where they might be lucky to get a minute or two's exposure unless they paid huge sums to be on the winning cars. It was unbelievable. We'd already got the biggest increase in land-speed-record history – and no new sponsors. Only Sterling Software, who employed our Internet webmaster, Jeremy Davey, took up our challenge in the closing stages. The truth was that the public were much more interested in what we were doing than the corporates, who ignored it at their peril. If they lost touch with their public, that was their funeral.

Just before nine o'clock in the morning Jayne began the countdown to our most crucial run to date, and at eight minutes past the hour she announced that *ThrustSSC* was rolling. There it came, the big black express. That day in particular I kept saying to myself, 'God help us, let's hope it's going to be all right. Please let us make it.' I took a deep breath as Andy thundered through the mile, making one hell of a noise, and then, once he was through, I felt I could relax, as if once he'd got through the measured mile everything was going to be all right.

Then we heard the sonic boom cracking across the desert. The team cheered, and cheered again when Petrali told us what we so badly needed to know: speed: 759.333 m.p.h., Mach 1.015. We were halfway there, but could we get back within the hour?

This time there had been no problems with the parachutes, and just after Craig Breedlove had sportingly joined us, Jayne announced, '*SSC* with Firechase rolling. Clear supersonic. Clear supersonic.' It was four minutes after ten. We were bang on target.

The second run was almost worse emotionally, and again there was this awful feeling: 'Are we going to make it? For God's sake don't let us have an accident.'

Then Andy came hurtling past. This time we didn't hear the sonic boom, but those near the timekeepers, a quarter of a mile closer to the track, already knew

Craig Breedlove reached 636 m.p.h. in Spirit of America – Sonic Arrow.

what Petrali would soon tell us. They knew ten miles away in Gerlach, too, where the sonic booms had thrown plates and pictures off dresser shelves and walls, where the fire-extinguisher sprinkler-caps in the school had been shaken off, where the postmistress became distressed. I hadn't taken out insurance against supersonic booms, but fortunately there were no claims.

'Your speed through the mile was seven six six point six zero nine m.p.h.,' Dave said, and after an agonizing delay, 'Your Mach number was one point zero two.'

We'd made it! Both ways. Within the hour. The world's first supersonic land-speed record. Sally and I hugged each other. It was one hell of a moment. Of course everyone wanted to know how I felt. I remembered what Donald Campbell had said when he broke the land-speed record back in 1964: 'I'm just glad we've got the bastard.' At that moment I knew exactly what he meant. All I could say at first was, 'We bloody did it! Thank God it's over.'

The average speed across both runs, the new official land-speed record, was 763.035 m.p.h. Our second run reached a peak of 771 m.p.h., Mach 1.03. It was a fabulous achievement.

Andy got back to the team at the pit station before I did. By the time I arrived with the media crowd, which was clamouring for the story, he'd already voiced the conclusion I had privately come to. He was all too aware that we were getting this enormous drag increase at the far side of Mach 1, and that the car really wasn't going to go much faster. On top of that we had an organization that was exhausted, one that had already started to lose people. Andy simply stood up and said, 'That's it, I'm going home.' I thought, Great, that's absolutely fine by me.

Andy Green gives a press conference.

RON AYERS

'The real sound barrier wasn't technical. It was psychological.

'About a week before our final run we peaked at Mach point nine nine. There had been plenty of performance in hand. Extrapolating from that point, it looked as though we could get fairly comfortably up to about Mach one point zero five or thereabouts. We were beginning to talk quite glibly about whether we should try for eight hundred m.p.h. But as soon as we got over M equals one, over our initial barrier, we suddenly found it was like hitting a wall. The drag was going up enormously just around the point when the drag coefficient should have been levelling off. At the time we didn't know why this was happening. It may have been that the transonic drag rise hadn't actually reached its peak. The other explanation was that the ground was being pummelled by the shock waves and creating a twelve-foot-wide ploughed field instead of four separate wheel tracks. Ploughing such a field at seven hundred and sixty m.p.h. would clearly take an enormous amount of energy, and the wheels would then be running in a kind of fluidized bed instead of on the smooth, packed surface.

'The shock wave was much as I'd envisaged it, fanning out at the front of the car, but I hadn't expected to get flow visualization. Various people up on the spur said they could see the shock wave suddenly spreading out like a pair of wings. Quite incredible.

'Immediately after setting the supersonic record my reaction was nothing. Well, not much. There was relief that we'd succeeded before the weather, or lack of money, had stopped us. And there was certainly relief that we hadn't had an accident, because even with all the precautions and research, we could only minimize the risk. We could never totally eliminate it.

'It may sound arrogant, and I don't mean it to, but I wasn't surprised at our success. I had worked on the project for five and a half years; I'd thought deeply about it and was totally confident in the underlying design philosophy. If at any point I'd lost that confidence I would have called a halt. We had cautiously approached the speed of sound in small steps, checking everything as we went. Two days earlier we had just missed the supersonic record. We had persevered, and now we'd succeeded. That seemed like justice. We had simply achieved the target we had set for ourselves.

'The reaction came later, when I saw the effect on other people. As we returned with *ThrustSSC* to pit station after the final run, we were mobbed.

As if by magic, that remote desert wilderness was now full of people shouting and cheering. Some were even crying. One man was bellowing, "This is the greatest day of my life – I've seen history made!" Then there was the message from the prime minister, and one from the Queen, and the thousands of e-mails and faxes, and the millions of Internet hits. So after all the setbacks and lack of financial support, the world really did care about what we had done. Then, suddenly, I felt very proud.

'It had worked. But if it had gone wrong and we'd suffered a fatal accident, there would have been no shortage of people to say, "I told you so." Most technical experts were constructive and helpful, if understandably cautious. But the worrying ones were those who would say categorically that travelling supersonically on land was stupid and impossible, and I was irresponsible to risk someone's life in the attempt. When pressed, these critics weren't able to identify weaknesses in the design, or say why our quest was impossible. Their objections were always vague and sometimes demonstrably wrong, but they remained implacably critical anyway. Their comments reminded me of the navigational charts of the Middle Ages. The known world in the centre of the sheet was surrounded by pictures of mythical beasts, with the stark warning to unwary mariners, "Here Be Serpents." We had pressed on despite these pessimists and we had succeeded, but it was certainly a great relief to feel that they could not now boast of their prescience. I had still to learn that they would instead say, "See, it wasn't so difficult after all. Come to think of it, your twin-engined design with active suspension was pretty obvious, really."

'As I said, the real sound barrier wasn't technical. It was psychological.'

Craig Breedlove sportingly joined the celebrations after we went supersonic.

OTHER VOICES

GLYNNE BOWSHER

'It just felt good. Some people said it couldn't be done, but the booms were there on the film, there for the timekeepers and there to be heard by history.

'*ThrustSSC* did what we designed it to do. I like to think that Ron's concept was proven. It doesn't mean to say that a different concept won't do the same thing. But it was our concept that did the job. There were difficulties. I will say that rear-wheel steering worked well enough for Andy to set two world records, even though he had to work hard. A front-wheel-steered car may have been better, but that wasn't possible within our layout.

'In all fairness, Ron, Richard and Andy never stopped supporting what I was doing, which was tremendous. There was never a shortage of people coming to tell me what a lot of rubbish rear-wheel steering was, and that it couldn't work – but they didn't and they stayed with it, Andy most of all. He made it work for me.'

Pit station had become bedlam, with everyone shouting and laughing and wanting to shake Andy's hand and know how it had felt to create history. People were hugging each other and slapping backs, and champagne was flowing. Even before Andy could finish speaking one of the microlights was airborne, trailing a sign saying 'M1', and an air ambulance was doing low passes and waggling its wings in celebration. All the spectators who had so faithfully camped out along the road to Soldier Meadows came pouring down onto the playa, anxious to add their own tributes and offer congratulations. We had beaten the world, and everyone wanted to share a historic moment.

Suddenly it was all over. All the years of hope, strain, fatigue and uncertainty were finished. We had succeeded, and done what people had said was impossible. We had claimed the world's first supersonic land-speed record, and to the watching world we had made it seem easy. It was only ten thirty on a glorious morning, and I wondered what we were going to do for the rest of the day.

But one or two people in the team wanted to push on towards 800 m.p.h. 'Richard, you know, that's the wrong

Atop Rob Hemper's shoulders, Andy relishes our success with a triumphant salute.

decision,' Rod Barker said to me. 'We should have stuck with it. We should have changed to the 205 engines and pushed on.' The 205s had another 2,500 pounds of thrust in each of them, 5,000 total. That would have made quite some difference to the 42,000 pounds we had to begin with. But we were in an area of complete and utter uncertainty, and we just didn't know whether the drag would lessen if we could only go a little bit faster, or whether it would simply increase.

Ron's view was that we were generating so much damage to the desert that the rolling drag was accounting for a tremendous amount of power. We already had a problem with fuel capacity. It was also possible that the extra power might accelerate the car faster and get it to the mile quickly enough to ensure the fuel didn't run out. Ron thought that, providing we'd been able to get the car up to that speed without running out of fuel, the extra 15 per cent power might have been absorbed, just creating more drag with only a minimal increase in speed.

Then there was the extraordinary situation where Jerry's data system was showing that we had good aerodynamic download on the front suspension, so no problem there, but that the wheels were underspeeding. So how the hell did you explain that? Jerry's data system was extremely clever and accurate and incredibly reliable, so you had to believe it. What was happening? It was only worth further risk if we could reach 800 m.p.h., and we seriously doubted we could get to that figure. Anything less was academic after the sound-barrier success.

There was one hell of a party in Gerlach afterwards. Andy rode his motorcycle straight into several of Gerlach's bars, with Jayne riding pillion. The celebrations lasted until late. The risk in pressing on simply wasn't worth it. We'd achieved what we went to Black Rock for, and most of the team were very happy with that. In photographs showing the shock waves I subsequently saw a detached wave ahead of the car on its supersonic run. That was something we hadn't expected, and which would need investigating were we to continue.

Frankly, hardly anybody in the team wanted to carry on. We were absolutely right to stop when we did.

When you've broken the sound barrier on land, you can get away with most things! Crew members Ian 'Radar' Dennington and Chris Cowell congratulate Andy as he and Jayne Millington ride his motorbike into the Miners' Club in Gerlach on the day the record fell.

OTHER VOICES

ANDY GREEN

'On that penultimate run I ended up fifty feet off line with ninety degrees of steering lock. And looking at another white line altogether. I would have shut it down there and then had I crossed it; had I needed more than ninety degrees of steering to slow down the yaw rate. On the tape you can hear a note of concern in my voice, but then I said, "On the wrong line. It's coming back. I'll worry about that later." And that was simply because I'd already recognized that I was driving up a line I would need for my second run. But I knew that then I'd be running over it with the parachute out, slowing down, and, in fact, on the return run I just steered very slightly round it. No big deal.

'Always the doubt throughout the project was, "Where was the money going to come from?" Richard is the one man who never gave up. He kept going and kept going, and kept pestering companies. He kept going to convince them that we did know what we were doing, and that we really were going to do it.

'I can fully understand any company not wanting to get involved with something that's not fully guaranteed, and for which they had to take our word. There were six land-speed-record teams when we started; five of them had to be lying about winning the race, but the companies that came with us trusted that we were telling the truth and that we were going to win! Very great credit to them. We went out and our aim was to show the whole world that British technology and British engineering and British cars are still the best and the fastest in the world.

'One of the things that always gave me such confidence in the project was that the team made really difficult things look easy, even when they were working very hard, under pressure. I knew how hard they were working and it just didn't show. That's a sign of how professional they were.

'I was really pleased that I'd been able to put so much into it, but it was only the same as Ron, Glynne, Jerry, Richard and all the rest of the team

Sign here please, sir. Andy obliges as Dick Myers of the Bureau of Land Management gives him a mock citation for speeding on the desert.

putting in their effort over the years. But the greatest pleasure was to be a part of a bunch of guys who did something remarkable. That's not just a glib line. If I'd gone round telling them what to do, yes, I'd have felt tremendous satisfaction. That it was my car and they all worked for me. But it didn't work like that. We all had our own bits to do. And if you'd taken any one of those guys out of the equation, it wouldn't have happened. It was tremendously satisfying, but I can't say, "Yeah, I made a huge input to the supersonic land-speed record." We all did. The team created that record and we all had an essential part to play in it. That was the satisfying bit. It still amazes me that we did it.

'I only ever took one decision about running the car without having first agreed it with the rest of the design team. That was the decision to stop. I had spoken in depth to every member of the design team about further runs and how things were holding up – they were all getting concerned about the battering *ThrustSSC* was taking. Not one of us said so, but I could see in each person's eyes the thought that we had reached a sensible limit and it was time to stop. Even Richard had offered me the chance to stop as soon as I wanted – it was the first time I had ever heard him express any negative sentiments about running the car. It was a sign of just how concerned he was becoming. I knew they would all back me when I stood in front of the press and told them we were finished. It was over.

'Later somebody came up to me just after I'd made that announcement and said, "We stopped at the right time – we did just the right number of runs." And my reply was immediate: "No, we did two runs too many." We had been very close to the edge.

'People have asked me what it will mean if others go faster, but does it matter? Even if Craig Breedlove took all his friends to the top of the land-speed Everest and had a massive dinner party, when he gets there he'll still find the Union Flag flying at the top, because we were there first.'

JEREMY BLISS

'To be honest, my first reaction when we finally got the supersonic record was, "Thank fuck we don't have to run that thing again!"'

'Looking back, I think the real credit has to go to Richard. It was always clear that he had no intention of carrying it on beyond 1997. I knew that in January. The project took a lot out of him, and he was the one who kept all the momentum going all the time, when others were flagging. He has taken so much stress over this. OK, he can be a bit bonkers occasionally, but you can't really hold that against him. He has shouldered enormous pressure.

'I liked Richard's idea of having a one-level organization. If we were going to have problems, he wanted us to talk about them internally and present a united face to the outside world. Others didn't agree.

'I really began to respect Richard a lot when he would come into meetings and say, "Right, it's shit. We're in the pooh, we've got no money, we're x thousand in debt." Once he stopped all this, "I can feel it, it's coming right," stuff and just said, "This is the situation, it's not very good, this is what we've got to do," I just thought, Yeah, that's the way it should be done. And he would go out and do it. When we went to Black Rock, up until the point when the record was broken, we were living on fumes. The little black bag he carried around was all we had left. That was the finances.

'I have a lot of respect for him. He can be a real wanker at times, and he's very strange like that. He thinks of six impossible things before breakfast, and some people reckon that he acts thoughtlessly. But a lot of it is extremely calculated. He plays games, but he usually wins by just bulldozing on. And people do get pissed off by that, but he gets the job done, and there aren't enough people like him who do that.'

JAYNE MILLINGTON

'I was surprised to feel complete elation. At the start of the project I hadn't been that turned on by land-speed record-breaking, but over the years of involvement it had begun to grow on me more and I'd got really excited at the thought of breaking the sound barrier. There was a feeling of relief when it was all over, not because I felt, Thank goodness, now he's not putting himself

The ThrustSSC team.

in danger. That wasn't it. It was relief because all the effort hadn't been in vain. It was such a brilliant achievement.

'I will never forget the feeling that I experienced on that last run, with the sonic boom rocking pit station. Had I not seen the car, I would literally have thought there'd been an explosion, because that's what it sounded like, and that's what the force was like. It's a trite phrase maybe, but It was completely awesome.

'It was an excellent place to stop. It had been very hard work over the three years, and we could now go back to concentrate on our day jobs. I had a training course at RAF Boulmer only days later. Andy and I were lucky that we had our primary careers to go back to, but it was bizarre in a way. I had five minutes of thought when I was sitting down in the classroom at eight o'clock on that Monday morning, thinking, Good heavens, forty-eight hours ago I was in Nevada, and we'd just made history. It didn't take long to come back down. But it's still lovely, every now and then, to think, Good heavens, we did it! Nothing will ever erode that feeling of incredulity that Adam, Jack (Trackmaster) and I experienced in pit station.

'Even today, I still have a feeling of elation, thinking back. Nothing really makes me leap into the air very much, but that's exactly what I did, and I couldn't believe I'd done it at the time! I can still physically feel the effect of that sonic boom, and that is remarkable because I don't tend to be motivated to superlatives very often. It really was an awesome experience.'

ThrustSSC's shock wave is clearly visible,
fanning out from the front wheels.

22 EPILOGUE

It's now six months since *ThrustSSC* made its last supersonic run. We ran its engines for the last time in Farnborough in December 1997 and now the car is complete, but will never run again. Andy Green is back happily flying RAF Tornados, and the *ThrustSSC* team has disbanded. The FIA certificates have long arrived and our records have been fully ratified. But there is still huge interest in what we achieved. Our website is still running at 140,000 hits a week, and we may have created the first Internet legend.

A lot of people have asked where this leaves the world land-speed-record. To be competitive now any challenger has to have safe supersonic performance, with all that implies. The hurdle is now much higher but hopefully plenty of contenders will come forward. Whether the wide car with the twin-engine layout is the way to go remains to be seen. Certainly Craig Breedlove and Rosco McGlashan plan challenges as I write this, using different types of vehicle, and collectively we are all going to learn a great deal more.

But when someone does come forward with a faster car than *ThrustSSC*, and it will surely happen one day, the point to remember is that we were the first to achieve the supersonic land-speed record. Being the first at anything is one hell of an achievement because you've done something the critics said was impossible. Everyone remembers that Charles Lindbergh was the first to fly solo across the Atlantic, but nobody remembers who did it second. The same is true of Edmund Hillary and Sherpa Tenzing, who were the first to climb Everest, or Neil Armstrong, who was the first man to set foot on the moon. I borrow Ron's expression whenever people ask me about *ThrustSSC* – 'We've pioneered a trail, and from now on anyone who travels it will simply be tourists.'

One of the astonishing achievements of the *ThrustSSC* team was to capture the supersonic record on a budget of just £2.8 million over six years. In corporate terms this is an accounting-error figure, and when we are asked how this was achieved, the answer is very simple: we had a highly motivated and very determined team. Nothing was wasted and most people worked very long hours, in a very intense manner.

Ask anyone in the team why they did it, and they'll tell you we wanted to reposition Britain, and British engineering, on the world map. We belong to a great country and we're fed up with underachievement. We did it to make a point.

The public response has been nothing short of incredible, not only in scale but also in duration. When Andy took *ThrustSSC* to his home town of Norwich late in 1997, 9,000 people turned out, blocking all the roads and reducing the *ThrustSSC* merchandising team to taking orders on scraps of paper. Coventry was just spectacular. I'm told that more than 30,000 people turned out to greet the *ThrustSSC* team over the two days we were there. Certainly 15,000 went to see *ThrustSSC* in the Museum of British Road Transport in one day. That is almost 25 per cent of its usual total of annual visitors. The City Council sent us on a ceremonial tour round the whole of Coventry with the team in an open-topped bus and *ThrustSSC* on its transporter behind. John Coppinger, one of the Mach 1 stalwarts, spotted what was really special about the occasion. 'Do you know what I am seeing, Richard?' he asked as he stood next to me on the bus. When I asked him what he meant, he said, 'Well look at those people. They have smiles on their faces. You don't see people in the streets with smiles any more. They're smiling and they're cheering.'

It was the same when many of the *Thrust* team were invited to attend the annual dinner dance of the British Racing Drivers' Club. I was very nervous during my speech because I was condemning tobacco sponsorship in front of the very people who benefit most from it. But again there was a standing ovation. Andy got one too at the Guild of Motoring Writers' dinner, where they voted him Driver of the Year, and again when he and the team received honours at the Autosport Awards just before Christmas.

We came home with substantial financial liabilities which it was our first objective to clear. Formula One team owner Frank Williams, who is also sponsored by Castrol, invited the team to visit the Williams factory, and gave the project a £10,000 donation. The BRDC gave us £25,000. These were fantastic and moving gestures. With a huge effort from selling our merchandise and making public appearances, we cleared our six-figure debts within five months.

Early in the new year, the Rolls-Royce board invited Andy, the design team and myself to a private black-tie dinner in their Boardroom. Towards the end of the meal, Sir Ralph Robins made a speech. 'I want you all to know that the Rolls-Royce board considers this to be a very great achievement and we are delighted that the supersonic record was achieved with our engines,' he said. And then he presented us with a solid-silver Spitfire model.

Not everyone sees it this way. After we had broken the *Thrust2* record the *Sun* did a big spread, stating that *ThrustSSC* was about as useless as the Royal Yacht. What can you say to that?

The Times correspondent Peter Barnard was clearly not a fan either. Before our first success he wrote: 'I have always had difficulty with speed for its own sake…' And he went on: 'I cannot for the life of me work out what the Land Speed Record is all about. The question is whether the *Thrust* team have got the aerodynamics right to the point where *Thrust* will exceed seven hundred miles an hour without leaving the ground. If so it will prove nothing whatsoever that matters to me. They will have contributed nothing to the development of land vehicles as we know them. The driver of *Thrust* has as much of a connection to the ordinary driver on the road as Bishop Roddy Wright has to moral rectitude.'

Nor was he much impressed with arguments about man naturally aspiring to go faster, higher and further, arguing that our goal was not a legitimate aim, as the conquest of Everest or the four-minute mile had been. He ended: '*ThrustSSC* may be an object of our curiosity, but it can never enter our consciousness as an object of pride or excitement.'

It was a shame that he could not have been with us on the desert as we stood on the threshold of history, or in Coventry or Norwich. But as Andy so often says, you'll never understand the land-speed record if you have to ask for an explanation.

I would have tried to explain to Peter that this was never about trying to do something practical for motorists. It was about spirit and determination, teamwork, commitment and courage. And restoring a nation's pride in its abilities.

Despite such features, the project exceeded its media objectives in style. The sponsors were to benefit from five television documentaries, and an estimated cumulative live global television audience of one billion. In the UK alone there was one column kilometre of press coverage, and we made the headlines in almost every country around the world. We achieved 56 million hits on the Internet, which in its best week reached 11 million hits. We had fulfilled our promises to the sponsors.

They seemed reluctant to cash in on the vast global media exposure. Perhaps they felt that, given such a huge publicity bonanza, there was no need. But others did. In the UK Volvo screened a prime time advertisement about a team member picking up a brake parachute which had come from a long, thin, black land-speed record car. The car was in fact American Al Teague's *Spirit of '76*, a 400-m.p.h. car which holds a wheel-driven record, but everyone who has seen the advertisement congratulates us. The test is whether Volvo would have screened the ad without *ThrustSSC*, for they had absolutely nothing to do with our project. When we have explained this to some viewers their reaction is usually considerable anger and concern, which may not be conducive to impulsive Volvo ownership. Sally and I responded by immediately putting our Volvo up for sale.

Audi's double-page press ad had a car belting across a desert and a slogan saying, 'The sound will be along later.' The copy began with the words, 'Thrust from Audi.'

When approached, neither the Independent Television Commission nor the Advertising Standards Authority appeared to have any concerns about the advertisements' apparent association with the project. The Audi ad was subsequently banned on the grounds of encouraging motorists to drive fast. This effectively means that in the UK it is perfectly acceptable to benefit from a very tough, high-risk, expensive and high-profile project, without the inconvenience, expense or risk of actually sponsoring it.

Right after our successful, but penniless, return to the UK, we were approached by a City bank which appeared to demand the ultimate in low-risk retrosponsorship. They wanted their name on *ThrustSSC* and were prepared to pay heavily for it. I couldn't believe that they thought we were so stupid. I explained that they would have been most welcome if they had approached us when we were in deep trouble, but that right now we would be trading our way out of our financial difficulties.

Early in 1998, we had the farewell lunch for the Mach 1 Gold Members. This was a very sad experience, for over the years these members had supported the project through thick and thin and we had all made many friends. And of course the entire Mach 1 membership was the project's largest sponsor. It became clear that they had no intention of letting it die. There we were, explaining that this was the end of the Mach 1 Club and that a cheerful goodbye was better than a lingering death, and there they were talking of forming themselves into regional groups and keeping the thing going. I've lost count of the number of people who told us, 'We really enjoyed being a part of all this, and we really don't know what we are going to do. We've lived with this for the last four years and the *ThrustSSC* team has really given us something special in our lives.' It was truly wonderful: the Mach 1 Club had evidently worked really well for its members.

We emptied the project coffers to give the team a huge pre-Christmas party in our Farnborough hangar, which true to form ran all night and into the next day. With the last of the fund we gave all the full-timers a bonus and each of the part-timers a huge one-twentieth scale model of *ThrustSSC*.

In the period immediately after the supersonic project, I was seriously unhappy.

There were the inevitable post-record blues when you know that a truly magic team has to disband. But there was also the mountain of debt administration and the huge volumes of correspondence that greeted us on our return home. We needed to sleep for a month, but *ThrustSSC* would not let go and as a priority we needed to get out of debt. The correspondence flowed in far faster than we could answer it. We were deeply grateful for the flood of merchandise orders because it all helped to turn the financial tide. But there were times when I felt as if I'd become a glorified shopkeeper. It was quite clear we were no longer in control. People demanded the car here, there and everywhere for shows and displays. And we just had to respond, to meet the debt.

The whole thing about record-breaking is that you're out of business at the very moment of your success. Finding a course to pursue beyond that can be a serious difficulty. There is something very special about working as a member of a small, dedicated, highly motivated and ultimately successful team that makes it extraordinarily dissatisfying to go back to working in the outside world, with its inefficient tall pyramids and its politics. It had been difficult enough for some of the *Thrust2* team, though the average age was a lot older and many were happy to take well-earned retirement. But the *ThrustSSC* team were younger and they really suffered because they weren't ready for this to be the pinnacle of their lives. It was like the Battle of Britain pilots. One moment you are a great hero then suddenly the war is over and what you have achieved appears to count for little. But once that feeling wore off and they were rested again, they began to suffer the most appalling withdrawal symptoms. Some just couldn't settle. The intensity, teamwork and bonding of the *ThrustSSC* project had been so great. Now they were casting around for something to take its place, and it was proving difficult. It was hard to know what to do other than get a new project up and running and get them back on the payroll again.

One of the first things I did when we made it back to the UK was to write to Tony Blair with a complete list of the team members and their contributions, so that he would know who had done what. He had, after all, sent us messages of congratulation on both the 714-m.p.h. and supersonic records. I got a very friendly and understanding personal letter back.

I did this because of what happened after the *Thrust2* record. When you get an official award, such as an O.B.E., you receive a letter which says, 'Will you accept this award? If so, you are not allowed to talk to anyone about it.' When I got my O.B.E. I duly kept quiet and simply assumed that John Ackroyd had got something too. We were absolutely shattered at the time, but keeping mum was the wrong thing to do. I was appalled when I discovered later that John hadn't got anything. I quickly got a letter off to Mrs Thatcher, recommending John for the O.B.E. and reminding her that the *Thrust2* record was just as much his achievement as mine. My letter was ignored.

So what happened this time? Andy got the O.B.E., which seems light for such a huge and popular achievement, for a man who risked everything time and time again for his country. I got the O.B.E. for driving at 633 m.p.h.: Andy took a far greater risk than I did, in a far more difficult car, and raised the record by 130 m.p.h. And he drove through the sound barrier, for God's sake! He achieved a major world first for Britain.

Without Ron Ayers, the whole project simply would not have worked. That is not to denigrate the efforts of the other team members in the slightest. But without Ron it could not and would not have happened. It was Ron's quiet assurance, his vast aerodynamic expertise and the enormous amount of work he put in which was decisive. The whole project depended on him. And he wasn't recognized. He stood up to be counted for his country, with six years' very hard work at an age when most people are enjoying their retirement, and his country let him down. Words fail me.

In Britain we seem to have a tremendous problem in promoting engineering. We don't seem to be attracting the young and the universities are finding it difficult to fill their engineering slots. The profession has an old and stuffy image, and does little to inspire. Early in 1998 I was invited to make a major dinner speech in front of 400 engineers. Margaret Beckett, President of the Board of Trade, was also there. I really let them have it. 'This is absolutely ridiculous! *ThrustSSC* is a huge global engineering success, and you guys just aren't using it,' I told them. 'The important thing you have to understand is that everyone in the team did it for Britain. That's why they did it. Ask Brian Palmer, Rob Hemper, Nick Dove, Glynne Bowsher, Chris Cowell, Jerry Bliss, Jeremy Davey, Peter Ross. Ask any of them. That's why they did it! Then, when you see that Britain doesn't make use of it, you wonder what the hell is the point.'

So what happens now? *ThrustSSC* will continue to live in Farnborough for as long as DERA can accommodate us, and there are all kinds of spin-offs from the project that can be turned into valuable revenue-earners. Businesses seem to be particularly interested in the teamwork and the flat-pyramid concept. Use that in your business and nobody need go to work with a gloomy outlook. But any organization taking that on has to make very fundamental changes.

I am already deep in research into the next project. A tremendous industrial opportunity is now becoming apparent and we need a new very fast-moving high-technology product. The project is still in its infancy but it is gaining ground and I'm going to give it everything to see whether we can develop it into a market winner. Whenever I fly my own Super2, I think of the ARV battle we fought and lost, and I know that there is unfinished business.

I suppose my philosophy is very simple. I just believe that provided you have researched and planned your work, and really believe in what you are trying to accomplish, if you build a strong team and give your project everything you have, then you might just earn that little bit of luck that will help your team through to success.

You only get one spell on this wonderful planet, and it's up to you to make the very best of it. If it benefits other people as well, then so much the better. It's a hard grind and you can't expect anything other than that. Why should you? You shouldn't lead yourself, or any one else for that matter, to expect that you are going to get an easy ride. It doesn't happen that way. Lunches never come free.

You make your own progress and your own luck. By determination, commitment, refusal to give up or be straitjacketed by convention or the short-sightedness of others – describe it as you will – you are the one who creates the airflow beneath your own wings.

ACKNOWLEDGEMENTS

I would like to explain our failure to produce an acknowledgements page. We tried very hard, but these projects all depended on huge numbers of people and on their generous help and enthusiasm. The original list came to some 300 plus names, and every night we would all remember more. In the end we came to the conclusion that we could name at least a thousand people and still we would forget some who were key to the success of the projects.

Rather than offend our friends, I decided that it is more important for the reader to understand that these projects depended totally on enthusiastic personal commitment and that every one of our friends and supporters has an absolute right to call the success of these projects their own. They know who they are!

We had a huge workload creating this book, which would have been heavier still without David Tremayne's outstanding writing and sheer hard work and persistence. David is a world-recognized authority on record-breaking history; he wrote the limited-edition story of our *Thrust2* record in 1983 in little more than two weeks, and virtually from memory once we had decided to publish it ourselves. This time round he attended our trials at his own expense, such was his determination to see the story told, and he has excelled himself by turning my late-night ramblings into a very accurate and readable book.

We also dragged others into this process, namely my wife Sally, Jayne Millington, Ron Ayers, Jerry Bliss, Glynne Bowsher, and the greatest and coolest land-speed driver of them all, Andy Green. All of them have had to read the manuscript many times, frequently with deadlines that interrupted their busy lives, and each rose to the occasion with commensurate enthusiasm and attention to detail. I'd also like to thank John Ackroyd and Craig Breedlove for their valuable contributions.

This book would never have happened without the vision and wisdom of our editor, Adam Sisman, whom we befriended after achieving the supersonic land-speed record, and our publisher, Transworld. Six months into a tremendous association we are indeed proud to be published by Transworld and, on behalf of the writers and contributors, would like to thank them for the huge effort they have invested and for their faith in our ability to deliver. I personally should acknowledge Transworld's tolerance as the work progressed and other projects made it impossible to meet every deadline!

I should like to dedicate the book to Mary Noble, who worried during the *Thrust2* project, and who sadly never lived to enjoy the huge success of *ThrustSSC*; Sally, Miranda, Genevieve and Jack Noble, who lost six years of normal family life to the *ThrustSSC* project; and to Andrew Noble for all his help.

To everyone who helped with the land-speed-record projects, I make a solemn promise: we were without doubt fortunate to achieve our objectives, and to do so without injury. We achieved a world first and that is it – we are never going back!

If you want to contact us, write to PO Box 77, Hampton, TW12 2XN, UK.

THRUST RECORDS
(APPENDIX 1)

DATE	DRIVER	CAR	SPEED (m.p.h.)	RECORD	VENUE
24/25.09.80	Richard Noble	*Thrust2*	116.470	1 Mile standing start	Greenham Common
	Richard Noble	*Thrust2*	149.570	1 Kilo standing start	Greenham Common
	Richard Noble	*Thrust2*	259.740	Flying Quarter Mile	Greenham Common
	Richard Noble	*Thrust2*	255.060	Flying 500 Metres	Greenham Common
	Richard Noble	*Thrust2*	251.190	Flying Kilo	Greenham Common
	Richard Noble	*Thrust2*	248.870	Flying Mile *	Greenham Common
10.10.81	Richard Noble	*Thrust2*	418.118	British car and driver	Bonneville Salt Flats
21.10.81	Richard Noble	*Thrust2*	463.683	British car and driver – Mile	Black Rock Desert
21.10.81	Richard Noble	*Thrust2*	468.972	British car and driver – Kilo	Black Rock Desert
03.11.82	Richard Noble	*Thrust2*	575.489	British car and driver – Mile	Black Rock Desert
03.11.82	Richard Noble	*Thrust2*	575.562	British car and driver – Kilo	Black Rock Desert
04.11.82	Richard Noble	*Thrust2*	590.551	British car and driver – Mile	Black Rock Desert
04.11.82	Richard Noble	*Thrust2*	590.843	British car and driver – Kilo	Black Rock Desert
21.09.83	Richard Noble	*Thrust2*	606.469	British car and driver – Mile	Black Rock Desert

British Land-Speed Record

04.10.83	Richard Noble	*Thrust2*	633.468	World LSR – Mile	Black Rock Desert
04.10.83	Richard Noble	*Thrust2*	633.468	US Unltd	Black Rock Desert
04.10.83	Richard Noble	*Thrust2*	633.468	Int Cat C Group Jet	Black Rock Desert
04.10.83	Richard Noble	*Thrust2*	633.468	Nat Cat C Group Jet	Black Rock Desert
25.09.97	Andy Green	*ThrustSSC*	714.144	World LSR – Mile	Black Rock Desert
25.09.97	Andy Green	*ThrustSSC*	713.990	World LSR – Kilo	Black Rock Desert
25.09.97	Andy Green	*ThrustSSC*	714.144	Int Cat C Group Jet – Mile	Black Rock Desert
25.09.97	Andy Green	*ThrustSSC*	713.990	Int Cat C Group Jet – Kilo	Black Rock Desert
25.09.97	Andy Green	*ThrustSSC*	714.144	Nat Cat C Group Jet – Mile	Black Rock Desert
25.09.97	Andy Green	*ThrustSSC*	713.990	Nat Cat C Group Jet – Kilo	Black Rock Desert
15.10.97	Andy Green	*ThrustSSC*	763.035	World LSR – Mile	Black Rock Desert
15.10.97	Andy Green	*ThrustSSC*	760.303	World LSR – Kilo	Black Rock Desert
15.10.97	Andy Green	*ThrustSSC*	763.035	Int Cat C Group Jet – Mile	Black Rock Desert
15.10.97	Andy Green	*ThrustSSC*	760.303	Int Cat C Group Jet – Kilo	Black Rock Desert
15.10.97	Andy Green	*ThrustSSC*	763.035	Nat Cat C Group Jet – Mile	Black Rock Desert
15.10.97	Andy Green	*ThrustSSC*	760.303	Nat Cat C Group Jet – Kilo	Black Rock Desert

BLACK ROCK DESERT RUN LOG, 1997

(APPENDIX 2)

RUN	DATE	PEAK SPEED (m.p.h.)	MILE AVERAGE	KILO AVERAGE
39	08/09	148	0	0
40	08/09	50	0	0
41	10/09	306	0	0
42	10/09	428	0	0
43	10/09	517	0	0
44	11/09	550	0	0
45	11/09	624	600	600
46	13/09	550	0	0
47	20/09	410	0	0
48	20/09	554	553.970	553.931
49	22/09	650	618.556	634.77
50	22/09	689	687.941	689.347
51	23/09	697	693.507	696.863
52	23/09	721	719.137	721.358
53	25/09	706	700.661	697.95
54	25/09	731	728.008	730.784
55	03/10	560	389.483	374.194 ABORTED
56	03/10	628	0	0 ABORTED
57	06/10	721	714.427	720.428
58	06/10	732	727.860	730.546
59	07/10	750	0	0
60	07/10	170	0	0 TRANSIT BACK TO PITS
61	13/10	750	749.687	749.139
62	13/10	766	764.168	762.937
63	13/10	761	760.135	758.102
64	13/10	200	0	0 TRANSIT BACK TO PITS
65	15/10	763	759.333	756.742
66	15/10	771	766.609	763.718

TEAM LISTS
(APPENDIX 3)

LONDON–CAPETOWN, 1971

Susie Bond	Maria Duda	Mark Masefield
Sally Bruford	Jane Forster	Richard Noble

CAPETOWN–BOMBAY–LONDON, 1972

Judy Hodson	Fi Mills	Dieter Pickhardt
Nick Hodson	Richard Noble	Clara Wigboldus

THRUST1 TEAM, 1977

Simon Chapman	Richard Noble	Mark Rasmussen
George Myers	Sally Noble	

THRUST2 TEAM, 1983

Birgit Ackroyd	Mick Chambers	Ninetta Hearn	David Tremayne
John Ackroyd	Richard Chisnell	Andrew Noble	Trish Tremayne
Brian Ball	Lorraine Culkin	Charles Noble	Simon Walmsleys
Mike Barnett	Eddie Elsom	Richard Noble	John Watkins
Ron Benton	Gordon Flux (deceased)	Sally Noble	George Webb
Gordon Biles	John Griffiths	John Norris	
Glynne Bowsher	Peter Hand	Ken Norris	
David Brinn	Mike Hearn	Ian Robinson	

ARV AVIATION TEAM, 1988

Mike Barrett	Bruce Giddings	Simon Kingdon Butcher	Nick Sibley
Andy Betts (deceased)	Alan Green	Paul Marfleet	Ginger Squibb
Colin Butler	Mark Harris	James Morton	Nick Valente
Alan Chaplain Orman	Reg Hobbs (deceased)	Richard Noble	Pat Ward
Richard Dove	Peter Hogan	Andy Pavey	Keith Winter
Don Ellis	Steve Horner	Ian Proudfoot	
Glen Fitch	Hugh Kendall	Peter Smith	

ATLANTIC SPRINTER TEAM, 1991

Michael Campbell	Adrian Hamilton	Sally Noble	John Scott-Scott
Pat Dellard	Robin Knox-Johnston	Sara Newhouse	Erbil Serter
Martin Francis	Dai Morgan	John Robertson	Ted Toleman
David Green	Richard Noble	Dick Sarre	

THRUSTSSC TEAM: BLACK ROCK DESERT, 1997

Robert Atkinson	Eddie Elsom	John Lovatt	Leigh Remfry
Ron Ayers	Jack Franck	Jayne Millington	Paul Remfry
Rod Barker	Andy Green	Andrew Noble	Robin Richardson
Jeremy Bliss	Mike Hearn	Jack Noble	Pete Ross
Glynne Bowsher	Ninetta Hearn	Richard Noble	Ruth Stringer
Chris Cowell	Rob Hemper	Sally Noble	Steve Wiltshire
Jeremy Davey	Mike Horne	Adam Northcote-Wright	
Martyn Davidson	Robbie Kraike	Steve O'Donnell	
Nick Dove	Suzy Kraike	Brian Palmer	

PEGASUS MICROLIGHT TEAM

Simon Blacker	John Fack	Richard Meredith-Hardy	Bill Sherlock

MACH 1 CLUB PLATINUM MEMBERS AT BLACK ROCK

Jim Cavanagh	Steve Francis	Jason McCann	Sarah Tilley
Jim Clark	Duncan Garrett	Roger McCann	Clive Tucker
John Coppinger	David George	Barbie McSean	Stanley Tucker
Matthew Cole	Steve Georgii	Fred Patrick	Allan White
Rob Coy	Damien Hawkins	Allan Reid	Andrew Whyte
Mike Dempsey	Bob Ibbertson	Doug Spence	
Ian Denington	Jonathan Lee	Robin Spence	
Anthony Edwards	Damien McCann	Brian Taylor	

UK SUPPORT TEAM

Nick Chapman	Neal Fletcher	Nigel Grant	Rob Hazell

THRUSTSSC BRAND SPONSORS, 1997

BTR plc	Kidde-Graviner Ltd
Castrol International	Mach 1 Club
Chase Technology plc	*Paris-Match*
City of Coventry	Permabond Europe
Cytec Aerospace Ltd	Space Air Conditioning plc/Daikin
DERA	Sterling Software Ltd
Dunlop Aviation Division	Survirn Engineering
HeavyLift-Volgadneper Ltd	Taxan (Europe) Ltd
Inbis Group plc	TI Group plc

THE LAND-SPEED RECORD
(APPENDIX 4)
1898–1997

DATE	DRIVER	CAR	SPEED (m.p.h.)	VENUE
18.12.98	Gaston de Chasseloup-Laubat	Jeantaud	39.24	Acheres
17.01.99	Camille Jenatzy	Jenatzy	41.42	Acheres
17.01.99	Gaston de Chasseloup-Laubat	Jeantaud	43.69	Acheres
27.01.99	Camille Jenatzy	Jenatzy	49.92	Acheres
04.03.99	Gaston de Chasseloup-Laubat	Jeantaud	57.60	Acheres
29.04.99	Camille Jenatzy	Jenatzy	65.79	Acheres
13.04.02	Leon Serpollet	Serpollet	75.06	Nice
05.08.02	William K. Vanderbilt	Mors	76.08	Ablis
05.11.02	Henri Fournier	Mors	76.60	Dourdan
17.11.02	Augieres	Mors	77.13	Dourdan
17.07.03	Arthur Duray	Gobron-Brillie	83.47	Ostend
05.11.03	Arthur Duray	Gobron-Brillie	84.73	Dourdan
12.01.04	Henry Ford	Ford Arrow	91.37*	Lake St Clair
27.01.04	William K. Vanderbilt	Mercedes	92.30*	Daytona
31.03.04	Louis Rigolly	Gobron-Brillie	94.78	Nice
25.05.04	Pierre de Caters	Mercedes	97.25	Ostend
21.07.04	Louis Rigolly	Gobron-Brillie	103.55	Ostend
13.11.04	Paul Baras	Darracq	104.52	Ostend
25.01.05	Arthur Macdonald	Napier	104.65*	Daytona
30.12.05	Victor Hemery	Darracq	109.65	Arles-Salon
23.01.06	Fred Marriott	Stanley	121.57	Daytona
08.11.09	Victor Hemery	Benz	125.95	Brooklands
16.04.10	Barney Oldfield	Benz	131.275*	Daytona
23.04.11	Bob Burman	Benz	141.37*	Daytona
24.06.14	L. G. Hornsted	Benz	124.10**	Brooklands
17.02.19	Ralph de Palma	Packard	149.875*	Daytona
27.04.20	Tommy Milton	Duesenberg	156.03*	Daytona
17.05.22	Kenelm Lee Guinness	Sunbeam	133.75	Brooklands
06.06.24	Rene Thomas	Delage	143.41	Arpajon
12.07.24	Ernest Eldridge	Fiat	146.01	Arpajon
25.09.24	Malcolm Campbell	Sunbeam	146.16	Pendine Sands
21.07.25	Malcolm Campbell	Sunbeam	150.76	Pendine Sands
16.03.26	Henry Segrave	Sunbeam	152.33	Southport Beach
27.04.26	Parry Thomas	Babs	169.30	Pendine Sands

28.04.26	Parry Thomas	Babs	171.02	Pendine Sands
04.02.27	Malcolm Campbell	Bluebird	174.883	Pendine Sands
29.03.27	Henry Segrave	Sunbeam	203.792	Daytona Beach
19.02.28	Malcolm Campbell	Bluebird	206.956	Daytona Beach
22.04.28	Ray Keech	White Triplex	207.552	Daytona Beach
11.03.29	Henry Segrave	Golden Arrow	231.446	Daytona Beach
05.02.31	Malcolm Campbell	Bluebird	246.090	Daytona Beach
24.02.32	Malcolm Campbell	Bluebird	253.970	Daytona Beach
22.02.33	Malcolm Campbell	Bluebird	272.460	Daytona Beach
07.03.35	Malcolm Campbell	Bluebird	276.820	Daytona Beach
03.09.35	Malcolm Campbell	Bluebird	301.129	Bonneville Salt Flats
19.11.37	George Eyston	Thunderbolt	312.000	Bonneville Salt Flats
27.08.38	George Eyston	Thunderbolt	345.500	Bonneville Salt Flats
15.09.38	John Cobb	Railton	350.200	Bonneville Salt Flats
16.09.38	George Eyston	Thunderbolt	357.500	Bonneville Salt Flats
23.08.39	John Cobb	Railton	369.700	Bonneville Salt Flats
16.09.47	John Cobb	Railton	394.194	Bonneville Salt Flats
05.08.63	Craig Breedlove	Spirit of America	407.450***	Bonneville Salt Flats
17.07.64	Donald Campbell	Bluebird	403.100****	Lake Eyre
02.10.64	Tom Green	Wingfoot Express	413.200	Bonneville Salt Flats
05.10.64	Art Arfons	Green Monster	434.020	Bonneville Salt Flats
13.10.64	Craig Breedlove	Spirit of America	468.720	Bonneville Salt Flats
15.10.64	Craig Breedlove	Spirit of America	526.280	Bonneville Salt Flats
27.10.64	Art Arfons	Green Monster	536.710	Bonneville Salt Flats
02.11.65	Craig Breedlove	Spirit of America – Sonic 1	555.483	Bonneville Salt Flats
07.11.65	Art Arfons	Green Monster	576.553	Bonneville Salt Flats
13.11.65	Bob Summers	Goldenrod	409.277****	Bonneville Salt Flats
15.11.65	Craig Breedlove	Spirit of America – Sonic 1	600.601	Bonneville Salt Flats
23.10.70	Gary Gabelich	The Blue Flame	622.407	Bonneville Salt Flats
04.10.83	Richard Noble	Thrust2	633.468	Black Rock Desert
21.08.91	Al Teague	Spirit of '76	409.986****†	Bonneville Salt Flats
25.09.97	Andy Green	ThrustSSC	714.144	Black Rock Desert
15.10.97	Andy Green	ThrustSSC	763.035*****	Black Rock Desert

Not recognized by European Authority

** *First mandatory two-way run*

*** *First pure-jet figures, recognized by motorcycle authority not car (three-wheeler)*

**** *Wheeldriven record (after 1963)*

***** *First supersonic record (Mach 1.0175)*

† *Not universally accepted*

INDEX

Picture credits

Associated Press: page 291
Castrol: pages 1, 7, 85, 146, 177, 182, 184–5, 190, 192, 194, 195, 196, 202, 207, 208, 215, 216, 220, 221, 225, 227, 234, 238–9, 243 (landscape), 245, 247, 248, 250, 252, 253, 255, 256, 257, 259, 260, 281, 284, 285, 286, 287, 295
Alain Ernoult/*Paris-Match*: pages 2–3, 4–5, 210, 211, 231, 243 (portrait), 254, 255, 258, 261, 262, 263, 267, 268, 273, 274, 275, 278, 279, 282, 283, 290, 292, 293, 305
Richard Meredith-Hardy: pages 280, 296–7
Marilyn Newton/ *Reno Gazette-Journal*: pages 12, 289, 304
Popperfoto: pages 13, 14, 38

The remaining pictures are taken from the private collections of the authors. Every effort has been made to trace the copyright owners, but anyone who feels his or her copyright has been infringed is invited to contact the authors c/o the publishers.

The diagrams are based on sketches by Ron Ayers except where otherwise indicated.